Communicating Emotion

D1376547

This thoughtful and informative book addresses questions about communication and emotion that are important to theory and to everyday life. How important is emotion in everyday interaction? How does communication help us find meaning in traumatic events? How do emotional messages communicate moral meaning?

Emotion is not just a biological endowment; it is also the sophisticated capacity of human beings to coordinate with others. Sally Planalp demonstrates that although emotions can sometimes be problematic and difficult to control, they also complement nonemotional thought by orienting people to important personal, social, moral, political, and cultural concerns. Presented here are seven dichotomies in scientific and folk theories of emotion that stimulate exploration of emotions and help to enable their functions and complexity to be understood. Innovative research involving people's recognition of others' emotion is drawn upon, as well as a wide interdisciplinary selection of up-to-date literature from communication, psychology, sociology, management, philosophy, and anthropology, to show how emotion serves as a basis for social connections, as a locus of negotiation between individuals and society, and as a glue that holds people together in cultures.

Sally Planalp is a professor in the Department of Communication Studies at the University of Montana and an adjunct professor in the Department of Management Communication at the University of Waikato, Hamilton, New Zealand.

STUDIES IN EMOTION AND SOCIAL INTERACTION
Second Series

Series Editors

Keith Oatley
University of Toronto

Antony Manstead
University of Amsterdam

This series is jointly published by the Cambridge University Press and the Editions de la Maison des Sciences de l'Homme, as part of the joint publishing agreement established in 1977 between the Fondation de la Maison des Sciences de l'Homme and the Syndics of the Cambridge University Press.

Cette collection est publiée co-édition par Cambridge University Press et les Editions de la Maison des Sciences de l'Homme. Elle s'intègre dans le programme de co-édition établi en 1977 par la Fondation de la Maison des Sciences de l'Homme et les Syndics de Cambridge University Press.

Titles published in the Second Series

The Psychology of Facial Expression
Edited by James A. Russell and José Miguel Fernández-Dols

Emotions, the Social Bond, and Human Reality: Part/Whole Analysis
Thomas J. Scheff

Intersubjective Communication and Emotion in Early Ontogeny
Stein Bråten

The Social Context of Nonverbal Behavior
Edited by Pierre Philippot, Robert S. Feldman, and Erik J. Coats

For a list of titles in the First Series of Studies in Emotion and Social Interaction, see the page following the index.

Communicating Emotion

Social, Moral, and Cultural Processes

Sally Planalp
University of Montana

CAMBRIDGE
UNIVERSITY PRESS

& Editions de la Maison des Sciences de l'Homme
Paris

PUBLISHED BY THE PRESS SYNDICATE OF THE UNIVERSITY OF CAMBRIDGE
The Pitt Building, Trumpington Street, Cambridge, United Kingdom
and EDITIONS DE LA MAISON DES SCIENCES DE L'HOMME
54 Boulevard Raspail, 75270 Paris Cedex 06, France

CAMBRIDGE UNIVERSITY PRESS
The Edinburgh Building, Cambridge CB2 2RU, UK   http://www.cup.cam.ac.uk
40 West 20th Street, New York, NY 10011-4211, USA   http://www.cup.org
10 Stamford Road, Oakleigh, Melbourne 3166, Australia
Ruiz de Alarcón 13, 28014 Madrid, Spain

First published 1999

Printed in the United States of America

Typeface Palatino 10/13 pt.   *System* DeskTopPro$_{/UX}$® [BV]

*A catalog record for this book is available from
the British Library.*

Library of Congress Cataloging-in-Publication Data
Planalp, Sally, 1950–
Communicating emotion : social, moral, and cultural processes /
Sally Planalp.
p.   cm. – (Studies in emotion and social interaction)
Includes bibliographical references and indexes.
ISBN 0-521-55315-6 (hardcover). – ISBN 0-521-55741-0 (pbk.)
1. Expression.   2. Emotions.   3. Interpersonal communication.
4. Emotions – Social aspects.   I. Title.   II. Series.
BF591.P57   1999
302.2 – dc21   98-49524
                                                CIP

ISBN 0 521 55315 6 hardback
ISBN 0 521 55741 0 paperback
ISBN 2 7351 0795 7 hardback (France only)
ISBN 2 7351 0816 3 paperback (France only)

This book is dedicated to my mother and father, within whose love I have always lived.

Contents

Acknowledgments

Thanks go above all to the many scholars of emotion and communication whose work is the foundation of this book. Because it is impossible to be comprehensive, I have relied on others' reviews in order to capture the range of connections and rich possibilities for further research at the interface of emotion and communication. I have taken the risk of being a dilettante in the interests of raising a variety of issues and exploring a number of topics that I believe have great heuristic value. What I write should be taken as only an initial excursion. Besides, in an area that is growing as fast as this one in many academic disciplines, research changes year by year, article by article, conference by conference.

For many reasons, I owe thanks to the students who have studied emotion with me. For some years now, I have taught "Communication and Emotion" to graduate students and undergraduates at several universities, and I have learned that simply studying emotion can be a liberating experience. Students feel reassured that they can understand their feelings rather than just being compelled by them. They learn to appreciate people in their lives who have given them emotional support. They are relieved to learn that when no one can listen to their troubles, they can always turn to diaries. They learn how to manage feelings but also the limits of control. They are relieved to know that happiness does not depend on increasing material affluence and, in fact, may be quite independent of it. Students are intrigued by the idea that the emotional lives of people in other cultures may differ from their own in ways that they have to struggle to understand. They think of emotions as their own private experiences and problems, and they have a *very* hard time thinking in terms of shared or socially enacted emotion. They believe me when I say that shared emotions make sense, but their worldview is deeply individualistic so that collectivist thinking does not come easily. I hope that they learn to live emotionally fulfilling and creative lives as individuals and that they try to relegitimize emotion in the lives of others.

The Department of Speech Communication at the University of Illinois was more supportive of my work than I fully realized at the time. The University of Colorado gave me the opportunity to study emotion with excellent graduate students and supported my sabbatical, for which I am grateful. During my sabbatical I visited the Institute for the Study of Motivation and Emotion at the University of Amsterdam at the invitation of Nico Frijda. It was the first time I had been around a group of scholars who study emotion, and it was quite stimulating. Nico has a passion for emotion, is able to penetrate to the heart of issues in amazing ways, and is a role model for open-minded curiosity. For the last half of my sabbatical, I received support from the Mondragón Cooperatives, especially the people at Otalora, in the form of a room with a breathtaking view, gourmet lunches, much peace to write, and the opportunity to know them a bit. During the final stage of editing this book, I visited the Department of Management Studies at the University of Waikato in Hamilton, New Zealand, and enjoyed it so much that I am continuing as a part-time Adjunct Professor there. Finally, I want to thank the Department of Communication Studies at the University of Montana. My colleagues are dedicated, caring, and fun-loving people who communicate curiosity and compassion to their students. The shared good feelings enrich our daily lives, and we live in Montana, a state that holds on to some emotional values of bygone eras that I hope will never be lost. Montanans have not transferred their affections altogether to goods, pleasure, or status; they retain an abiding devotion to the land, to other creatures, and to each other.

Several colleagues and friends provided extremely valuable feedback on drafts of this manuscript, and I have tried my best to do their suggestions justice. Daena Goldsmith, Brant Burleson, and Julie Fitness gave me very helpful advice and suggestions. Special thanks go to Nico Frijda, who challenged and expanded my thinking, and to Keith Oatley, who was so encouraging. Thanks to George Cheney, who, ironically, has been the person to help me most to think beyond the dyad and whose support never wavered in the long process of writing. My sister Susan helped me purge the draft of jargon, inconsistencies, and confusion.

In writing this book, I have tried to overcome the dry academic style to which I have been socialized. I am losing patience with it. Instead, I am trying to make research more accessible to a wide range of readers, including advanced students and interested laypersons, without sacrificing its scholarly integrity and precision. It is a difficult road. Please forgive me if I come only partway.

Introduction

Ironically, we probably know more about the rings of Saturn than
the emotions we experience every day.

(Lindsay-Hartz, 1984: 689)

With a burst of new interest, scholars in the social sciences and the
humanities are talking about emotion, and the public is joining in.
There are several reasons. Sheer intellectual curiosity compels us to
try to understand whatever is mysterious, and emotions are mysterious to most people. They are complicated physical, mental, social,
moral, and cultural phenomena that provide new frontiers for human
understanding. Feelings may be especially mysterious to many middle-class European Americans (academics in particular) because suppression has become something of a way of life (Stearns, 1994). Emotions have been ignored, denigrated, and cut off from the rest of social
experience in much of the Western philosophical tradition (Solomon,
1993). They are viewed as beastly, infantile, crazy things that must be
controlled for society to operate smoothly and rationally, or so everyday talk and practices suggest. Academic investigation, however, is
all about challenging accepted truths and opening up new possibilities. As Woodward (1996: 774) puts it: "Scholars in the humanities
and social sciences have been working assiduously to rescue the emotions from cultural contempt."

The world is also forcing us to come to terms with emotion. Carmichael (1991: 185–186) writes that "This century, more than any other
in human history, has brought us a terrifying awareness of the dark
and evil capacities of human nature. . . . It has been the realization that
rationality and reason have failed that shocked us." Today's papers
have news about massacres in Mexico and Algeria; not long ago they

1

were in Bosnia, Rwanda, and El Salvador. Emotional problems surround us – road rage, epidemic levels of depression, homicidal jealousy, suicidal love, and genocidal hatred and fear. Rationality does not seem to be an effective antidote, so perhaps the solution lies in understanding emotion on its own terms.

Emotions need to be recognized and respected in everyday talk and interaction because emotion is meaningful and meaning is emotional, whether we like it or not. By emotional meaning, I do not mean the kind of abstract, derived meaning that we find in dictionaries, but the meaning by which people live their lives. It is the kind of meaning we refer to when we say "He'll never know how much he meant to me" or "Do you know what it means to lose your job?" or more trivially "You know what it will mean if you don't clean your room." It is meaning with emotional force and with practical implications. It is also moral meaning, the meaning of how we *do* live our lives and the meaning of how we *should* live our lives. Finally, it is meaning founded in interaction, the meaning that we share in varying degrees, some of us as members of the same culture and all of us as human beings on the same planet.

Each chapter of this book deals with a different issue related to emotional meaning, and to some extent the arguments and evidence of each chapter set up those that follow. For example, the emotion process that is described and analyzed in Chapter 1 is used throughout to organize other topics. At the basis of each chapter is also a false dichotomy that oversimplifies our view of emotional meaning and neglects its full richness and complexity. One of the gems of wisdom that comes from traditional cultures is that great insight and profound connection can be found in dualities such as male–female, life–death, good–evil, yin–yang, and energy–matter. More recently, we have learned that particles and waves are united as integral and inseparable parts of the whole. It was Niels Bohr who said that "profound truths [are] recognized by the fact that the opposite is also a profound truth" (cited in Wurmser, 1995: 5). The trick is not to try to resolve dualities but to explore and appreciate the complexities that they reveal.

The problem with dichotomies is that when we get beyond our initial intuitive conceptions of emotion, it becomes harder to take sides. First, one position is recognized as extreme, then the other is, and our conceptions of emotion bounce back and forth with this argument, that piece of evidence, or yet another scholarly trend. Scholars lose patience, the dichotomies themselves begin to blur, and it becomes clear that emotional communication does not admit to such simple characterizations. Rather than assuming inconsistency between extreme positions, it becomes more fruitful to struggle to find a way of thinking about emotion that broadens our thinking and admits both. We have learned a great deal from considering the dual nature of emotion as both corporeal (bodily) and cognitive (Damasio, 1994; Leavitt, 1996), as both rational and irrational (de Sousa, 1987; Solomon, 1993), and as both individual and social (Averill, 1986; Parkinson, 1995).

Chapter 1 addresses the issue of how important emotion is in everyday interaction. We have long assumed that if we could just be rational rather than emotional, social life would be calm and we would make better decisions. Now we are starting to recognize that emotion may be good for social life and decisions, perhaps even essential. Two dichotomies underlie this chapter: the dichotomy between emotion as rare or pervasive and the dichotomy between irrational emotion and dispassionate reason. If we think of emotion as rare and inherently irrational, we will try to minimize emotion in conversations, except perhaps in the unusual case of loving, intimate talk. Alternatively, if we think of emotion as rare in its most dramatic manifestations, but also pervasive throughout social interaction, we will try to tune in to the emotional aspects of *all* conversation and understand how it guides us in making decisions, relating to others, and living our lives. Moreover, if we think of emotion and rationality as mutually dependent, rather than as opposites, we will try to understand how the two work together.

Chapter 2 addresses the question of how and why emotion is communicated. How do you let someone know that you're angry? You just, well, get angry. You yell, you stomp your feet, you use bad words, you pout. There's no explaining it; that's just how it happens. And when someone gets angry with you? You either get it or you don't. If you don't get it, there is no way to understand why you didn't. In any case, it was probably the other person's fault; after all, he or she is not being reasonable. Besides, if you ignore it, it may just blow over. That is one way of looking at communicating emotion. Another way is to view emotional exchanges not only as understandable, but also as requiring substantial skill to handle well. Emotions do not just "come out that way"; they are communicated in ways that are more or less accurate, more or less subtle, and accomplish goals to varying degrees. Moreover, we can work to develop our skills in communicating emotion effectively in order to manage a wide variety of social situations.

The dichotomy that underlies this chapter is between emotional communication as easy or as difficult. There are dangers at both poles. If you believe that communicating emotion is easy, you may believe you will be in touch with other people's feelings automatically and you may become complacent. If, on the other hand, you believe that communicating emotion is difficult, you may give up the hope of really communicating your own feelings or understanding the feelings of others. In fact, many skills are both easy and difficult. The rudiments are easy; anyone can use them without special training, and most of the time they work well enough. But you do not have to throw up your hands in despair if communicating emotion does not come easily. You can build the knowledge and skills that make it possible to connect with others' emotions in a variety of ways.

Chapter 3 addresses the question of whether emotional communication is spontaneous or strategic. We talk about emotions being expressed – "pressed out" like espresso coffee. Fear of public speaking, for instance, might creep into your tone of voice, leak out in your gestures, or show up in your choice of words. Even if you can control whether and how they come out, you cannot control the feelings themselves, and you would not want to if you could. They are your genuine feelings. But then again, maybe they aren't. Emotion is a complicated process with many components that are alterable in a variety of ways. What's more, you can use your emotions strategically to pursue many different kinds of social goals. You do it every day whether you realize it or not, and many of our social institutions encourage you. You rein in your anger at your child's spilled milk or you put on a happy face for the customer.

Within Chapter 2 lies the dichotomy between the spontaneous and the strategic. We assume that emotions are either genuine, real, and expressed spontaneously or that they are phony, artificial, and manipulated strategically. Spontaneity is, of course, honest and good; strategy is deceptive and bad. But, again, we see that the dichotomy does not hold up. Regulation is built into the very substance of the most genuine feelings. In addition to deciding consciously to feel this way and act that way, we also automatically and unconsciously orient our feelings to our goals and adapt to other people. Spontaneity and strategy blend seamlessly into one another such that they become virtually impossible to disentangle.

Chapter 4 addresses the issue of how emotional meaning is constructed through communication. The usual metaphor here is one of illness or disease. When will he ever "get over" her? It's been three years since the accident, and she seems all right physically but still hasn't "recovered" emotionally. If she would just "let it out" she would feel better (like vomiting up spoiled food). But this is not the best way to think of emotion. Communicating emotion is not a matter of purging, but of constructing meaning from lived experience. Powerful feelings are not so much a sign of trouble as a way of keeping up the pressure to understand an emotionally charged experience and reconcile it with other beliefs about the world and ways of living.

The dichotomy underlying this issue is that feelings are in themselves either therapeutic or debilitating. It comes in many different versions. One is that feel-good emotions (happiness, love) are therapeutic, but feel-bad emotions (guilt, anger) are debilitating. Another is that intense emotions are crazy, but moderate emotions are normal. Yet another is that certain emotions are unpleasant but necessary (grief comes to mind), and others are just plain bad for you (guilt is a good candidate). In any case, you need to figure out which emotions you should cultivate and which you should discourage to promote your own well-being. In place of the therapeutic versus debilitating dichotomy, however, you can think of strong emotions as a sign that you need to find new meanings and make adjustments. Emotions are neither good nor bad in themselves, but they give you important information about how you are orienting toward the world. Grief promotes readjustment to loss, and love promotes changes in the way you relate to others, but grief is not necessarily bad and love is not always good.

Chapter 5 addresses the simultaneously personal and social nature of emotional meaning. One side says that your emotions belong to you; they are your business and nobody else's. You may show them to others, but they are yours to show or to hide. Invading others' emotional space is invading their privacy. The other side says that a good deal of our emotional life is shared. We react to each other emotionally ("I'm ashamed of you"), we share common emotional experiences (the football game last weekend), we socialize children emotionally ("Look happy about your gift!"), and we negotiate emotions together ("Please don't be mad at me. I'm sorry"). In a similar way, emotion is ghettoized in the private, personal sphere. It may not be proper at work, but you can let loose at home. In fact, emotion is a more proper topic for academics to study in the context of personal relationships than it is in the context of work relationships or public affairs. (In support of this claim see Andersen and Guerrero's 1998b *Handbook of Communication and Emotion*, but for an exception see Fineman's 1993 *Emotion in Organizations*).

The false dichotomy that underlies Chapter 5 is that emotions are *either* private and located in the individual *or* public and located in the social world. Generally speaking, Americans do not even hesitate on this one. Of course, emotions are inside you. It doesn't even make sense to think of emotions as out there between people; at least it didn't until several writers came along to make a case for the social. My favorite is Parkinson's (1996) article with the direct and unambiguous title "Emotions are Social" (also McCarthy, 1989). But why do we have to choose? Can't emotion exist inside us *and* in the social world that we share? Can't they be both private and public, both secret and shared, or at least some of each? When you feel awe that a man walks on the moon, is it a personal or a social experience? When you feel embarrassed when you trip onstage, is it personal or social? Well, really, it is both.

Chapter 6 addresses the issue of how emotional messages communicate moral meaning. A common view is that love (or jealousy, sadness, or disgust) is what it is. You can't condemn people for how they feel any more than you can condemn them for their headaches or the size of their ears. Besides, how would we go about evaluating emotions? The answer is – we do it all the time. We say "You shouldn't be jealous of your girlfriend's study partner" or "You should feel guilty about cheating on your taxes" or "How can you do that – it's disgusting!" Indeed, we are very generous in evaluating other people's emotions whenever we believe that our own interests or the common good is at stake. How and how much we should judge each other's emotions is a moral issue in itself, but emotions do not and cannot hide from moral judgments.

The dichotomy that underlies Chapter 6 is between the "is" and the "should be." You can operate in either the realm of the real or the realm of the ideal, but moving back and forth is a hard road traveled mainly by saints and philosophers. And emotions are clearly real, not ideal. Real as they may be, however, they are founded in ideals. What is anger without something gone wrong, often some form of perceived injustice? What is shame without expectations for proper behavior? What is sadness without some recognition that what was lost was and should be valued? What kind of society would we have without compassion for other people, regret for wrongdoing, horror at atrocities, or disgust at the unclean?

Chapter 7 addresses the issue of how well we can understand emotions across cultures and across historical periods. When we go to an exotic place and see the local people, we often assume that we know how they are feeling. If they are smiling, they are happy; if a loved one dies, they cry; if they go along with things without protest, they are agreeing to what we want. Are we right? Well, not entirely. Nor should we assume that their emotions are completely incomprehensible to us. Even though all humans share the same emotional capabilities, and probably some of the same expressions and tendencies to act, emotional meaning is more variable and subtle than most people realize. We may be able to comprehend the outlines of their feelings, but the details and subtleties require deep knowledge of the culture as well.

The dichotomy that underlies Chapter 7 is between the universal and the relative, a permutation of nature versus nurture. Either all humans have the same emotions or they have completely different ones. We seem to want either to assimilate new information into what we understand already or to view it as completely alien (Eiser, 1990: 53–76). But if we have learned anything from the protracted nature versus nurture controversy in other domains, it is that most forms of human behavior are a combination. The more interesting question is *how* nature and nurture combine to produce our emotional lives and *how well* we are able to communicate emotion across cultures.

The issues and dichotomies represented in these chapters are not just academic ones. People who know nothing about the scholarly literature still use their own implicit theories of emotion to guide their action and talk, although largely at an unconscious level. When the chair of a committee asks members to "be reasonable" instead of getting angry, she is opposing emotion in favor of reason. When one person defends an insulting remark with "I was just saying what I felt," he is assuming that expressions of emotion are amoral and are not subject to criticism. When we look at the smiles of international students and conclude that they like our classes, we are assuming that emotional communication is universal. The stances toward emotion that are held by nonscholars no doubt have more impact on how the world works than do scholarly debates. Nevertheless, everyday and scholarly biases often coincide, either because everyday conceptions of emotion guide how scholars think or because scholarship influences popular thinking. I have chosen to pursue both scholarly and practical issues in this book in the hope of addressing both audiences and exploring gaps that may be found between popular and scholarly notions about emotional communication.

1. How Important Is Emotion in Everyday Interaction?

> A world experienced without any affect would be a pallid, meaningless world. We would know that things happened, but we could not care whether they did or not.
>
> Tomkins, (1979: 203)

What role does emotion play in everyday talk? One view is this: You're having a perfectly normal conversation, and everything goes along just fine until some emotion disrupts things. You're talking about work with a friend and you happen to mention a sensitive topic (such as how he just lost his job), and he gets upset. He says something insulting to you (such as how you don't really deserve yours), and you have a hard time maintaining your composure. Another person enters the room and tells you that he has been offered a job (though one you know is not very good). He is thrilled. Talk to him? Forget it. There is no way you can carry on a rational conversation now. He is too emotional.

As Cochran and Claspell (1987: 2) say: "Emotion lurks about upsetting well-ordered lives, disrupting rationality, and dividing a person with paltry and degenerate demands.... An emotion is a commotion." Most of the time we are free of emotion; it rarely occurs in everyday conversation, and blessedly so. When an emotion does occur such as when one person yells at another, someone "breaks down" in tears, or laughs "hysterically," it is a BIG DEAL! "Tears are stupid, tears are childish, tears are a sign of weakness, important people don't cry, clever people don't cry" (Carmichael, 1991: 186). Normal patterns of interaction stop when emotion erupts, and everyone responds one way or another. We may confront the feelings, try to cope with them, or try to pretend that they didn't happen (as we do with many social

9

disruptions). What we are unlikely to do, however, is to take the emotion into account and continue to talk, make decisions, and go about our business.

Yet there is another view of the role that emotion plays in everyday conversation. Emotion is what gives communication life. A conversation between emotionally involved partners is bright and lively, but a meeting without feeling is deadly dull. Without feelings, we might be like Mr. Spock, the Vulcan on *Star Trek*, who has no emotions and participates in conversation rationally, but more likely we wouldn't care enough to participate at all. We would be without pathos – *apathe*tic. If other people had no feelings, they would care no more about us than they care about the chairs we are sitting on; they would be without com*passion* or em*pathy*. Without emotion, nothing makes any difference; we are indifferent. Life goes on, but we are removed from it. We feel like spectators in our own lives, not participants. Conversation does not touch us; it is removed, as if it is taking place on another plane of existence or happening to someone else.

In fact, people who have injured parts of their brains that are associated with emotion or have gone through experiences that have left them emotionally drained report exactly what I have described. Emotionally impaired people seem normal on the surface and are pleasant in conversation. Their emotions are not inappropriate; they simply don't exist. These people approach life as "uninvolved specta-tors" (Damasio, 1994: 44). For people who are emotionally drained, any feelings, even feelings of anguish and pain, are often preferable to no feelings at all (Cochran & Claspell, 1987: 118). Fortunately, this is a rare state, so most people take feelings for granted.

Social life is sometimes described as a fabric, with the threads of individual lives woven together through interaction. The social fabric can be tightly woven, loosely woven, or even torn by misunderstand-ings or intentional disruption. If society is a fabric, then emotion is its color (Lazarus, 1991: 19). We can imagine a primarily gray social fabric interspersed with occasional bursts of color (bursts of emotion) or we can imagine a fabric suffused with color (emotion) interspersed with rare streaks of gray. Which fabric we imagine depends on how we think about emotion and, either way, we can find theorists and re-searchers who agree with us (Berscheid, 1990). In either case, emotion is an important part of the fabric of daily life and its colors are woven into everyday talk. Emotional colors enliven and give meaning to the lives that we weave together. The metaphor of social life as fabric, communication as weaving, and emotion as color will be used throughout this book to explain and explore a number of implications about emotional communication.

For example, if we think of emotion as the occasional and problematic burst of color, advice about how to handle emotion in interaction can follow the troubleshooting model (that is, if X goes wrong, try Y). Deal with it, and maybe it will go away. Cope with it, and things will return to normal. But if we think that emotion is an ongoing quality of conversation, we can observe the constant ebb and flow of emotion as conversation unfolds. And maybe it is always there because it is serving some useful purpose. Rather than "dealing with" or "coping with" emotion, perhaps we should be listening to and appreciating it. Better yet, perhaps both perspectives are valid. To explore how they might be understood and reconciled, we turn to process theories of emotion.

Emotion as Process

Process theories of emotion can be formally represented in several ways – with diagrams of prototypes, flow charts, or simple verbal descriptions – but they all describe emotion as a process made up of several definable subparts or components that operate together to produce emotion. Although theorists may disagree about what specific components are essential to emotion, five appear in most theories in one form or another: (1) *objects, causes, precipitating events*, (2) *appraisal*, (3) *physiological changes*, (4) *action tendencies/action/expression*, and (5) *regulation*.

A prototype of sadness is a good starting point for illustrating all five components (Shaver, Schwartz, Kirson, & O'Connor, 1987). The emotion process starts with an event that precipitates the emotion. For sadness it is an undesirable event such as losing a loved one, being rejected, or not getting what you want. To produce sadness, the event must be appraised not only as negative but also as one that you cannot do anything about (otherwise it might be anger or fear). Characteristic actions and expressions are sitting around, slumping, talking little or not at all, withdrawing from contact, and a host of others. Physiological changes produce a less aroused state, reflected in being tired, rundown, low in energy, and lethargic. Regulation processes include talking to someone about the sad feelings or events, taking action, looking on the bright side, or trying to act happy.

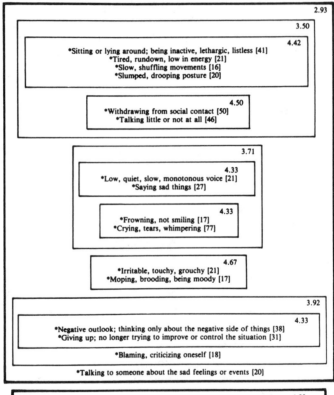

Prototype of Sadness, reprinted from Figure 5 in P. Shaver, J. Schwartz, D. Kirson, and C. O'Connor (1987). Emotion knowledge: Further exploration of a prototype approach. *Journal of Personality and Social Psychology, 52,* 1077. Copyright © 1987 by the American Psychological Association. Reprinted with permission.

Alternative versions of process theories emphasize different components, but the basic elements are roughly the same. For example, action tendencies are central to Frijda's process theory, emphasizing the fact that the *urge* to act in certain ways (or not to act, in the case of sadness) is more characteristic of emotions than action is (or lack thereof) (Frijda, 1986; Frijda, Kuipers, & ter Schure, 1989). Stein, Trabasso, and Liwag's (1993) formulation emphasizes the many steps in appraisal and the planning and goal-directed nature of action and regulation. Ekman (1993) emphasizes expression, especially in the face.

Process theories handle discrete categories of emotions by specifying what precipitating events, appraisals, action tendencies, actions and expressions, physiological reactions, and regulation processes characterize the basic categories of emotion such as sadness, joy, or fear. But they also can handle an almost infinite variety of other emotions, including subtle differences between similar emotions (the difference between guilt and shame over ignoring a panhandler), blended emotions (blends of joy and fear when your son leaves home), and emotions for which we have no name (the feeling of being socially overwhelmed – the opposite of loneliness). They capture our sense that emotions are processes that occur over time, ranging from the brief rush of fear when a car drives too close to your bike to the enduring joy of watching your child grow up (Frijda, Mesquita, Sonnemans, & van Goozen, 1991).

Process theories also give us ways to understand experiences that are emotionlike but not exactly emotions. Moods, for example, do not have *objects*. We don't say, "I'm really moody at my boss today"; we say, "I'm not angry at my boss, I'm just in a bad mood." Other than having no object, bad moods are much like emotions. They are pleasant or unpleasant (*appraisal*), they sap our energy (*physiology*), they make us inclined to snarl and complain (*expressions and action tendencies*), and we try to control them as best we can (*regulation*). Another example is a sentiment, such as love, which describes a disposition to *appraise* an *object* (the loved one) in a particular emotionally relevant way (Frijda et al., 1991). Only in its most intense form is love a full-blown emotion (including *expression, physiological* reactions, and *regulation* processes); much of the time it remains a sentiment.

Process theories help us understand how emotions can be seen both as rare and as pervasive. On the one hand, textbook cases of emotions (complete with object, appraisal, physiological changes, expression, and regulation) occur rarely in conversation. How often, for example, do you feel full-blown anger, such as you feel when someone (*object*) criticizes your report unfairly (*appraisal*), making your heart rate go up (*physiology*), making you want to throw your coffee at him (*action tendency*), but in response to which you say instead (*regulation*) in a firm but irritated voice, "Perhaps you should reread the third paragraph on page three" (*expression*). It happens, but rarely. On the other hand, we have emotionlike experiences (such as slight irritation or boredom) almost all of the time. If a conversation feels uncomfortable, there may be no clear object, just a general sense of unpleasantness, expressed through a slight frown, and a vague desire to be somewhere else. Or if you are interrupted, you may react physiologically, but you may not interpret it as either good or bad and you may not respond. In both of these cases, only some of the components are present, so they are not true *emotions*, but enough of the components are there to be emotionlike.

Components of the Emotion Process

The most important feature of process theories is that they enable us to take apart the components of emotion, study them in detail, and put them back together again. In the section that follows, each component is analyzed in the context of face-to-face interaction, drawing on current theories and research to explain how it works.

Objects/Causes/Eliciting Events

Most often when you have an emotion it is *about* something – it has an object. You are happy *about* making plans to go boating; you are afraid *of* hearing the doctor's report; you are sad *that* your friend has to work all weekend. When feelings or moods are detached and free-floating, they feel strange. They are difficult to understand, to do something about, or to explain to others. It is tempting to direct the feeling toward some convenient object just to have it make sense. It is hard to be angry at the world and life in general but very easy to direct that anger toward your roommate's dirty dishes.

The Problem with Causes. One of the biggest problems for researchers studying emotion and for people experiencing emotion is how to determine its object or cause. If we define the object as the situation or event toward which the emotion is directed, we can analyze it by looking to the other components of emotion. We know that Joan is angry at you, not me, because she thinks you are being unfair, not me, and she is yelling and swearing at you, not me. But, of course, even that is not simple. She could be thinking you are unfair because she loves me and cannot admit to herself that I am the one who treated her badly. She may yell and swear at you, not because she thinks that you are unfair, but because I am more powerful and yelling at you is a way of getting to me indirectly. So *you* may be the object of Joan's emotion from Joan's point of view, but with some extra information, we may understand that *I* am the real cause.

To complicate things further, *neither* you *nor* I may be the real cause of Joan's anger. She may be angry because her puppy dirtied her rug this morning, making her late for work, and she had too much caffeine before meeting us. *We* didn't make her angry because if these things had not happened, she wouldn't be angry at all. In this case, the object of Joan's emotion is different from the cause, as it may be in many cases. Aligning object and cause is no small feat, for Joan or for anybody else. In fact, years of psychotherapy may be devoted to searching for the true causes of feelings. Nevertheless, we are usually able to direct our emotions toward objects in more or less appropriate ways (if not in completely flawless or insightful ways).

The literature on emotion does not provide a full account of how objects of emotion are determined, but there is an extensive literature on causal attribution that helps. Several processes probably operate. For example, whatever is salient is likely to be seen as the object of an emotion (Taylor & Fiske, 1975). For example, after Joan arrived at work, she was still physiologically aroused and irritable, but she forgot about the dog. When we changed her schedule, however, the arousal and irritation were directed at the objects of her attention – us. In addition, Joan (like all of us) has certain beliefs about what causes emotions that she uses to find the appropriate object (Kelley & Michela, 1980). Helpless little puppies are not appropriate objects of anger, but people who change your schedule are. And for reasons indicated earlier, you are a better target than I am, so you become the object. Moreover, Joan noticed that she was angry right after she heard about her schedule being changed, so she inferred that her anger was caused by the schedule change. She also knows that having their schedules changed usually makes other people angry as well (Kelley, 1967).

Notice several things about this example. Even though it is may be impossible for Joan to determine the true cause of her emotion, she has several heuristics available for making a reasonable judgment about it. Those same heuristics may serve as a basis for two or more people to discuss causes. For instance, if Joan blames me, I might say, "You know, I just read about a study linking coffee drinking to anger," to which Joan might reply, "But I wasn't angry until I heard about this schedule change and everyone else is angry about it too, whether they were drinking coffee or not," to which I might reply, "They weren't nearly as angry as you were," and so on. Thus, in a very real sense, causes make emotions discussible, negotiable, and perhaps changeable. By contrast, nothing is quite so frustrating as someone closing down discussion by claiming to be "just in a bad mood."

Because the issue of causality is so complicated and indeterminate, emotion theorists often employ terms that dance around the term *cause* (for an exception, see Lazarus, 1991: 171–213). Various possibilities are: emotion-provoking or emotional stimuli, antecedents, emotion-eliciting events, precipitating events, and situational conditions.[1] Because no event in itself is capable of causing emotion without the other components playing their parts, events rarely if ever count as exclusive causes. An earthquake might provoke, elicit, precipitate, precede, or set up conditions for fear, but unless someone appraises the situation as dangerous and is inclined to run, hide, freeze, or do *something*, there is no fear. Generally these terms refer to *apparent* or *perceived* objects or causes, usually determined either by asking people to describe the emotion (including its object) or by assessing what events or conditions precede and co-occur with emotion. That is probably as close as we can come to determining true causality, so careful theorists avoid the term *cause*, although avoiding the term does not solve the problem.

Causes of Emotion in Conversation. It is especially difficult to determine the objects or causes of emotion or feelings in conversations because emotions can be about or caused by practically anything. In conversation, objects of emotion can be verbal (jokes or even the topic of

---

[1] Frijda (1986) refers to *emotional stimuli*; Lazarus (1991) to *situational conditions*; Stein et al. (1993) to *precipitating events*; Summerfield and Green (1986) to *emotion-eliciting events*; Izard (1991) to *antecedents*, *causes* (psychological or phenomenological), *elicitors*, and a variety of other terms.

conversation), nonverbal (gestures), people (your partner or yourself), thoughts (daydreams), or even emotions themselves (*guilt* about *enjoying* the ethnic joke or *anger* about your partner's *jealousy*). They can be something as microscopic as a compliment, an insult, an interruption, or a touch or, alternatively, something as macroscopic as a stressful interview, an exciting argument, or a lifetime of frustrating interactions.

In analyzing communication patterns, we distinguish between the *content* of a message and its *relational* meaning, a distinction that is useful in analyzing the causes of emotion (Watzlawick, Beavin, & Jackson, 1967). The content level carries information about the topic or subject of the conversation; the relational level carries information about the relationship between speaker and hearer. An emotion may seem to be caused by the content of a message when in fact it is a response to relational meanings. That is sometimes why we overreact to what appear to be trivial incidents. On a relational level they are anything but trivial. "The Cadbury Egg Incident" reported by a student of mine is an excellent example. At Easter, her sister sent her a basket full of jellybeans, various goodies, and one Cadbury egg. Her boyfriend came over, looked eagerly at the basket, and asked if he could have the Cadbury egg. She casually told him no, that her sister had sent it to her and that there was only one Cadbury egg. He was joking around, not taking her answer seriously, and started to unwrap the egg. She yelled at him to knock it off. He laughed and took a bite. She then "lost it," began ranting, and screamed at him to leave. Now, was this all worth it for one Cadbury egg? Obviously not. But later she realized that the issue was not the Cadbury egg (the content of the message and apparent cause), but rather whether she had authority over what was rightfully hers and whether her boyfriend respected her wishes (the relational issue). What's more, the incident was part of a pattern of behavior by her boyfriend. Now, *that* may be worth anger, confrontation, and relational negotiation.

Social Situations as Eliciting Events. In order to be comprehensive, research on causes or objects of emotion in interaction tends to analyze general types of causes rather than details. We know that emotion flourishes in social situations (Andersen & Guerrero, 1998c: 57–64). For example, U.S., European, and Japanese students reported experiencing joy, sadness, anger, and fear most often when they were with one other person, second most often when in a group, and least often when alone (except for fear, which was experienced about equally often in all three situations) (Scherer, Wallbott, Matsumoto, & Kudoh, 1988: 18). Relations with others were the most commonly reported antecedents of joy, sadness and anger (but not fear) in Japan, Europe and the United States (Scherer et al., 1988: 12). Residents of Glasgow representing a variety of occupational groups reported that other people's actions were the most likely elicitors of their own happiness, sadness, anger, disgust, and fear (with the only close second being fear elicited by one's own actions) (Oatley & Duncan, 1992: 271).[2] But not all types of social situations are equally evocative of emotion. People with whom one has a close relationship are more likely to evoke emotion than are strangers. Friends, in particular, are important to students. Students from eight countries reported feeling joy most often when meeting friends (not relatives or strangers), feeling sadness most often when they had problems with friends, and feeling anger most often when friends failed them (although traffic accidents provoked more fear than anything friends did) (Summerfield & Green, 1986).

From other studies, we can piece together some ideas about what happens in interactions to elicit emotions. Threats of social rejection elicit fear. Loss of relationships, rejection, exclusion, and disapproval elicit sadness. Insults elicit anger. Receiving esteem, praise, love, liking, or affection elicits joy. Exceptionally good communication elicits love (Shaver et al., 1987). Many kinds of speech events can be hurtful – accusations, evaluations, advice, and simple information, to name a few (Vangelisti, 1994). Some of these examples illustrate an important problem that researchers confront in trying to find more specific causes of emotion. Causes may not be logically separate from the emotion being caused. For example, threats of social rejection may be interpreted as threats at least in part *because* they elicit fear. A threat is not a real threat unless it is scary. On the other hand, many speech acts that take the form of a threat are not really threats. For instance, if I "threaten" to dismiss class early unless students do the readings, it is not a threat if they don't believe I will do it or if they would be happy if I did. Or saying that "exceptionally good communication"

---

[2] Other categories were (1) self's action, (2) something remembered, (3) something imagined, (4) something read, seen on TV, etc., (5) not caused by anything, and (6) other elicitors.

elicits love may be nothing more than saying that we define communication as exceptionally good if it elicits love.

All this is to say that most events in the social world are impossible to disentangle from their interpretations, leading some theorists (such as Lazarus, 1991; Parkinson, 1995) to leave out causes and deal only with appraisals. There are few "brute facts" in social interaction, that is, facts that speak for themselves (Buck, 1984: 12–13; Searle, 1969: 50–53). Instead, most of what occurs in social interaction is meaningful only as it is interpreted through an elaborate system of personally and culturally defined meanings, and these meanings lie at the heart of emotion just as they lie at the heart of language, cognition, and culture. Making attributions about causes or objects of emotion is only the beginning; they must also be given emotional meaning. Mesquita and Frijda (1992: 183) use the term *event coding* to describe the process of relating particular events to event types that are socially shared. For example, bereavement seems to be a universal event type related to the death of a loved one, but shameful events can vary considerably from exposing bare feet or back of the hands to covering (not *uncovering*) the breasts (Parrott & Harré, 1996: 54).

Appraisal

Emotional meaning is given to events through appraisal processes. Emotion does triage, directing our formidable cognitive and physical capacities toward stimuli in the environment that warrant our attention. That is why we would be not just cold without emotion; we would also be lost and bewildered. We would not know where to turn or how to prioritize. Simple as it may seem, determining what stimuli or events in the environment warrant emotion is a complicated process. To understand it, we turn to several theories of appraisal, where a number of common themes can be found but where controversies and unresolved issues also make things lively.[3]

Concerns. In the most general sense, emotion is generated by events that are important for our well-being or that relate to our concerns.

---

[3] For a brief history, see Frijda (1993); other recent influential papers are Ortony, Clore, and Collins (1988); Smith & Ellsworth (1985); Scherer (1988); Roseman, Spindel, and Jose (1990); all of *Cognition and Emotion, 7*, Issues 3 and 4.

An astute reader will think, "That could include almost anything," and in principle it could. Most of us couldn't care less about the 1,000th grain of sand that runs through our fingers, but a yogi might discover the essence of joy there. This is possible but not likely. In fact, human beings in large measure are moved by the same basic concerns – concern for our own physical well-being (tied to fear), concern for knowing what is going on (tied to surprise or anxiety), concern for close ties to others (tied to sadness, shame, love, jealousy), concern for achieving goals (tied to joy, anger).[4] Some of these concerns are so generally agreed upon that we might as well say that the events themselves elicit the emotions – but not always. For example, the loss of a loved one produces a strong emotional reaction in Americans, Europeans, Japanese, Balinese, and almost any other culture we can imagine. On the other hand, personal experience tells us that losing a job produces more emotion in some people than in others, depending on the meaning attached to the loss. If you lost a job that meant a lot to you, you would have strong feelings; if you lost a job that was of little concern to you, you would feel very little or nothing.

Concerns are tied to the goals and plans that we pursue in life, from basic goals such as physical survival and social belonging to more specific goals and plans such as making a friend or completing a project (Mandler, 1984; Oatley, 1992; Stein et al., 1993). Emotions occur when there is a significant change in the status of our plans, and they alert us to the need to adjust accordingly. Significant changes can be positive (We just won the race! – Joy), negative (I can't seem to get this computer to work – Anger), or neutral (Who's knocking at this hour? – Surprise). On the other hand, if our goals and plans proceed as usual, we do not feel much of anything, and we should be thankful for that. We cannot be continually on the alert. Lord Byron (whose name is almost a synonym for passion) said, "There is no such thing as a life of passion any more than a continuous earthquake, or an eternal fever. Besides, who would ever *shave* themselves in such a state?"[5]

The inability to sustain powerful emotional states has interesting implications for communication, especially in close personal relation-

---

[4] Concerns include drives, interests, and goals, but the term *concerns* best captures a wide range of biologically, culturally, and individually determined factors.

[5] Letter, 5 July 1821, to the poet Thomas Moore (published in *Byron's Letters and Journals*, Vol. 8, 1973–81). Cited in *The Columbia Dictionary of Quotations*. (1993). New York: Columbia University Press.

ships. Everyday communication has little capacity to move us, which is probably just as well; it saves our energy for when we really need it. Novel information commands our emotions, such as getting fresh news or giving your first speech. Eventually, though, you get used to it, a phenomenon that emotion theorists call *habituating* – making it a habit (Berscheid, 1983; Mandler, 1984). A couple's first kiss, first big fight, commitment to drop all rivals, and help in a crisis are all common turning points in relationships, but after a while they start to be taken for granted (Baxter & Bullis, 1986; Siegert & Stamp, 1994). You no longer feel passion at a regular old kiss, get hysterical over the usual argument, feel thrilled that your partner is free on Saturday night, or feel gratitude that he listens sympathetically. Habituation can make your feelings for your partner pretty bland (usually called "taking him for granted"). You may start to conclude that you do not love him anymore. What you may not realize is that because your joint communication patterns are so well oiled, he has tremendous capacity to disrupt them and produce powerful feelings. Your feelings for him are latent, not absent. If he leaves, you may be completely distraught when you are struck by the painful absence of normal kisses, evenings together, sympathetic talks, and even the usual arguments (Berscheid, 1983).

In fact, the more familiar things become to us, the less capacity they have to arouse us emotionally. That may be why conflict-habituated couples can have horrendous and ongoing arguments (described by one man as a "running guerrilla fight") that are perfectly normal to them but make others' blood curdle (Berscheid, 1983: 159–160). Habituation may also be the reason we can witness so many fictional and even real deaths on TV without being awfully disturbed. Similarly, benevolent links among people – trust, mutual concern, fair treatment, mutual respect – are so widely assumed that they form the foundation of social life. When they are disrupted, we experience not just powerful emotions, but trauma. Challenges to your beliefs about a close friend's honesty, loyalty, or commitment to stay in contact produce powerful emotional reactions (Planalp & Honeycutt, 1985; Planalp, Rutherford, & Honeycutt, 1988). Yet these pale by comparison to the betrayals of human decency that are a part of violence, sexual abuse, and other physical and emotional torture.

Some goals and concerns are human universals; others are specific to personal circumstances; and many are of universal concern but more salient to some people than to others. Appraisal theories can handle both commonalities and differences among people by taking into account themes and variations in what events mean to people. Consider how you might feel, for example, if you were very close to your mother and she had just died of lung cancer. There are any number of emotions you might feel, depending on your appraisal – anger (if you blamed her), guilt (if you blamed yourself for not convincing her to stop smoking), fear/anxiety (if you can't imagine getting along without her), or sadness (if you know she is gone and nothing can be done about it). Under certain circumstances you might feel relief (if she was suffering terribly), pride (if you helped her find meaning in her death), or happiness (that she is in a better place). Such a wide range of emotions is possible not only between people, but within the same person feeling the mixed emotions that occur with complex appraisals (Dillard, 1998: xxi).

Appraisals Unfold Over Time. Some theorists divide appraisal into primary appraisal, which determines whether and how the event is relevant to one's well-being, and secondary appraisal, which is concerned with one's resources and options for coping (Smith & Lazarus, 1993). It is only sensible that primary appraisal precedes secondary appraisal because determining the extent and nature of the event logically precedes assessing how one can cope. Other models postulate somewhat different processes. For example, one could start at an even more basic level (when something novel happens), divide the unfolding appraisal process differently (into four parts), or add an additional type of appraisal (such as compatibility with internal or social norms) (Scherer, 1988). Most theories do agree, however, that the early stages involve relatively simple judgments that are made very fast and usually automatically (that is, without conscious awareness or control) (Lazarus, 1984; Zajonc, 1984).[6] Later stages of the process may be more complex, slower, and often involve conscious thought processes. Finally, appraisal seldom occurs instantly and is over and done with; instead, as time goes by, as new information comes in, or as we think and talk about emotionally charged events, the appraisal process con-

---

[6] Frijda (1993) comments on the early stages of appraisal being linked to causes or antecedents, whereas later stages elaborate an already operative emotion. As Frijda says, the two "coalesce into a sense of reality," but this raises the interesting question of whether we would have worked ourselves up into a frenzy about the trials and tribulations of do-it-yourself carpentry without the original, very simple impetus – hitting one's thumb with the hammer.

tinues. Appraising an event that is as intense, complex, and important as the death of your mother may go on throughout the rest of your life.

Whether appraisal occurs instantly or takes longer, there is no doubt that it commands resources that have been developed over one's lifetime – knowledge, beliefs, experiences, plans, and sense of self and others (see Lazarus, 1991, for knowledge; Markus & Kitayama, 1991, on self and others; Oatley, 1992, on plans and experience). Your feelings about your mother's death draw on all the knowledge that you have about her life, on your deepest beliefs about the nature of life and death, on your experiences together, on your thoughts about your relationship with her, on your plans for a future without her, and on your sense of self as your mother's son or daughter. If you are very young, her death can shake the foundations of your social world, undermining your confidence that people are responsive to your needs (Bowlby, 1969a, 1969b). It is hard to capture these complexities except to say that emotional appraisal draws on the deepest aspects of our beings. Appraisal is not only a matter of deciding whether an event is good or bad, your fault or mine, frightening or manageable; it is also the process of understanding the meaning of events in the broadest and deepest sense.

Appraisal processes also give us a way of viewing emotion as social (Van Hooft, 1994). Meaning is not created by people living on their own private planets; it is created by people who talk with one another, live in groups, and experience a social world in part inherited from their forebears. We live in societies that offer us ways of interpreting life. The meaning of your mother's death, for instance, may be found in talking with your father, your siblings, or other people who knew her. It may be found by reading a religious text, by consulting a shaman, or through a culturally based ritual such as a funeral. It may be found in a renewed appreciation for your own children or in a commitment to cure cancer.

Appraisal in Conversation. With this brief sketch of appraisal processes, we can begin to address the question of why social interaction is such a ripe domain for emotion. Several theories start emotion with novelty – something new happens, new information comes to light, or the world is seen in a new way. By its very nature, conversation is supposed to be about something new. Conversations develop as new information is added to what is already taken for granted, and you violate a basic conversational rule if you tell people things they already know (Clark, 1992; Grice, 1975). Sometimes we do talk about the same old things, but that is to maintain social bonds, to try to find a new angle on an old issue, or perhaps just to avoid silence. But, let's face it: those are not our most emotionally charged conversations.

Emotion also comes from events that are relevant to our concerns. And since we can talk about anything, we can talk about our deepest concerns and have the intense feelings that come with them whenever we want. Of course, sometimes we choose to do this and sometimes we do not, as anyone who is grieving can tell you. Sometimes the weight of feelings is too heavy to bear, and a little light-heartedness is needed. Emotions are involving, to be sure, but they can also be draining.

What makes conversation especially rich in emotion, however, is the simple fact that it involves two people who have to coordinate with one another and whose concerns may or may not be the same (Oatley & Larocque, 1995). When the topic of discussion is an important concern for everyone, the conversation can be an emotionally powerful one, as it often is in important decision-making meetings or in support groups. But when one person dominates the conversation with issues that are of concern only to herself, the conversation is boring to the other (Jones, Hobbs, & Hockenbury, 1982; Leary, Rogers, Canfield, & Coe, 1986). If each person has important concerns that compete and interfere with the concerns of others, the conversation can be charged with anger or hostility. And this assumes that people's concerns are set in advance, which they obviously are not. One person can bring on guilt, jealousy, love, hate, or joy by bringing up old concerns or by producing new ones.

Coordination between partners in conversations occurs at many levels, and they are all grounds for emotion. Partners have to coordinate the chance to talk and to listen, which in itself is no small task and can lead to feelings of frustration if one person is constantly interrupted, never gets a chance to say anything, or cannot get his or her partner to talk (Wiemann & Knapp, 1975). Partners have to coordinate understanding and being understood, which is such a basic goal of interaction that, again, success can be exhilarating and failure can be painful, especially if the misunderstanding is about issues of great concern. As illustrated in the example about one's mother's death, the range of appraisals that are possible is wide, so the chance of misunderstanding is great.

Moreover, a virtually limitless range of other goals can be pursued through conversation, and we know that emotions are tied directly to goal facilitation and interference. Goals that are typically pursued in conversation can be grouped into three basic categories: accomplishing a task, presenting oneself in certain ways, and managing social relationships. To complicate matters, all three goals are pursued simultaneously in most conversations – a coordination nightmare in itself. Tasks range from figuring out who will take out the garbage to deciding the fate of nations, and all can be facilitated or impeded by conversation. Conversations in which tasks are accomplished can be joyous (think of productive meetings); conversations in which tasks are impeded can be disappointing (think of having a proposal rejected); and conversations in which no progress is made can be frustrating or boring (think of unproductive meetings).

When people converse, they also risk their selves and their social identities. The self is nearly always bound strongly to emotion (Higgins, 1987), and support of or challenges to self-image and self-esteem occur almost constantly in everyday conversation. When we receive praise we feel proud, when we are blamed we feel guilty, when we are complimented we feel joyous, when we are insulted we feel angry. We apologize to try to forestall or mitigate the anger of others. In conversation, we try to present ourselves in a certain light – as competent, likeable, or powerful (Clark, Pataki, & Carver, 1996; Jones & Pittman, 1982). If other people respond as we wish – if they admire us, like us, or fear us – all is well. But if not, our very selves may be on the line, evoking strong emotions.

When you realize that emotion is grounded in the fate of personal goals, it is easy to see why close relationships command such profound and enduring emotions. Close relationships, by definition, require coordination on many issues of mutual concern over long periods of time (Kelley et al., 1983). Relationships that facilitate or interfere with so many important, long-lasting concerns are capable of evoking powerful emotions and are sources of our greatest delights and distresses. When they go well, they go very well. Friends, family, and other close connections are our greatest source of happiness, and love is a peak experience in life (Argyle, 1987: 14–15, 130). When they go badly, they are horrid. Conflict is dreaded, disruption is traumatic, divorce takes from two to four years to get over, and social isolation can be debilitating or even fatal (Atkins, Kaplan, & Toshima, 1991; Sillars & Weisberg, 1987; Wallerstein & Blakeslee, 1989; Weiss, 1975; Wilmot & Hocker, 1998).

Yet it is important to remember that events are not appraised for emotional meaning just so that we can feel good or bad about them. If emotion stopped at appraisal, emotions would just roll around inside to no real purpose. We appraise events so that we can *do* something about them or at least make an informed choice not to do anything. The active side of emotion is to ready the body, to prioritize action, and to express this state to others.

Physiological Changes

Emotion produces changes in the body that are far too extensive and complicated to consider at length here. For a sampling, there are changes in heart rate, blood pressure, blood flow, respiration, sweating, gastrointestinal and urinary activity, secretion, pupil dilation, trembling, hormonal reactions, brain waves, and muscle tension (Frijda, 1986: 124–175). Such physiological changes have long been considered an important component of emotion, but controversy still rages over just how important it is (Candland 1977: 22–39; Cannon, 1929/ 1984; James, 1884/1984). It is tempting to consider physiological change (especially arousal) *the* defining feature of a true emotion for several reasons. First, it produces a clean distinction between emotions and other related entities like thoughts, moods, and attitudes. Everyone knows that emotion is embodied, so if bodily changes occur, that's emotion. Second, physiological changes provide very reliable, high-quality data. The data are so pure that they can (and sometimes must) be gathered by machines, completely unsoiled by human hands. Third, early influential experiments showed that injections of epinephrine (adrenaline) could be interpreted as anger or euphoria, depending on the circumstances. Arousal produces emotion, so arousal must be the essence of emotion (Schachter & Singer, 1962).

If only it were that simple! First, physiological changes may distinguish emotion from cognition, mood, and attitudes, but they don't distinguish emotion from the effects of exercise, drugs, or sex (Berscheid, 1990; Cannon, 1929/1984; Reisenzein, 1983). Physiology saves us from some quagmires but gets us into others. Second, physiological data turn out to be much less solid than we would hope. Physiological changes may occur in some situations that evoke an emotion, but not others or in situations that evoke different emotions. They may occur in some people but not in others. They can be controlled, at least to some degree (as biofeedback instructors assume). And there are no completely reliable or pure indicators of emotion (Frijda, 1986: 124–175). Third, early arousal-based theories have been criticized on a number of grounds, an obvious one being that emotion is not usually produced by shots of adrenaline in everyday life. If you adopt the process model, you can argue easily that arousal-based theories lop off the part of the emotion process that gives emotional meaning to events in the first place.

It seems then that physiological changes have no special status as indicators of emotion and instead must find their place among other components within emotion theories. Ideally, we would find a distinct physiological profile for each basic emotion that we could use to discriminate among different emotions. Reviews of the evidence show mixed results. Emotions have somewhat distinct profiles, but they are not distinct enough to discriminate neatly, and they are too variable within each emotion to fit the ideal (Frijda, 1986: 161, 164; Lang, 1988: 180–181). At the least, arousing emotions (like anger) should be different physiologically from those that make the body less aroused (like sadness). Unfortunately, volumes of studies on arousal have failed to pin arousal down to a general, diffuse, and unitary physiological arousal. The best that can be said is that the jury is still out, awaiting further data (Lazarus, 1991: 75–78).

A coherent theory of physiological change as part of the emotion process probably also awaits a firmer connection between physiology and emotion. Depending on the theory you consult, physiological changes may precede other components, may feed into action tendencies, or may be largely epiphenomenal. There can be little doubt, however, that physiological responses to emotional stimuli have their own dynamics. For example, the body may become accustomed or habituated to an emotional stimulus and weaken over time, or it may become sensitized and strengthen over time. Physiological responses may take time to come on and time to go away; worse yet, how long they take to go away may depend on factors that change (Frijda, 1986: 141–142).

Physiology in Conversation. Certainly there are many communicative situations in which physiological reactions play major roles – intense speech anxiety, marital quarrels, or episodes of passionate love (Leary & Kowalski, 1995: 128–155; Levenson & Gottman, 1983). Some people argue that emotion occurs only when physiology plays a role, but others argue that this is emotion only in its fullest, most prototypical form. Emotionlike experiences, such as moods and feelings that do not produce dramatic physiological changes, probably occur more often, especially under mundane circumstances such as talking about the events of the day (Levenson, Carstensen, & Gottman, 1994).

Physiological reactions may be an important factor, however, in the more subtle, emotional or emotionlike processes by which people adjust to each other's nonverbal cues indicating involvement. Several theories of communication, including expectancy violation theory (Burgoon & Hale, 1988), discrepancy arousal theory (Cappella & Greene, 1982), and arousal-labeling theory (Patterson, 1983) address physiology from somewhat different perspectives, but for all, arousal is central to explaining approach and avoidance tendencies in moment-to-moment interaction (Cappella, 1981). In one study, for example, when one person in an interaction changed from moderate involvement to either high (e.g., closer distance, more touch, more smiling and nodding) or low (pulling away, avoiding eye contact, or facing away), the other person registered this violation of expectation as a change in physiological arousal (as measured by heart rate and skin temperature) (Le Poire & Burgoon, 1994). Whether people are aware of feeling excited, anxious, or just uneasy is unclear, but they do tend to adjust their behaviors in response to those of the other person.

No one really knows exactly what physiological responses communicate to others. Many changes, such as changes in heart rate or changes in levels of adrenaline, are perceptible only from within. Others, such as changes in blood pressure, are not perceptible at all without special equipment. Neither of these two types of physiological response can be communicated directly to other people (except when lovers come close enough to hear each other's heartbeats or feel cold chills, for example). Other physiological responses, such as pupil dilation or sweaty palms, are too subtle to have widespread effects on social interaction (except in cases such as staring another down or shaking hands). Some physiological reactions, however, are blatantly obvious and may communicate important messages. Blushing, for example, may serve as an "involuntary remedial display," indicating to others that you know you have made a faux pas and feel embarrassed about it (Leary & Meadows, 1991), or it may indicate that you feel ambivalent about the attention you are getting when someone praises or flirts with you (Frijda, 1986: 167–168).

It is very likely, however, that the primary function of physiological change is to prepare for action (communicative or otherwise) and sometimes inaction. Anticipating an important public speech, for instance, gears up the body in ways that can be used for good or for ill. One important mission for teachers of public speaking is to help students guide their physiological arousal toward dynamism rather than debilitation. Conversely, sadness gears down the body in ways that seem to be counterproductive but that may help to conserve and restore resources until priorities can be reassessed and new meanings found in renewed activity (Cochran & Claspell, 1987; Klinger, 1975, cited in Lazarus, 1991). But on the whole, it seems that physiological changes per se are less important than how they prepare us to act.

Action Tendencies, Action, and Expression

Emotion wouldn't be emotion without the urge to act and express (or the urge not to act, in the case of sadness). At best it would be lively cognition, but not anything that truly *moves* us, as the term *e-motion* implies. Because of emotion, we may be inclined to move toward or away from someone, to act or give up, to cry or sing, to help or hide. Action tendencies may exert subtle influences on communicative behavior that are not as overt as the more prototypical expressions of emotion such as facial expressions. For instance, the tendency to move toward or away from others has its communication counterpart in responsiveness (Davis, 1982), immediacy (Andersen, 1985), interpersonal warmth (Andersen & Guerrero, 1998a), communication apprehension (McCroskey, 1982), or shyness (Crozier, 1990). We can see the tendency toward hyper- or hypo-activity in animated or relaxed communicator styles (Norton, 1983). For instance, dynamic stage performers may have a whole cluster of tendencies that include nervous energy, enthusiasm, and extraversion.

Action tendencies are also manifested more concretely in communicative behaviors such as variations in eye gaze (toward or away), interpersonal distance (close or far), voice volume (loud or soft), amount of talk (loquacious or reticent), and any number of others. But such communicative behaviors are multifunctional and thus do not indicate action tendencies (and emotion) unambiguously (Patterson, 1983). Someone could stare at you, move closer, and yell because she is angry or because the party is noisy and she doesn't think you can hear her.

Approach and avoidance behaviors are a normal part of family life, but their meanings are not always straightforward. In one study (Kahlbaugh & Haviland, 1994), normal children aged 7 to 16 showed nonverbal behaviors of approach toward their parents (measured as a combination of smiling, face orientation, head nod, eyebrow flash, touch, symmetry, and body orientation). They differed by age group, however, in avoidance behaviors (measured as a combination of covering face, gaze aversion, self-manipulation, self-inspection, contempt expressions in face and body, disgusted expressions, closed arms, and backward lean). Young adolescents (11–13) showed more avoidance toward their parents than did younger children (7–10), and older adolescents (14–16) showed outright contempt toward their parents, as did their parents toward them (leaning away from each other, crossing their arms across their chests, sneering, and rolling their eyes). As any parent knows, avoidance behaviors can be interpreted in either a positive or a negative light. They can be intended as (and interpreted as) displays of self-assertion in the context of strong attachments or as indicators of stress and conflict.

From a communicative point of view, action tendencies can be known only through actions or expressions. For example, if you experience an emotion, you may know that you have suppressed the urge to yell, but someone observing you can never know this directly. She might be able to pick up subtle cues, like a strain in your voice, but that in itself is an expression. You might tell her that it's all you can do to keep from yelling, but the telling is an expression. You may report her to her boss – an action you think will solve the problem – but the action may be interpreted as an expression of your emotion.

Action tendencies may also be manifested in behavior that might not ordinarily be thought of as emotional. I may go for a walk because I need exercise, but that is not emotional. When I have an urge to walk away after someone said something to me (object) that I interpreted as an insult (appraisal), I felt my body tensing (physiological change) and wanted to get away from him (action tendency), that is emotional. If I get up and walk away during a conversation, it is difficult to say whether that urge is emotional or not; we can interpret it as such only if we have more information. This may be the case for many behaviors considered earlier as manifestations of action tendencies. Nevertheless it is often clear that certain communicative behaviors are expressions of emotion – because they fit the typical profile of how people express anger, sadness, or joy (such as jumping up and down, smiling, and hugging people) or because they occur under conditions that normally produce those emotions (such as winning the lottery).

Whether manifested overtly in expression and action or not, action tendencies are pervasive in social interaction. Seldom are we inclined neither to approach nor to avoid others, neither hyper- nor hypo-activated, neither interested nor uninterested. Someone without action tendencies is someone who is unresponsive to the social environment, and people are seldom unresponsive. On the contrary, they seem to be constantly responding and adapting to one another in a variety of ways.

Regulation

Emotion regulation is not just a matter of stopping action tendencies before you do something stupid, much as you might stop the urge to have a chocolate eclair if you were on a diet. Rather, regulation is an integral part of the entire emotion process and is built into all four other components of the process – object, appraisal, physiology, and action tendencies/expression. We can regulate emotions by dealing with the object (avoiding the car in our path), managing appraisal (plenty of room to spare!), managing our physiological reactions (deep breathing), or managing action tendencies (nothing to be gained by screaming).

More often than not, we regulate emotions unconsciously and automatically, having started regulation early in life when we learn that mothers don't always respond when we cry, nor do fathers always smile when we smile (Bowlby, 1969a, 1969b). We regulate our emotions for ourselves as well as for others when we try to feel better after a disappointment or try to contain our love until our partners reciprocate. We regulate by toning down feelings (such as controlling fear in an emergency when action is required) or by amplifying them (such as throwing a tantrum to get our way). We can make feelings more positive (looking on the bright side) or more negative (finding the worst in people).

Clearly, regulation in its most conscious goal-directed form is rare. Only rarely to do we think to ourselves, "I should not show X that I really like her" or "I should act as if the consequences of this plan really scare me, or the committee may vote for it." But, of course, conscious, goal-directed regulation is just the tip of the regulation iceberg. Subtle, unconscious, habitual regulation of emotion goes on below the surface but probably plays an even bigger role. We regulate emotions in order to manage our own emotional states (staying calm), to advance our goals (studying when we don't feel like it), to influence others' emotions (being cheerful for the kids' sake), to facilitate common goals (making passionate arguments), to maintain social norms (not getting overwrought about an issue), to live within the law (refraining from vengeful murder), and so on. You might say that such regulation is second nature, but perhaps it's not even second; it may be in our very nature as humans not to be at the mercy of our emotions.

Social interaction may also be a vehicle for controlling emotion. One study found that people who respond strongly to stimulation (augmenters) engaged in less arousing (and less social) activities (reading, writing letters, watching TV) compared to people who respond less strongly to stimulation (reducers), who sought out emotional stimulation in more arousing (and more social) activities (team sports, playing cards/board games, going to a party) (Larsen & Zarate, 1991). People who were told by an experimenter that they would receive an electric shock preferred to wait with others, especially others who were also receiving the shock (Schachter, 1959).

Emotional Experience

There is a final aspect of emotion that is not one of the key components of process models or even necessary for an emotion to occur: the subjective experience of emotion. Clearly, *having* an emotion and *feeling* an emotion are not the same thing. For instance, we do not hesitate to say that infants are happy, even though we know nothing about their subjective states. We also do not hesitate to challenge other people's reports of their subjective feelings – "You're more upset than you're willing to admit to yourself." Sometimes we may admit in retrospect that we were anxious or lonely, although we did not realize it at the time. Sometimes others may tell us that we look and act happy, embarrassed, or sad even though we don't really feel that way.

There are many possible reasons for these discrepancies. Your attention may be so riveted on the object of emotion (such as when a child runs in front of your car) that you simply are not aware of how you are appraising the situation, how your body is responding, and how you are deciding what to do. Focusing on yourself is a luxury that must wait until later. Bear in mind, too, that all the processes that make up an emotion are largely unconscious and often are realized in behavior at an unconscious level. An astute observer may see a pattern in your behavior that you don't. For instance, if you always speak in admiring terms of someone, appear really excited whenever you see her, and try to be around her as much as possible, an observer may say you are in love, but you may not have noticed. Or you may have noticed the pattern, but you don't interpret it the same way – it's simply interest in her work. Or you may find the feeling uncomfortable and try to regulate it before it reaches a conscious level. You may also have the subjective experience of feeling an emotion such as love or fear without giving off any signs – visible or hidden. Some people feel fear but act calmly, show no physiological symptoms, and make no attempt to escape or avoid the object of fear. In general, however, discrepancies between subjective feelings and observable states are most likely to occur at intermediate levels of fear rather than when it is very intense or very mild, but whether all the signs of fear converge also depends on how emotion is regulated (Rachman, 1990: 3–11).

Some people also seem to be more tuned in to their own emotions than others (Booth-Butterfield & Booth-Butterfield, 1990, 1994, 1996). Salovey and colleagues (1995), for example, developed the meta-mood scale to measure the extent to which people attend to, understand, and try to regulate their moods. They found that depressed people were more likely to pay attention to their emotions but less likely to feel that they understood them and more likely to believe that one could not repair negative moods (p. 141). Conversely, people who reported being usually very clear about their feelings were more likely to rebound from bad moods (pp. 143–144). Pennebaker and Roberts (1992) also found that women were more likely to rely on appraisals for cues to their emotional states, whereas men were more likely to tune in to physiological cues. This led them to suggest that "Educating women about relevant physiological signals and men about important situational cues may de-escalate emotional conflict and enhance an appreciation of the other's perspective" (p. 209).

On the other hand, when people can sit back and reflect on their experiences of emotion, they reveal elaborate knowledge of what it means to be angry, sad, joyous, or frightened (Shaver et al., 1987). This knowledge helps us understand our own emotions, but perhaps more important, it gives us a basis for imagining (and sometimes accurately understanding) the emotions of other people. For example,

Fitness (1996) found that people had two levels of emotion knowledge – knowledge about emotions for relationships in general and knowledge about specific emotions within their own close relationships. For instance, someone may believe that jealousy is bad for close relationships in general but at the same time express jealous feelings to her own partner because for this couple it results in reassurance and positive outcomes (p. 205).

How does this apply to conversation? First, people seldom have the luxury to sit back and reflect on their emotions during conversations. They have to listen, talk, maybe take notes, maybe worry about whether their partners are bored or whether the plan is going to work. More likely, the phenomenon of having one's attention riveted on the object of emotion at the expense of being aware of the emotion itself is common in conversation, though to varying degrees. Our best conversations feel like *flow* experiences, in which we lose awareness of ourselves and become absorbed in the flow of events (Csikszentmihalyi, 1990). Only later do we realize how enjoyable the experience was. Contrary to the common belief that enjoyment is the pleasurable feeling that we have when indulging ourselves (such as when eating a banana split), in fact, people report that peak experiences are those in which they are deeply *involved*, often in challenging activities with other people. Only later do they appreciate how truly enjoyable the experience was.

We are also unaware of our feelings when the content of conversation is so important (as, for example, with suicide crisis lines) that our own emotions don't deserve attention until later. More likely, however, attention fluctuates among the many different aspects of conversation – the content, the process, the other people involved, our own thoughts, and our own feelings. Our own feelings get attention when they become more important or urgent than other concerns or when we sit back and reflect on them. Salovey (1992) has shown that when affect (either positive or negative) is aroused attention is turned toward the self. How often that happens during everyday conversation is an empirical question that is so far unanswered.

Putting the Process Back Together Again

How do all the pieces of the emotion process come together in the emotional states that are an integral part of everyday interaction? According to the theories reviewed earlier, emotion processes are continuous and ongoing, and often occur below the level of awareness both for the person experiencing the emotion and for anyone observing it. But occasionally these processes produce configurations that we recognize as anger, joy, or sadness. In Frijda's words:

> In emotional responding generally there is no succession of discrete events so much as flow of varying attitudes, acceptances, rejections, abandonments, and reserves; and that flow may be manifest in experience only. Only sometimes – when events are sudden or urgent and dealing with them is difficult, when control fails or is let go of – does the subject settle upon actually achieving, maintaining, or changing a given transaction, or is forced so to settle, or abandons it. Then fullblown, paradigmatic emotional response bursts loose, overtly or inwardly, and the subject has "an" emotion. (1986: 479)

Returning to the weaving metaphor, we might think of emotion processes as the color that is always present in fabric. Intuitively, we think of even the lack of color (black) as a color, just as we think of the lack of emotion as an emotion (one's darkest hour). From time to time, conditions are such that clear, primary colors are evident – the reds, yellows, and blues that we recognize easily. Those are akin to clear, recognizable emotions, especially the basic ones – joy, anger, sadness, and fear – but also shame, grief, love, envy, surprise, and others.[7]

Emotion is not only an integral part of conversation, sometimes producing a certain emotion is the main or only reason for having the conversation at all (Frijda & Mesquita, 1991). We may talk with others just to have fun, to enjoy ourselves and each other. In that case, the main purpose of the conversation itself is to produce good feelings, with the pleasant by-product of an increased sense of social solidarity. Sometimes we have conversations to persuade people to do things – to move them to action, and persuasion often (though not always) involves engaging feelings and emotions such as fear, hope, love, or anger. Other conversations are used to make decisions. These might, in principle, be emotionless, but we know that in practice they can be gut-wrenching experiences that involve the whole range of emotions. Sometimes we have conversations to work out problems, problems that must be dealt with because someone is angry or unhappy. Sometimes we have conversations to coordinate tasks; how emotional they

---

[7] These emotions are on the list of almost everyone who believes in basic emotions. For an interesting extended discussion, see Stein and Oatley (1992).

are depends on the task and what it means to both people involved. Negotiating who takes out the garbage can be either a boring ritual or a fight to the death (of the relationship) over power. Sometimes we have conversations just to understand one another, especially on an emotional level.

Valuing Emotion in Conversation

How important the role of emotion is in conversation depends in part on how big a role we *want* it to play and think it *should* play. It can be important in the dual senses of prevalent and valuable or unimportant in the senses of rare and worthless. Different speech communities recognize and value emotion to varying degrees, in different ways, and in different situations. For example, the emotional atmosphere of interactions among men in the working-class Chicago "Teamsterville" community studied by Philipsen (1975) seems to be emotionally stoic, where strong feelings are considered weak and perhaps even dishonorable. Action is more important. At the other extreme are the highly dramatic (and highly orchestrated) emotional performances on TV talk shows, where openness is the norm and reserve is considered silly, selfish, and certainly uninteresting. The techno-strategic discourse of defense intellectuals functions to keep feelings out of military decisions (Cohn, 1987), but the Nukulaelae islanders of Polynesia make other people's emotions the focus of their gossip (Besnier, 1995c).

A widely held belief is that women's talk is more emotion-laden than men's, and after reviewing the literature on gender differences in emotion, Manstead (1992: 380) concurs. Indeed, "with the exception of situations likely to provoke aggression, males tend to be less expressive and more physiologically responsive than females," but not by much. That is, women may be more outwardly emotional than men (except for anger) and men may have more internal bodily reactions, but the differences are not great. Norms for appropriate emotions also differ from one situation to the next. People strongly agree, for example, that when a bouncer throws you out of a bar, you should feel embarrassed; when you sing to an infant, you should feel happy; and when you appeal to a state trooper, you should feel nervous (Heise & Calhan, 1995) – regardless of whether you are male or female.

What you *should* feel, however, does not necessarily correspond with what you *do* feel. In American middle-class culture in general, the most acceptable and most common emotional stance is a mild but positive "impersonal, but friendly" tone (Stearns, 1994). Intense emotions should be neither seen nor heard, and are considered infantile and embarrassing. It is best to be "cool." In addition, "the positive emotions alone are regarded as being useful; the negative emotions are cast as dangerous and destructive, emotions to be avoided" (Sommers, 1984b: 214). Specifically, American students prefer to hide anger, jealousy, fear, and guilt, and even positive emotions require regulation if they are too intense (euphoria, surprise) (Sommers, 1984a). To prepare to interact with a stranger, students reported adjusting their own mood toward the norm of neutrality (Erber, Wegner, & Therriault, 1996).

Another reason to keep strong emotion out of conversation is the belief that emotion is not just different from reason but antithetical to it – positively irrational (Parrott, 1995). Solomon (1993: 3) observes that since the time of Socrates and Plato, emotion has been seen as a threat to reason. "One of the most enduring metaphors of reason and emotion has been the metaphor of master and slave, with the wisdom of reason firmly in control and the dangerous impulses of emotion safely suppressed, channeled, or (ideally) in harmony with reason." Nonemotional, eminently reasonable talk can also be used to conceal one's true emotional interests. If you desire passionately to attack Iraq, you might better accomplish your goal by keeping a low emotional profile and arguing that it is the only reasonable thing to do (N. H. Frijda, personal communication, February 17, 1998).

Because emotion is presumed to be irrational, many scholars feel compelled to defend emotion. Oatley (1992: 130–177), for example, makes the point that emotion may have its problems, but reason isn't perfect either. Neither emotion nor reason is a guaranteed guide to perfect action. Parkinson (1995: 292) argues that emotion works for us when "the local or general moral or rational order breaks down or simply loses relevance" and social expectations must be realigned. When following the rules violates your rights, you may get angry as your only recourse. In a book devoted to the issue, de Sousa (1987: 172), argues that emotion is certainly *not* antithetical to reason; on the contrary, emotion is absolutely essential to reason. Emotions set the agenda, "spare us the paralysis" of not knowing what is important, and tip the balance between competing motivations. Recent developments in neurology (Damasio, 1994; Vogel, 1997) suggest that de

Sousa is right. In Kosslyn's words (cited in Vogel, 1997: 1269), "emotion apparently is not something that necessarily clouds reasoning, but rather seems to provide an essential foundation for at least some kinds of reasoning."

Parrott (1995: 82) argues that "academic discourse emphasizes emotion as adaptive, but in everyday discourse it is seen as dysfunctional." Certainly academics defend emotion as valuable, but often in a very intellectualized and rarely impassioned voice. That is the academic way because, like all professionals, "we associate authority in this society with an unemotional persona" (Smith & Kleinman, 1989: 56). Emotion might creep into talk, to be sure, but to keep discourse rational, we should keep feelings out. Feelings might be appropriate in bedrooms but not in boardrooms. Why, then, would we ever value emotion as a part of everyday interaction?

Here is why. Emotion has value "as a way of orienting us toward things that matter rather than things that simply make sense,'" to quote Lutz (1988b: 5). Remember the Cadbury egg? It didn't make sense, but it did matter. If we purge conversation of emotion, we will not know what concerns other people deeply and what is likely to move them to action. We will not know how the topic engages their subconscious, their bodies, their lived experience (Lazarus, 1991: 152–159). If we try to understand people's thoughts without trying to understand their feelings, we will only scratch the surface of meaning.

A lot of things make sense, but fewer of them really matter. In an age of information overload, we need emotion to help us orient to what is important and to set priorities. "By making the emotional claim that something matters, you draw other people's attention to your concern" (Parkinson, 1995: 292). Consider the difference between bland euphemisms and their emotion-laden counterparts. Even though they both make sense, "collateral damage" doesn't matter much; "slaughter of civilians" does. "Countervalue attacks" need not concern us, but "incinerating cities" must (Cohn, 1987: 691). Regardless of whether you think emotion is essential to social interaction or interferes with smooth social relations, it is important to learn how to communicate emotion effectively. That is the topic to which we turn next.

2. How and Why Is Emotion Communicated?

Sometimes a scream is better than a thesis.

Ralph Waldo Emerson

At first glance, communicating emotion seems easy. Foreigners, small children, and dogs seem to have no trouble picking up on fear or sadness (Plutchik, 1987; Thompson, 1987). Sometimes it takes only a quick look, a few words, or a subtle quality of the voice. But not all emotions are that simple or easy to communicate. How do you convey the emotions of the experience of childbirth or of being a prisoner of war? Simple words, tears, or screams fail. Even poetry does not quite seem to capture it. Even someone who has been through the same experience cannot fully understand yours. So emotion appears to be both easily expressed and inexpressible.

When you express your anger, I know what anger is, you know what anger is, and we communicate in ways that are standardized enough for me to know that you're expressing anger and not, for example, fear. Yet at the same time, your anger draws on your lifetime of experience, on your concerns, and on your goals, in ways that I cannot understand fully because I am not you. Thus the paradox. Notice that in setting up the paradox, I have introduced two theoretical perspectives on communication. The first is what we will call here *communication as exchanging messages*, and the second is *communication as coordinating meaning*.

Communication as Exchanging Messages

"If we could only communicate" is often heard, as if communication itself could fix all manner of problems. Or "We have a breakdown in communication," as if a telephone line were down and all that is needed is for the line to be spliced back together again. This sort of everyday talk reflects a message exchange perspective on communication, or, put more crudely, a *boxcar* theory (Shannon & Weaver, 1949). According to this type of theory, information is loaded into a boxcar (encoded), sent on its way on some track (channel), and unloaded at the other end (decoded). If someone takes the trouble to send a message, things go fine so long as the track remains undamaged and free of obstructions (noise). All the receiver has to do is to unload the right boxcar, unless, of course, he or she is distracted and "doesn't pick up on it" or he "just doesn't get it." In any case, the receiver can send back another boxcar, keeping the exchange going indefinitely.

This metaphor captures many of our intuitions about communication. At any moment, one person's efforts are focused on sending messages, while the other person's efforts are focused on receiving them. Some messages "get through" well, and others get "derailed" because the room is too noisy or because there is some problem with "getting the message." The whole process of sending messages back and forth takes time, and generally nothing much will happen unless one person takes the trouble to "launch" a discussion. And the whole process of sending and receiving messages is pretty simple.

But there are also some serious limitations to the metaphor. It assumes that only one boxcar can go at a time or there will be some sort of collision, and this is only partly true. People can talk at the same time and still understand each other, up to a point. The boxcar metaphor assumes that the cargo either arrives intact, as sent, or it doesn't (it might leak, but it doesn't get transformed or distorted on the way), and we know that this is completely false. Messages are commonly interpreted in ways that make sense to the listener, often leading to distortions (Coupland, Giles, & Wiemann, 1991), as is illustrated by the well-known "rumor" exercise. Start a rumor at one end of a crowded room and see how it turns out by the time it gets to the other end. Usually the original message is barely recognizable. The boxcar metaphor also assumes that information comes in bits piled into a heap (perhaps like coal), and clearly it does not; messages are highly organized (van Dijk & Kintsch, 1983). The boxcar metaphor assumes that once a message is sent, the sender no longer has it, which is not so. You remember what you just told me. The boxcar metaphor assumes that loading and unloading messages is relatively unskilled labor, and it isn't (Parks, 1994; Spitzberg & Cupach, 1984). Yet, despite its many limitations, the boxcar metaphor guides much of our thinking and plays a major role in how we understand communication (both in everyday life and in research). But it has been greatly elaborated and other theories have been developed to compensate for its weakness. These theories we might call *theories of communication as coordinating meaning*.

Communication as Weaving Meaning

Instead of a boxcar, we might appeal to the metaphor for communication that was introduced earlier – weaving a fabric together. Communicating with one another is like weaving the fabric of social life together, using a wide range and varying amounts of color (emotion). Weaving a rich and colorful fabric is much more creative and demanding than sending and receiving boxcars. Two weavers can coordinate to varying degrees; they can do relatively separate patterns or joint patterns, although a certain amount of coordination is required to make anything at all. We have all experienced the double-monologue type of conversation, but more commonly we have true dialogue. The pattern to be woven may be decided in advance (perhaps derived from models from the weavers' culture), or it may develop as the weavers go along, using whatever materials and dyes are available. Some conversations are scripted, and others are impromptu (ceremonies and bull sessions). Fabrics can range from extremely simple to very intricate designs (simple or complex conversations). Different fabrics are made for different purposes – from dishcloths to elaborate costumes (conversations to buy groceries and conversations to reunite with a long-lost friend). No fabric is perfect, but each shows the unique skills, interests, and talents of its makers. Of course, it takes a lifetime to develop the skills to weave well, and some exceptionally talented people can create masterpieces. But even if you never create a masterpiece, the act of weaving is itself enjoyable, gratifying, and compelling.

Obviously, this is a quite different view of communication from that of the boxcar. With the boxcar, messages either arrive intact or they don't; most often they do unless there is some technical interference. With weaving, "intact" doesn't really make sense. There can be problems that make the communication process "unravel," but usually it holds together. Ordinarily, messages are judged as "more or less" – more or less powerful, more or less coordinated, more or less appropriate to their purpose, more or less skillfully produced. More-over, we produce messages for many different purposes. For some purposes, any old message will do well enough ("Pass the salt"), but for others, great care is taken to make it just right (the State of the Union Address). Clearly, some people have more talent and better-developed communicative skills than others, but all draw on the re-sources of their culture. These include the language, standard mes-sages patterns (like interviews or informative speeches), routines for coordinating (like turn-taking procedures), and other resources too numerous to mention.

Consider communication during conflict as a case in point. Accord-ing to the boxcar metaphor, I should be able to get the message across that I want to see *Schindler's List*, and you can send back a message that you want to see *The Wizard of Oz*. *Schindler's List* is new, we've talked about seeing it, and I don't want to miss it, so I get angry when you suggest something else. You tell me, however, that you are al-ready sad and you don't want to go to a depressing movie tonight. So my anger boxcar is colliding with your sadness boxcar and there is a tendency for one to give way to the other, depending on who has stronger feelings, arguments, or power to intimidate.

Alternatively, I may be able to get the basic message across that I want to see *Schindler's List*, but communicating the subtleties of my feelings is quite another matter. I may have to weave a story about how much I love really good films and how much they lose on video. I need to explain how moved my friends were when they came back after seeing it. Then, again, you will have to explain that you are sad because your friend just moved away, and my movie is too relevant to be an escape, and you are afraid that you will be too upset to talk to your friend if you see *Schindler's List* tonight. Then we might decide that both of our feelings are powerful and legitimate, so that I should go to the movie and you should not. If we both are skillful in describ-ing our feelings and listening to each other, and if there is a good solution available, it all works well. But if I cannot explain why I am so angry, if my feelings make no sense to you even when I do explain them, if I want my way at all costs, or if the decision is about a more complex and important matter, communication can be much more difficult. For example, if your friend has to decide whether to stay in a war-torn country (remaining loyal to her homeland) or leave (to get the education she cannot get there), it is truly a matter of life and death. The processes of explaining, understanding, or empathizing with feelings such as love of country, guilt about leaving, hope for the future, and fear of never seeing loved ones again do not fit so well with the boxcar theory. Communication is a complex tapestry based on themes woven from each person's life.

Communicating Emotion and Communicating Emotionally

Normally, we think first of communicating *emotion* – letting another person know that we are angry, sad, or happy. The emotion itself is the substance or topic of the message, like weaving color for its own sake. In addition, we communicate *emotionally*. In this case, the emotion itself may not be the substance of the message, but rather a property of the message, like using color to create a pattern. We could talk about nuclear war fearfully or about a baby's first step joyfully. Of course, the emotional substance and the emotional tone of a message need not coincide. A person may say she is *not* angry using a very angry tone of voice or speak of her great sadness in a very bland, apathetic way.

What difference does it make in everyday life if we concentrate on communicating emotion or communicating emotionally? During a conflict, for instance, messages about emotions in themselves might be the substance of the conflict (e.g., How dare you laugh when I embarrass myself!). In that case, it is important to send and receive the emotion message accurately – to distinguish joy from embarrassment. But the emotion may not be the main source of conflict; it may be about something else that produces the feelings. Then it is important to get both messages across. If you are lonely because you are being ignored, it is important to communicate not only that you are lonely but also that you want attention. On the receiving end, the other person needs to understand the loneliness, the request for attention, and how they go together. The problem is not neglect + loneliness; they are inseparable. You would not be lonely if it weren't for the neglect, and the neglect would not be a problem if you weren't lonely. If either the emotion or the cause of the emotion becomes the focus by itself, the complete message is not getting through.

Tools of the Trade: Cues to Emotion

What resources are available to weave an emotional message? Most of the research in this area is organized by types of cues or channels (e.g., Lewis & Haviland, 1993), which might be likened to different types of thread that are available to make the pattern that we want (e.g., silk, cotton, linen, or wood fibers). *Cues* to emotion refer to the specific observable behaviors (verbal or nonverbal) that communicate people's emotions to others. Smiles, yells, pounding fists, harsh words, tears, and wide eyes are examples of cues. *Channels* refer to the sensory modes through which cues are communicated, such as the visual or auditory channels. In the review that follows, cues are organized into the following categories: facial cues, vocal cues (which include properties of the voice, excluding speech), gestures and body movement, physiological cues (which include internal physical changes), action cues, and verbal cues (which include words only) (following Planalp, DeFrancisco, & Rutherford, 1996: Table 1). Although people use several cues in combination to judge emotions, researchers begin by isolating types of cues in order to study each in greater depth.

Facial Cues

We see emotion in each other's faces. If you run into an old friend at the airport unexpectedly, your eyes widen, your mouth drops open in surprise, and you smile with joy. Then you may become angry because she did not call you before coming, and you show your anger with brows pulled forward, eyes squinting, and lips pressed together. Scholars knew how important facial expressions are to emotion even before Darwin described them (Bell, 1844, cited in Darwin, 1872/ 1965). There is more research on facial cues to emotion than on any other type, and facial expression is clearly one of the most important ways of conveying emotion (Camras, Holland, & Patterson, 1993; Ekman, 1993).

Most of the research has centered on the distinctive facial configurations associated with discrete emotions like anger, sadness, fear, surprise, joy, and disgust. Some research has given us descriptions so detailed that specific muscle changes can be isolated. The eyes are widened by surprise and narrowed by anger; the nose puckers with disgust; the mouth turns up with joy, down with sadness, and tenses with anger. Eye gaze can be riveted in anger or avoided in shame. Scholars debate, however, whether people express coherent facial patterns for distinct emotions (e.g., lowered brows, staring eyes, and raised upper lip for anger) or whether they give only some of the standard cues (e.g., lowered brow only) and observers use these to fill in the full emotional pattern (Carroll & Russell, 1997).

When people see photos of actors posing the typical facial expressions for each emotion, they are able to distinguish one emotion from another at levels better than chance (Gosselin, Kirouac, & Doré, 1995). The evidence is less clear, however, for spontaneous, unposed facial expressions of emotion than it is for posed expressions (Motley & Camden, 1988). It is also easier to distinguish positive emotions (joy or happiness) from negative emotions (sadness, anger, fear, disgust) than it is to distinguish the negative emotions from each other.[1]

Vocal Cues

The voice may not be as well known as the face as a means of communicating emotion, but it is probably equally important (Banse & Scherer, 1996; Frick, 1985; Kappas, Hess, & Scherer, 1991; Pittam & Scherer, 1993; Scherer, 1986). We hear people's emotions in how loudly they talk, how high or low their voices are, whether their voices tremble, how fast they talk, whether they sigh or laugh, whether they talk at all, and, if so, for how long. People laugh when they are happy, scream when they are angry, wail or fall silent when they are sad (Bowers, Metts, & Duncanson, 1985; Planalp et al., 1996; Shaver et al., 1987; Wallbott & Scherer, 1988: 45–47). Whining voices rise and mourning voices fall in intonation. It is not known whether such changes in the voice are biologically innate features of emotional expression, messages sent intentionally, or simple by-products of other processes (such as not wanting to be heard when ashamed or being aroused when angry). It seems likely that all may hold true to some degree (Frick, 1985: 425–426; Pittam & Scherer, 1993: 194).

People can recognize emotion in each other's voices much better than you would expect by chance, with anger, sadness, and boredom most recognizable, followed by joy and fear, and with disgust and shame barely recognizable (Banse & Scherer, 1996; Pittam & Scherer, 1993: 189–190). Vocal expression is based on three basic dimensions – loudness, pitch, and time – which can be measured in people's voices or simulated electronically to determine how they are associated with anger, fear, sadness, and other emotions. Some patterns are apparent

---

[1] Motley and Camden found that judges could discriminate among posed facial expressions of six emotions with 81% accuracy but among spontaneous expressions with only 25% accuracy, a result not significantly different from chance except for happiness. Similar results were found by Wagner, MacDonald, and Manstead (1986) and are reviewed in detail in Russell (1994).

(such as high pitch preceding crying), but distinct vocal profiles corresponding to distinct emotions have not yet been found. Instead, the same vocal properties (higher pitch, loudness, and higher speed) tend to be associated with arousing emotions such as fear, anger, or joy and their opposites (lower pitch, quietness, and lower speed) with arousal-dampening emotions such as sadness (Pittam & Scherer, 1993). We know that the voice also carries information about whether emotions are positive and negative because, based on vocal cues alone, pride is more likely to be confused with elation, happiness, and interest than it is with the negative emotions (Banse & Scherer, 1996: 632).

Physiological Cues

Thanks to an early, very influential study by Schachter and Singer (1962), to many people emotion means physiological arousal. In a classic experiment, these investigators injected people with adrenalin and found that those who were put in a room with an angry companion interpreted their bodily sensations as anger, and those who were in a room with an elated companion interpreted the same feelings as euphoria (provided that their feelings were not attributed to the drug itself). More recent analyses challenge physiological changes as the sine qua non of emotion (Frijda, 1986; Reisenzein, 1983), but emotions clearly do produce physiological changes at least some of the time, some of which are perceptible to others and may serve as cues to emotions.

By *physiological cues* I mean manifestations of physiological reactions that are largely *uncontrollable* at the time they occur. For instance, people sweat, get tears in their eyes, urinate frequently, vomit, blush, breathe fast, and get the chills. While these physiological responses are almost certainly not primarily communicative, some (such as raised skin temperature or fast breathing) may be noticeable to people with whom we are physically close (especially if touching). Other cues, such as blushing or sweating, are all too apparent to everyone, especially when you want desperately to control or hide them. On the whole, however, even the person experiencing the emotion may be barely aware of physiological changes, and observers probably notice very few physiological cues (Planalp et al., 1996).

Gestures and Body Movements

Emotions are also embodied. People scratch their heads, clench their fists, shake, gesture wildly, hug themselves, pace the floor, lean forward, fidget in their seats, walk heavily, jump up and down, slump, or freeze in their tracks. Despite all the ways that we know people communicate emotion through their bodies, there is much less research on body movement than on facial or vocal cues. We know that people can recognize happy dances when all they can see are points of light placed at the dancers' main joints (Brownlow, Dixon, Egbert, & Radcliffe, 1997), and we know that people can recognize sadness, anger, happiness, and, to a lesser extent, pride from walks (arm swing, stride length, heavyfootedness, and walking speed; Montepare, Goldstein, & Clausen, 1987). We know that depressed people tend to gesture less and hold their heads down more than nondepressed people (Segrin, 1998: 226). Still, body movement is by far the most neglected type of cue. This is surprising considering that motion is an integral part of emotion, both linguistically and conceptually. The term *emotion* comes from the Latin "to move out," suggesting that emotions are manifested in bodily movement or action.

Action Cues

People report that when they are emotional, they may hide, hang up the phone, go running, fix dinner, throw things, bang things around, slam doors, kick things, bring gifts, sleep, eat, smoke, and drink. Their body movements are also directed toward, away from, or against others. People hug, kiss, caress, sit close to, squeeze, tickle, hit, kick, and slap each other. Actions, like gestures and body movements, have not received much research attention, except as ways of coping with emotional problems. Perhaps this is because actions are purposeful and based on choice rather than being spontaneous expressions of emotion.[2] The effects of emotion on choices of action is an interesting topic of research in its own right. For example, extremely arousing emotions may limit choice by making people revert to habitual behaviors that were reinforced in the past, including violence (Zillman, 1990: 200; 1993: 380).

Verbal Cues

Despite the common wisdom that nonverbal communication is the prime medium for emotion and despite the dominance of nonverbal

---

[2] Action is distinguished here from body movement by being goal-directed, (unlike adaptors, for example, that are not), but the distinction between goal-free and goal-directed movement is difficult to maintain, as is discussed in Chapter 3.

channels for communicating emotion in the research literature, the verbal expression of emotion is also very important. It is true that we seldom know what other people are feeling because they do not tell us in so many words. Coming right out and saying, "I'm angry" or "I'm feeling depressed today" is rare (Shimanoff, 1985, 1987). On the other hand, indirect verbal cues to emotion are common, roughly as common as facial and body cues (Planalp et al., 1996). Often we know what people are feeling because they say, "That son of a bitch!" "He screwed me over," "I want to kill him," "Let me tell you what happened," and so on. More subtle verbal indicators of emotion are word choice, language intensity, verbal immediacy, and restricted vocabulary (Bowers et al., 1985). The possibilities for verbal communication are endless, so it is virtually impossible to describe them comprehensively or to come up with estimates of how accurately verbal cues are interpreted.

No Cues at All

Decades of debate over whether one "cannot not communicate" have sensitized researchers to the possibility that the absence of emotional expression may be interpreted as meaningful if an expression is expected (Watzlawick et al., 1967; for recent versions, see debates in *Western Journal of Speech Communication, 54,* 1990, and *Communication Studies, 42,* 1991). Observers would be amazed to watch you eat imitation dog feces made of chocolate without showing disgust or parachute out of a plane for the first time without showing fear. But lack of expression does not necessarily mean lack of emotion or even admirable control. Victims of disasters or torture may have very bland facial expressions, which an astute observer will interpret as feeling overwhelmed rather than unmoved (Frijda & Tcherkassof, 1997).

Varieties of Cues

What is most striking about this research is the large number and variety of cues that express emotion. Why so many? There are several possible answers. First and most obviously, since emotion engages the whole person – body and mind – it makes sense that many different body movements and expressions of thoughts would be affected. This view implies that expressions of emotion are merely the varied external manifestations of what is largely an internal process.

A second possibility is that different cues communicate different information. To come back to the weaving metaphor, we might say that cotton threads, for example, are more amenable to certain colors than are silk threads. We could speculate that your voice alerts me to the fact that that you are feeling something, perhaps something strong and bad. Your face, then, may tell me that you are feeling anger. Your words may provide information about how you are thinking about the situation. Your body movements, posture, and actions may let me know how you are inclined to act. I probably don't need all these cues, and I certainly am not aware of piecing together all this information, but if I do use them all, I can have a very powerful, subtle, and rich image of your feelings.

A third view is that emotion expression serves a further purpose – to alert others to a person's emotional state so that they can choose to do something about it. If you are angry, I need to know it so that I can stop irritating you. In that case, different channels provide communicative flexibility. In weaving, if silk thread is not available, it is nice to be able to turn to nylon. For instance, before infants develop any verbal capabilities at all, they can turn toward or away from people, smile and frown, and, of course, cry. If the person they need is far away, they can scream. Adults can talk about their emotions (in great depth if necessary), but in an emergency, a clear verbal statement will not do – a loud cry for help is needed. If you are talking face-to-face with someone, you can smile and look into her eyes, but if she is turned away doing something else, you can use touch. If you are talking on the phone and can't touch, you may yell and slam down the phone. In any case, you can easily adapt to almost any circumstances.

Cue and Channel Combinations

After reading the research literature, you might get the impression that people communicate emotion through single cues and channels or, at best, by simple combinations of cues. We study amputated heads, decapitated bodies, voices without words, and words without voices. Almost all cues are studied outside the context in which the actual emotion occurs. This is not what researchers intend, but the complexities involved in understanding even a single cue (such as the voice) make the task of understanding how cues fit together seem daunting and perhaps even premature. Still, it is quite apparent that people do not send and interpret cues separately, and some researchers have lamented how little we know about how the various cues work together (Ekman, 1982: 11–126; Gallois & Callan, 1986; Pittam & Scherer, 1993: 195).

The problem is that nearly every study that tries to determine how cues go together comes up with the same answer – it depends. And it depends on almost everything it could possibly depend on.[3] Because combining cues to emotion is so complicated, many researchers let people do it on the grounds that humans seem to be better than computers (albeit human-programmed computers) at judging emotion (Gottman, 1993). Drawing again on the weaving metaphor, messages may be woven together from different types of yarn into a pattern that is even more rich and complex than it would be if made from a single type. What overall color (emotion) comes through depends on which threads stand out, blend together, present a consistent tone, or clash with one another in intriguing ways. The complexity of cues may be interpreted for what it is – a complex message.

Inconsistent cues (such as smiling while rejecting a kiss, for example) may reflect truly mixed feelings. In fact, this is very likely because mixed feelings are found frequently in social interaction (Oatley & Duncan, 1992: 264; Omdahl, 1995: 158; Planalp, 1998: 42). Even if their feelings are not mixed, people may want to equivocate in the interests of "strategic ambiguity" (Bavelas, Black, Chovil, & Mullett, 1990). For example, a wife might say, "Did you feed the cat?", with a negative tone implying that her husband probably forgot, to which he replies, "Yes I did," with a negative tone implying that she doesn't trust him (Noller, 1984: 146). The content is neutral but the tone is negative, making it possible for either or both people to engage the issue of distrust or let it go. If accused of mistrust, the wife can always say, "I never said I didn't trust you," which, of course, is technically correct. She is using ambiguity to communicate a subtle and indirect message for which she cannot be held completely accountable, as her husband is as well when he responds. Buttny (1993: 101) notes that nonverbal

---

[3] For some examples, there are contextual information (Carrera-Levillain & Fernandez-Dols, 1994; Carroll & Russell, 1996), gender, ethnicity, individual attributes of whoever is sending and whoever is receiving the message (Gallois & Callan, 1986), type of cue, channel, type or valence of emotion being communicated, what emotional situation is being communicated, whether deception is suspected, whether cues are consistent or discrepant with each other, and the informativeness of contextual information (Ekman, Friesen, O'Sullivan, & Scherer, 1980; Ekman & Oster, 1982: 167–169; Noller, 1984: 140; Wallbott, 1988a, 1988b).

cues are especially likely "to convey messages which would be too threatening to say verbally, such as implied meanings involving challenge, deference, dominance, and the like." In addition, mixed cues can be used to communicate the message "I don't like your behavior, but I do like you" (Noller, 1984: 136), or presumably, vice versa. The beauty of expressions of emotion, whether verbal or nonverbal, is that they have the power to raise important issues while their implications remain ambiguous and appropriate reactions remain flexible (White, 1990: 51).

Expressions Change Over Time

There is another sense in which the weaving metaphor captures how emotion is communicated better than the boxcar metaphor does. Cues are seldom all rounded up and sent simultaneously on the boxcar to the receiver. Emotion sometimes seems to come out of nowhere, to hit you with full force, then to be over as quickly as it came (what Scherer, 1994, calls "affect bursts"). It feels like a freight train of emotion hitting you (or perhaps sweeping you off your feet, in the positive version).

More common, however, is emotion that develops slowly over time and is expressed as it unfolds more gradually. One reason emotions unfold is that appraisals of the situation unfold, resulting in changing expressions (Scherer, 1992b: 156). The face might first express recognition that something unusual has happened ("I thought you wanted to go to that party!"), then unpleasantness ("We'll miss a lot of fun"), then a discrepancy with your goals ("I want to go"), then a sense of control or lack thereof ("I want to get you to go"). Observers are sensitive to subtle changes in facial expression (Edwards, 1998), and other types of cues to emotion are inherently dynamic and become meaningful only as they change – vocal cues, body movements, and talk.

Emotions also change in response to events that are themselves unfolding over time. As one respondent in a study wrote: "My roommate just got the mail and received two letters. She was visibly happy about one because she smiled and opened it quickly. The return address was her sister who just had a baby so she was eager for news about her nephew. She read the letter quickly and read some parts aloud. There were pictures and she showed them to us and her tone of voice was bubbly and excited" (Planalp et al., 1996: Case #24). As the episode unfolds from getting the letter, to opening it, to reading it and looking at the pictures, the woman's emotional expression unfolds in response.

Expressions change, too, because social expectations change. Fernandez-Dols and Ruiz-Belda (1995) watched the facial expressions of 22 Olympic gold medalists' during an awards ceremony. Even though they reported extreme happiness (at least 9 on a 10-point scale), only 4 smiled when waiting behind the podium, all 22 smiled while standing on the podium interacting with authorities and the public, and none smiled when looking at the flags and listening to the national anthems. You can express whatever you want backstage, but you have to smile when getting an award, and you have to be solemn when national pride is evoked.

Expressiveness

Communicating emotion is also complicated by the fact that all people are not equally expressive (Gross & John, 1997; Kring, Smith, & Neale, 1994). Tune in to any large group of people interacting, especially a diverse one, and you may see a wide range of emotional expressiveness. Some people will express anger by yelling, using profanity, gesturing wildly, and using intense language. Others will speak quietly in a controlled tone, express their concerns in neutral language, and walk away calmly. It is easy to jump to the conclusion that the people who are more expressive are also angrier about the issue, but this may not be so. Some people simply express emotion more intensely and others more subtly. It is difficult to say who is angrier.

A person's level of emotional expressiveness is guided by rules found in culture, in class, in gender roles, in family norms, in temperamental differences, and perhaps in other factors not yet studied (Halberstadt, 1991; Manstead, 1991). As we find ourselves in a rich cultural, class, and gender mix in the community and workplace, there is danger in assuming that all people express emotion in a similar manner. Highly expressive families tend to make their emotional messages loud and clear (like using an emotional megaphone), whereas less expressive families are sensitively tuned to subtle emotional messages (like having their emotional hearing aids turned up) (Halberstadt, 1986).

Emotional messages, then, come through accurately so long as highly expressive people talk with each other and inexpressive people talk with each other. But when inexpressive people try to communicate with highly expressive people, problems may occur. An inexpressive person listening to a highly expressive person may be compared to someone with her hearing aid turned up listening to someone talking with a megaphone; the emotional message could easily be overwhelming. By contrast, a highly expressive person listening to an inexpressive person may be compared to someone with his hearing aid turned down listening to someone whispering; it would be easy to miss any emotional message.

Indeed, highly expressive people may judge less expressive people as cold, unfeeling, and uncaring, whereas less expressive people may judge the highly expressive as volatile, emotionally uncontrolled, even crazy (Tannen, 1984). For example, the emotional expressions of African Americans are intense, dynamic, and demonstrative, which European Americans often judge as impolite, unrestrained or insensitive. Conversely, European Americans' expressions are more modest and emotionally restrained, which African Americans judge as lacking passion or as insincere (Kochman (1981: 106).

Commentary on the death in 1997 of Diana Spencer, former Princess of Wales, revealed some harsh judgments about the contrasting expressive styles of the Spencers and Diana's former in-laws, the Windsors. The inexpressive Windsors, particularly Prince Charles and Queen Elizabeth, were accused of being cold and uncaring. In contrast, after the highly emotional eulogy that Diana's brother gave at her funeral, he was accused of shamelessly exposing his feelings and violating public decorum.

Members of the African American church studied by Nelson (1996) took pride in being a "lively" congregation and labeled other churches that did not exhibit the same emotional fervor as "dead." As one member of the congregation said, "Once you taste [the goodness of the Lord], you cannot go sit in no dead, dry, cold church." The Hutterites, one of the oldest communal societies in the Western world, are known for their low levels of defection, but recently larger numbers have left for religious reasons – in order to embrace a personal rather than a communal relationship with God. The researcher who studied them writes:

> My informants who left the colonies for religious reasons view emotions as a very positive experience, as pure and natural. . . . Expressing emotion is an important part of their new religious experience. They criticize the colonies and the leaders for being unfeeling, rational, and unspiritual. Conversely, colony people say that the religious converts are out

of control. They have allowed themselves to be overwhelmed with emotion, have become irrational, and cannot make proper decisions. (Hartse, 1994:76)

Sillars and Weisberg (1987) examined some of the implications of expressiveness for managing interpersonal conflict in different ethnic and social class groups. For example, "the preferred Jewish communication style is sometimes taken for verbal aggression by non-Jewish family therapists," whereas "Native American and African American males may regard deep personal feelings as too personal to express openly" (pp. 158–159). The stereotype that southerners (living in warmer climates) are more expressive than northerners (living in colder climates) is widely held in the Northern Hemisphere (especially in the Old World). Those differences are real, as indicated by people's self-reports of their own expressiveness, but they are minuscule (Pennebaker, Rimé, & Blankenship, 1996). Besides, people who live in the Southern Hemisphere do not hold the same stereotype – in this case, that people from the warmer northerly regions are more expressive than those who live in the cooler southerly regions.

Varieties of Emotional Connection

If communication were all or none – either you get it or you don't – measuring how easy or difficult it is to communicate emotion would be no problem. We could easily compute a measure of how often people get it – 20% of the time, 50% of the time, or 90% of the time. If they get through most of the time, communication is easy; if not, communication is difficult. That is how we would think of emotional communication from the boxcar or message exchange perspective, but it does not represent the nuances and subtleties of weaving emotional meaning.

In everyday life, we seldom talk about "getting" another person's emotions, we talk about understanding them. We talk about feeling about, for, and with another person. Like communication itself, connecting emotionally with another person occurs by degrees. Some people (especially children) manage to connect with other people's feelings in only the simplest ways, and sometimes have difficulties in their social lives as a result. Most people (especially adults) manage to connect with other people's feelings as well as is necessary to get along from day to day, though they may feel challenged when they have to deal with others' grief, depression, or anger. A talented and skilled few are able to connect with others in ways that are more subtle, insightful, and creative than those we normally witness in everyday life.

Some complex connections presume and build upon more basic connections, though the progression is not neat. For example, we start with the basic skill of noticing that another person is experiencing an emotion. Without noticing an emotion, you cannot identify it accurately or understand it. Understanding may also come before recognition. If you know the other person's circumstances (he just made a blunder) and emotional inclinations (he is prone to anger) – that is, if you understand him – you may notice cues to emotion that others would miss. The ability to connect emotionally with others involves a complex configuration of sensitivities, skills, and knowledge that cannot be pulled apart and analyzed easily, much less laid out as a ladder of skills. With that caveat in mind, we turn to several types of emotional connections: recognizing *that* the other is feeling, recognizing *what* the other is feeling, recognizing *how* the other is feeling, feeling *along with* the other, feeling *as* the other is feeling, feeling *about* the other's feelings, and *responding* to the other's feelings.

Emotional Recognition

One of the most basic forms of emotional communication is to be aware that the other person is feeling emotion. You may not know what she is feeling, but you know that she is not emotionally neutral – she is feeling something. Going back to the weaving metaphor, you need at least to notice when another weaver starts to use color, even if you're not sure what color it is. The complementary skill is letting others know that you are feeling an emotion. Research tells us a little about this process, but we don't know much. In one study, parents of preschool children were found to agree on about 70% of their children's experiences of happiness and sadness but less well on anger and fear (Stein, Trabasso, & Liwag, 1991, cited in Oatley & Duncan, 1992: 286). In another study, women were asked to keep a diary of their own emotional experiences and their husbands were asked to observe them (Aitken & Stevenson, unpublished, cited in Oatley & Duncan, 1992: 284–185). Most of the same incidents were recorded (84%), but they were not always interpreted the same way. In one case, both husband and wife noted an incident of her practicing the guitar. He thought she was annoyed, but she said she was contented. He knew she was feeling something, but not what it was. In another study, observers were asked to observe other people who were watching emotionally loaded slides and to report when meaningful events occurred. Agreement among observers on the number of meaningful events was high ($r = .79$; Buck, Baron, & Barrette, 1982: 511).

These studies illustrate some of the issues involved in deciding whether it is easy or difficult to tell *that* someone is communicating an emotion. For instance, in studies of adults, it is assumed that they know when they are feeling an emotion, but in studies of children, their parents may be better judges. Some people also may be better at showing that they are feeling emotions than others are. Women, for instance, were seen as showing more meaningful emotional behavior than men, especially through their faces. People also noticed meaningful events more easily with practice (Buck et al., 1982). Whether you notice others' emotions or not probably also depends on factors such as how closely you are paying attention, how obvious and powerful the expression is, how well you can anticipate the emotion occurring, and many others.

Emotional Accuracy

Assuming that you are aware *that* the other person is feeling an emotion, the next issue is how well you are able to tell *what* emotion it is. In both common and technical language, this is called *accuracy*. You are accurate if you can discriminate anger from fear, joy from sadness, embarrassment from anger, or, more generally, positive feelings from negative feelings at levels better than chance. Or, alternatively, you will help other people perceive your emotions more accurately if you express sadness differently from fear or joy differently from guilt. Using the weaving metaphor, the question is how well weavers can distinguish each other's blue, red, yellow, white, and so on. Of all the factors in emotional connection, accuracy has been the most widely studied, and sometimes it seems to have the status of the bottom line in communicating emotion easily or with difficulty.

Accuracy, however, is not nearly as straightforward as it appears. First, there is the question of what standard to use. Do senders, receivers, or outside observers decide which answer is right? Following the boxcar model, only the person sending the emotion should be able to judge whether it got there intact. But using the weaving metaphor, anyone can judge whether a color is red, blue, or yellow; and it's not clear how to resolve disputes.

Similarly, whether you can pick the right emotion depends in part on how many choices you have. The easiest discrimination is between positive and negative emotions (even correcting for the 50:50 odds and even across cultures; Russell, 1994). This is no big surprise considering that knowing whether someone is feeling positively or negatively toward you is probably more important than what version of negative he is feeling. Choosing among a range of emotions (joy, anger, sadness, surprise, fear, and disgust, for example) is easier if the choices are few or if some of the alternatives are unlikely, as anyone who has taken multiple-choice tests knows. There also may be more than one correct answer, to the horror of multiple-choice test takers. People typically report feeling and observing more than one emotion at a time (Oatley & Duncan, 1992). Omdahl (1995:158) reports that 90% of the real-life stories of emotion that she gathered involved multiple emotions or blends.

Nevertheless, distinguishing between positive and negative feelings is complicated enough to produce interesting research. For example, married couples were asked to report how positive or negative the intent of their own messages was and how positive or negative the impact of their partner's messages was (either while talking or while viewing a videotape of their own interaction). Couples in distressed marriages showed a greater discrepancy between intent and impact, indicating a "communication gap" in terms of the positive or negative values of messages. The smaller the gap, the greater their marital satisfaction was 5 years later. Distressed couples tended to read more negative affect into messages than was intended and responded more negatively as well (Gottman, 1994: 345–346; Noller, 1984: 140–148). A similar slippage was found between the intensity of emotions that people thought they had sent spontaneously and what observers noticed. Senders thought they were much more expressive than observers did, and were quite surprised when they were shown the actual videotapes to see how much they had overestimated their own expressiveness (especially the women and even when they knew they were being watched). When they tried intentionally to communicate their feelings, however, their own ratings matched those of the judges better (Barr & Kleck, 1995).

Difficulties might arise for people who have very narrow emotional repertoires. Men who have been abusive toward their wives have been found to "funnel" negative emotions into anger even though their actual feelings may be shame, fear, or (even more likely) some combination of weak emotions (Retzinger, 1991). Women, on the other hand, may be unwilling or unable to express strong emotions like anger, or they may express them in tears so that they come through as more socially acceptable weak emotions such as sadness (Egerton, 1988). Children who have been abused or who have emotional problems show difficulties in producing and interpreting facial expressions of emotion, suggesting an intriguing and probably complex link between emotional accuracy deficits and social problems (Saarni, 1990: 150).

Emotional Understanding

If you assume that emotion is a process made up of several interrelated components, you would speak not of accuracy but of understanding. Understanding can be rich, deep, and complete or it can be poor, shallow, or sketchy. It involves exchanging messages about the basic components of another person's emotion: precipitating events and underlying causes, appraisals, physiological changes, action tendencies, actions and expressions, and regulation. If you fully understood what another person was feeling, you would be aware of what prompted her emotion, what underlying conditions facilitated it, what concerns of hers were tapped by the situation, how she was thinking of it (especially in terms of positive–negative valence, importance, and her ability to cope), how she was reacting, how she was inclined to act, what she was expressing verbally and nonverbally, how she was trying to manage her feelings, and how all of these components fit together into a coherent "story." And if you really wanted another person to understand you, you would communicate all these components to him. That is quite a tall order.

A more sketchy (and probably more realistic) level of understanding might involve knowing some of the components, but not all – knowing that she is feeling bad but not understanding why, or knowing what situation prompted the emotion but not understanding why she reacted as she did. Frijda and Tcherkassof (1997) present evidence that people understand facial expressions of emotion by orienting primarily to eliciting events and action readiness, especially the latter. For example, one person described a picture of a typical fearful face "as if she is looking at something with fixed attention, a game or something tense, two cars which almost get into collision, but nothing happens." That is, the observer tried to understand the expression by imagining the eliciting event. If this had been a "live" emotion instead of a picture, you can be sure that the observer would look or listen to find out what the event was. Another common type of response was "shielding herself from something, withdrawing from something, accepting or not accepting something, opening up to it or closing off from it, or some combination of these" – in other words, action tendencies (Frijda, 1953, cited in Frijda & Tcherkassof, 1997: 84).

Understanding varies not only in thoroughness, but also in validity. It fits the facts or the other person's interpretation of the facts to varying degrees. For example, you might believe that your child is upset because the neighbor's kid hit him, when in fact he is upset because the other kids wouldn't let him play with them (invalid understanding of the cause). Or you might think that your roommate feels disgust at the smelly garbage, but she actually feels angry that you didn't take it out (invalid understanding of appraisal). Deep, detailed, and valid understandings are also not necessarily better than shallow, crude, or invalid understandings. How good or bad they are depends more on how we evaluate the goals to which they are put than the understandings per se. Deep understanding can be used to aid or to manipulate others, to comfort them, or to fine-tune and intensify emotional cruelty. Misunderstandings can also keep you blissfully ignorant of things like how much other people dislike you. As Bob Dylan sang, "If for just one time you could stand inside my shoes, you'd know what a drag it is to see you."

Assuming that understanding is more common and less problematic than misunderstanding (which may or may not be the case), we might look for reasons for emotional misunderstandings. Often people disagree about what the provoking event means. In one study, researchers found that when one person made another angry, the person who provoked the anger tended to see the incident as a meaningful, comprehensible, and isolated incident ("You didn't deserve a raise this year"). The person who was made angry, however, tended to see the provoking incident as arbitrary, incomprehensible, and one incident in a general harmful pattern ("He never rewards me, and I don't understand why"). Moreover, neither side is aware that the other side sees things differently (Baumeister, Stillwell, & Wotman, 1990).

Another source of misunderstanding is the intensity of the emotion. Observers often either underestimate or overestimate the intensity of another person's feelings (Oatley & Duncan, 1992: 284, $r = .26$ between self and other ratings). Other possible sources of misunderstanding might be failing to understand how components, such as how precipitating events and appraisals, go together ("Why does that comment bother you so much?"), how the person's appraisal and action tendencies go together ("If you really like her, why don't you call?"), or how appraisals and expressions go together ("You said you cared about this issue, but you look bored"). One study found self-protective misunderstandings. Dating partners who were close and yet insecure about their relationship felt threatened when their partners evaluated highly attractive opposite-sex persons in their presence and were found to understand their partners' thoughts and feeling *less* well than did dating partners who were less close or more secure in their relationship. The researchers called this *motivated inaccuracy* (Simpson, Ickes, & Blackstone, 1995).

The key to emotional skill or talent lies in the ability to develop a rich and coherent mental model of the other's emotional state, taking into account whatever relevant specific information is available and building on one's own emotion knowledge. Having a sophisticated view of emotion in the first place probably helps. For example, if you believe that emotion always follows everyday logic, you might wonder why someone could be angry at a loved one for dying. If you realize, however, that we can get angry at people or events that thwart our goals even if they are not responsible (like getting angry at hitting your head on the kitchen cabinet), their responses make sense (Frijda, 1993). Similarly, you might wonder why someone would feel guilty for hurting another person in an accident even though there was absolutely nothing they could have done differently, and they knew it. Baumeister, Stillwell, and Heatherton (1994: 251–253) could tell you that it is common for people to feel guilty about events over which they had no control and for which no one would blame them (such as surviving when others died).

Understanding of one's own and others' emotional processes becomes increasingly sophisticated up through midlife. In general, it changes from an early emphasis on impulsiveness and maintaining physical comfort ("I just wanted to punch her out"), to more precise and more elaborate descriptions ("I was so charged up that everything I did was exaggerated"), to more awareness of connections among components of emotion, especially mental and physical processes ("The feelings stem from inside. Emotionally you feel the loss and intellectually you accept the fact that it's a sad feeling that you have") (Labouvie-Vief, DeVoe, & Bulka, 1989: 430).

Talking about your emotions with other people, even more than communicating with them nonverbally, opens up the possibility that you will not be just *describing* what you feel, but also *modifying*, or *negotiating* what you feel. Unlike the contents of boxcars, emotions are not fixed commodities that remain unchanged when they move from one person to another. Talking about your feelings can change what you *think* you feel and even what you *do* feel. When you tell someone why you are *upset* (an all-purpose, generic negative emotion word), you may realize that in fact you feel *angry*. Describing the situation in more detail may fuel the anger, making you feel absolutely furious. The person you are talking with may then agree that the situation is intolerable, leading you to feel downright indignant. On the other hand, the other person may say that you don't really seem angry, just hurt, and after talking it over, you may come to see it that way yourself.

Emotional Coincidence

The most obvious and perhaps most common form of emotional connection is when two people react with similar emotions to the same event. We both watch the same movie, and we both laugh, smile, and feel good. We see the car slide over into our lane, and simultaneously we feel a rush of fear. We both read about our alma mater's football victory and feel pride. We are connected emotionally only by the coincidence of responding to the same situation, not by any real communication. But perhaps calling this a coincidence is leaving too much to chance. We have chosen to go to the movie together; I yell when I see the car veering so that you look up; or I tell you about the football game.

Communication makes many, perhaps even most, parallel emotional responses more than just coincidence (Van Hooft, 1994). Most conversations are joint activities in which both people's attention is oriented to the same content and their thoughts about it are expressed. We talk about how gloomy the weather has been and – voilà – we are both down in the dumps. We have a meeting and discuss an exciting new project, and we are all hopeful. Jakobs, Fischer, and Manstead (1997) found that when people imagined experiencing an emotionally evocative situation together with a friend (such as winning the lottery with a ticket purchased together), how they believed they would feel about it depended in part on the friend's reaction. If the friend was cool about the lottery win, saying that it could have been bigger, the respondents believed the friend's reaction would decrease their own happiness; winning the lottery is more fun when both winners are enthusiastic. If the situation had been real instead of hypothetical, the chances are good that the friends also would have talked to one another, thus influencing each other's appraisals even more ("Yeah, just think of all the things we can do!" or "That's not enough money to quit our jobs"). In the same study, researchers found that if two friends learned together that a mutual friend was terminally ill and both reacted with sadness, they believed that their sadness would be intensified. The presence of the friend may be comforting, but the friend's expressions of sadness may make you more upset.

Emotional Contagion and Empathy

In addition to responding to the same situation, we pick up on each other's emotions. In the research literature, two terms apply – *emotional contagion* and *empathy*. Emotional contagion occurs when you "catch" the emotions of others from their expressions (as you might catch a cold). We even talk about contagious fear and infectious laughter (Hatfield, Cacioppo, & Rapson, 1994; Provine, 1997). Empathy occurs when you see the situation from the other person's point of view, leading you to feel the other person's feelings. You can imagine how someone feels when he loses his job so that you can empathize with his plight (Omdahl, 1995).

Empathy is a much more sophisticated process and involves a greater communicative challenge than does emotional contagion. Going back to the weaving metaphor, emotional contagion is like noticing that other weavers are using green thread and starting to use green yourself, probably without even being consciously aware of doing so. Empathy, on the other hand, would involve using green thread because you understand *why* the other weaver is doing so. Green may or may not have been the color you thought was best, but even if you want to persuade the other weaver to use blue instead, you can do that more effectively if you understand why she is using green.

Emotional Contagion. Many examples of emotional contagion are found in accounts of war, when soldiers infect one another with either fear or courage, and children pick up on either the fear or the courage of their parents. Rachman (1990) reports a correlation of .59 between the fearfulness of mother and child during air raids. Emotional contagion is a largely involuntary response to other people's emotional expressions, but the exact mechanism is unclear. It may come from mimicking or modeling others' expressions, but we do know that it cannot involve sophisticated mental processes because infants "catch" others' emotions so readily. Even newborns cry in response to the distress cries of other newborns. Toddlers will approach a new and potentially scary toy if their mothers smile but will shy away if their mothers' faces show fear (Thompson, 1987). Children pick up on their parents' depression and are likely to become less content and more withdrawn themselves (Downey & Coyne, 1990; Gotlib & Whiffen, 1991: 191–196).

To be true to the contagion metaphor, one person must be vulnerable to a stronger emotional force from outside. Infants and toddlers are generally more susceptible to their mothers' emotions than vice versa, though prolonged bouts of crying can distress even the most stoic parent. Highly expressive people influence less expressive people more than the reverse (Sullins, 1991). Powerless people are more susceptible to emotional contagion than powerful people.[4] People who are sensitive and responsive to others are more likely to catch emotions from others; people who are insensitive are more likely to infect others with their own feelings. Individuals are more susceptible to the emotional tone of groups than groups are to those of individuals (Hatfield et al., 1994). Closeness is also a factor, both literally and figuratively. Since contagion operates through emotional expression, the susceptible person must be able to observe the other's expressions, which is most likely when they are in physical proximity. Closeness in the sense of intimacy also facilitates emotional contagion; people who like or love one another are more likely to experience emotional contagion than are strangers or enemies (Hatfield et al., 1994: 167–174).

One of the problems with emotional contagion is that it is possible to be either too susceptible or too infectious. You can be so sensitive to others' emotions that you are more in touch with theirs than with your own. Nathanson (1987: 258) notes that "One of the little discussed phenomena of family dynamics is our willingness to accept the mood of the dominant member." You can be overwhelmed, buffeted about, and outright victimized by others' feelings. Developing skills

---

[4] Hsee, Hatfield, Carlson, and Chemtob (1990), however, present evidence contrary to the prediction that powerless people would be susceptible to the emotions of powerful people rather than vice versa, perhaps because the powerless person is distracted or unable to concentrate due to stress.

at countercontagion may be important to you (Cappella, 1995). On the infecting side, you can be so expressive that you overwhelm others and force your emotions on them. The trick, then, seems to be to achieve a balanced sensitivity to your own and other people's feelings and to be aware of the effects they are having.

Empathy. In fact, emotional contagion may be a more primitive form of empathy that lays the groundwork for later, more sophisticated developments (Barnett, 1987; Thompson, 1987). Both emotional contagion and empathy involve feeling *with* other people. In the case of emotional contagion, one person *catches* the other's emotions from his expressions and they become her own, but in the case of empathy, one person *imagines* herself in the other person's position and feels the emotions that go along with it.[5] For example, you may empathize with someone else's embarrassment when you see him being forced to sing the U.S. national anthem, "The Star Spangled Banner," but you know that you are identifying with his emotions. You are not feeling them directly yourself. You feel his embarrassment, but he is the one who is making a fool of himself (R. S. Miller, 1987).

Although newborns are capable of emotional contagion, true empathic abilities develop only when children come to recognize others as separate individuals with their own subjective states. So empathy begins to appear at ages 2 to 3 years, perhaps from the groundwork laid by emotional contagion (Hoffman, 1987: 51). The conditions that facilitate empathy are similar to those that facilitate emotional contagion – similarity, physical co-presence, and familiarity with one another (Barnett, 1987: 154–155; Hoffman, 1987: 67). It is easier to empathize with someone who is a lumberjack like you, is standing next to you, and has been your co-worker for years than it is to empathize with the foreman sitting in his office over there whom you have just met. In addition, expecting a cooperative interaction facilitates empathy, whereas expecting competition tends to make people counterempathic. If you think you will have to work with your co-worker but against your foreman to hammer out a contract, you will tend to empathize with the co-worker rather than with the foreman (Lanzetta & Englis, 1989).

---

[5] Lazarus (1991: 287), for example, considers empathy to be "not an emotion, but an emotional capacity" defined as "sharing another's feelings by placing oneself psychologically in that person's circumstance."

Like understanding, empathy involves imagining the other's situation, but it goes beyond understanding by including an emotional reaction (often measured as a physiological response or observed expression). With understanding, you know how he feels; with empathy, you imaginatively enter into his feelings. To use the weaving metaphor again, with understanding, you know how the other weaver is using color; with empathy, you adopt those same colors yourself. The power that empathy has beyond simple understanding is its emotional force – its ability to move people to action, especially prosocial actions (Batson & Oleson, 1991). In addition, empathy may be self-reinforcing if awareness of your own empathy makes you recognize that you value the other's welfare, which in turn leads you to continue to empathize (Batson, Turk, Shaw, & Klein, 1995). In general, when people empathize with others in distress, they tend to be more inclined to help, though not always and not always in ways that really do help. For example, in one study, some children responded to the distress of another child by helping, but others responded with aggression (hitting the person who made the baby cry) or avoidance (running away) (Barnett, 1987: 149; Klimes-Dougan & Kistner, 1990).

The basic skills of empathy are more complicated than those of emotional contagion; they involve imagining the other's situation so vividly and powerfully that you feel her emotions (or at least an approximation of them). This process can go wrong in several ways. Obviously, you may not have the imagination to conjure up a very vivid image of another person's situation. You have always been with loved ones, so you cannot understand what it is like to be alone, much less feel another's loneliness. It is hard for most of us to empathize with the feelings (or lack thereof) of a murderer (perhaps blessedly so), and many adults have forgotten the emotional turmoil of adolescence and so can empathize only so far. There is always the danger of projecting our own emotions onto others. Good acrophobic that I am, I remember watching workers walk onto a walkway outside of the eighth floor to wash the windows. I sat there with hands shaking, unable to concentrate, while they went happily about their business. I was projecting my own fear, not empathizing with theirs.

There is a skill to achieving the right level of empathy, too, as there is with emotional contagion. Someone who overempathizes can become as needy as the person who needs help. I am reminded of someone who fell on the ice and broke his arm. A good friend happened to see him and became so empathically distressed that the ambulance almost took away the uninjured friend instead. Workers in many helping professions have to walk a fine line between too much and too little empathy. As one clinical psychologist said: "Once you are in the shoes of your patient, you cannot possibly be of any help because he has been in his shoes all along, and obviously not done too well" (Pines, Aronson, & Kafry, 1981, cited in Miller, Stiff, & Ellis, 1988: 262). Those who are truly skilled at empathy seem to be able to develop an attitude of "detached concern" without true emotional contagion, which helps them retain enough perspective on the other's emotions to be responsive yet avoid emotional exhaustion and burn-out (Miller et al., 1988). It is easy to feel overwhelmed by your own vicarious distress and become self-absorbed or run away. It is also easy to cut yourself off from other people's feelings, blocking feelings that are painful. It takes courage and skill to feel another person's pain and respond effectively.

Presumably there is also a certain skill involved in inspiring empathy in others. Researchers know very little about what produces empathy, although one would suppose that describing one's situation in vivid terms that promote feelings of familiarity, liking, and mutual concern would be central. Being able to mobilize empathy is one of the characteristics of books such as *Uncle Tom's Cabin* or *Huckleberry Finn* that have influenced the course of history (cited as examples in Hoffman, 1987: 60).

Sympathy and Schadenfreude

Another type of emotional connection that is often considered in conjunction with empathy is sympathy. Whereas empathy is feeling *with* another person (feeling the other's feelings), sympathy is feeling *about* another person's situation (having your own feelings about the other person's situation, possibly including his feelings) (Wispé, 1991).[6] You may empathize with someone who has brought on her own sorrows (you feel her sorrow), but you may have no sympathy for her (her situation does not justify sorrow in you). It is also possible to feel sympathy but not empathy for someone who has lost a limb even though he reports being perfectly happy. You think it is a profound

---

[6] Wispé (1991: 79–80) distinguishes between empathy and sympathy on the grounds that "in empathy one person reaches out for the other person, whereas in sympathy the sympathizer is moved by the other person ... empathy is a way of knowing; sympathy is a way of relating." Her distinction comes closer to the distinction I have made between understanding and empathy.

loss, but he doesn't. You certainly do *not* empathize when you feel *schadenfreude*. This is a German word for which we have no equivalent in English, derived from the roots "damage" + "joy." It means to take pleasure in another's misfortune, especially that of your enemies. Batman fans take pleasure from feeling the Joker's anguish, and sports teams are delighted to see their defeated archrivals looking dejected.

Responding to Each Other's Emotions

When someone yells and screams at you, generally you do not think, "Well, that must be anger, rather than fear; I will try to understand it," at least not at that moment and perhaps never. Instead, you flinch, cower, or yell back. In the research literature, conscious communication processes have been emphasized over unconscious ones, even though we know that people *react* with preferences or inclinations toward or away from other people based on simple preconscious judgments such as novelty or familiarity (Burgoon, 1993; Zajonc, 1980).

Abram (1996: 80–81) describes how you can hear an emotional relationship in the voices of two friends who are unexpectedly reunited. "Each voice, each side of the duet, mimes a bit of the other's melody while adding its own inflection and style, and then is echoed by the other in turn – the two singing bodies thus tuning and attuning to one another, rediscovering a common register, *remembering* each other." Bodies, like voices, also perform duets of mutual attunement through smile, gaze, posture, gesture, and distance (Andersen, Guerrero, Buller, & Jorgensen, 1998). Mutual adjustments make up the bedrock of social interaction and go on continually, often below the level of conscious awareness. Sexual desire, for example, is often communicated through a subtle and continuous exchange of overtures, acceptance, rejection, and negotiation (Metts, Sprecher, & Regan, 1998). Interpersonal warmth is also communicated through subtle nonverbal messages as well as verbal ones. It develops as people respond to one another spontaneously (as Abram's example shows) and is closely linked to relational intimacy, closeness, bonding, and attachment (Andersen & Guerrero, 1998a).

Why Communicate Emotion with Others?

In a way, it makes no sense to ask *why* we communicate emotion. We do it for no apparent reason at all – because expression is an integral part of emotion. Joy is made up, in part, of smiles, quick steps, and spontaneous laughter. Depression is shown in slower speech, a monotonous tone, negative conversational topics, less eye contact, and other communicative behaviors (Segrin, 1998). We may also communicate our feelings in order to let other people know about them – to share our joy, sorrow, loneliness, or relief. Perhaps all we want is for someone else to listen and to understand. But perhaps we want more, even though we may not be consciously aware of it. We also communicate feelings to get other people to give us hugs, to change their irritating habits, to get out of the way of trains, to spend more time with us, and so on. Moreover, one reason for communicating emotion does not rule out another. We may communicate joy because we feel it, because we want to share it, and because we want to convince friends to go celebrate – all at the same time. It may be impossible to separate one reason from another because, in this case, they are all working together.

To use the weaving metaphor, we might say that we weave with colors simply because thread is colored, because we want to coordinate with others who are weaving the fabric with us, and because we are weaving fabrics to serve certain purposes or functions – to keep us warm, to inspire great deeds, to show off our haughtiness or humility. Although the goal may not be formulated or pursued consciously, and although it may even be worked out and adjusted as we go along, the weaving is not completely aimless even if we seem to be doing it primarily for its own sake.

The work of several scholars converges on these three models of emotional communication. O'Keefe (1988) wrote of expressive, conventional, and rhetorical message design logics for persuasive messages. Gallois (1993) applied a similar scheme specifically to emotional communication, as did Scherer (1992a). Frameworks such as Salovey and Mayer's (1990) *emotional intelligence* and Saarni's (1990) *emotional competence* also include elements of all three models, with emphasis on the latter two because they require more skill.

Frijda and Mesquita (1991) argue that when emotions occur in a social context, they are shaped by whatever purpose they are serving at that time. If you are talking about your worries to convince someone to help, the worry is not just expressed through talk – it is defined through talk. Watch children to see the transformation that emotions go through as their goals change. A child may wail in distress if Mom is nearby and might give comfort, but when other children appear who might ridicule him, suddenly he is just fine. To all appearances, not only does the expression change, but the feelings as well. Adults may be less aware of how their own emotions are shaped in similar ways, or perhaps they are just less willing to admit it because it implies a certain insincerity (more on this in later chapters).

It is also worth noting that the varieties of emotional connection discussed earlier (accuracy, understanding, empathy, etc.) are seldom if ever made for their own sake; they serve other functions. Recognizing another person's irritability will help you stay out of her way and avoid a confrontation. You will probably notice different aspects of someone's emotional expressions if you plan to marry him than if you plan to rob him. Understanding another person's emotions may help you figure out how to comfort her, how to handle the situation, and or how to influence her behavior. Fostering empathy tends to foster altruism, as discussed earlier, and you may purposely cultivate another's empathy in order to get help or suppress your own in order to avoid giving it. Even responding to one another's feelings on an intuitive, almost reflexive level serves the function of building rapport and interpersonal bonds, and your attunement with one another both reflects and shapes your relationship. To reiterate, goals need not be pursued consciously in most cases, but communicating emotion serves those goals nonetheless.

Communication scholars, in particular, have adopted the goal-oriented model and have explored how emotion is used in the service of one's own goals (e.g., embarrassing another person to discredit her; Bradford & Petronio, 1998), the other person's goals (e.g., alleviating another's distress; Burleson & Goldsmith, 1998), joint goals (e.g., being friends; Gaines, 1998), or widely held social goals (promoting health; Witte, 1998). The list of possible goals is endless, but some of the most common ones that have been studied are (1) solving problems (Lazarus, 1991), (2) persuading or influencing (Aristotle, n.d.; trans. McKeon, 1941; Bailey, 1983; Dillard, 1991; Jorgensen, 1998; Petty & Cacioppo, 1986; Witte, 1998), (3) eliciting comfort (Burleson & Goldsmith, 1998), (4) presenting yourself (Clark, et al., 1996; Graham, Gentry, & Green, 1981; Laux & Weber, 1991), (5) enforcing social standards (Baumeister et al., 1994; Miller, 1996) and (6) managing social roles, positions, or relationships (Feeney, Noller, & Roberts, 1998; Frijda & Mesquita, 1991; Guerrero & Andersen, 1998). How emotion is used to pursue those goals and is shaped by them is a topic that is pursued in depth in later chapters.

Emotional Communication Competence

Emotional competence has received much public attention recently due to the popularity of Goleman's best-seller, *Emotional Intelligence* (1995). Saarni (1990) and Salovey and Mayer (1990; Salovey, Hsee, & Mayer, 1993) developed the basic orientation described earlier, arguing that emotional competence or intelligence is required to function effectively in the social world. Both formulations make communicative skills central, including discerning others' emotions, realizing that expressions and experience do not necessarily match, knowing the cultural rules for displaying emotion, using the emotional vocabulary, feeling empathy, recognizing that your own expressions affect others, and using all of these skills in relationships with others. Communicating emotion effectively is a skill that is just as sophisticated as, say, reading a book, so it clearly merits the label *intelligence*. Intelligence, however, connotes a relatively unchanging aptitude rather than a skill that can be developed, so I prefer the term *competence*. We may not all be emotionally brilliant, but most of us are competent – we get along.

Ultimately, how well we get along depends on whether shared emotional meaning is "good enough." A newborn cries, and her father comes running. We do not know whether she is really experiencing fear or anger, a primitive physiological reaction or a full-blown emotion, what meaning the experience has for her, and neither does her father. He doesn't need to understand, empathize, or, for that matter, feel anything at all. He just needs to come to comfort her. They are weaving a cloth together, but if it makes only a crude diaper, that is good enough. At perhaps the other extreme, a person may enter therapy in order to change emotional patterns developed over a lifetime. Much more is required of the therapist to be "good enough." It requires sensitivity to cues, insight into the emotion process, awareness that self-reports of emotions may not be accurate, and, most important, the ability to understand, empathize, and create ways to transform an emotional life. Therapists need to weave a highly intricate cloth from threads with very sophisticated colors and textures. Effective therapy requires, most of all, control over the weaving process – knowing what colors to choose to create the desired overall pattern. Like weaving, communicating emotionally may appear to be spontaneous and haphazard (and perhaps sometimes it is), but more often, it is a complex, goal-oriented activity, whether the participants recognize it or not.

3. Is Emotional Communication Spontaneous or Strategic?

You learn to put your emotional luggage where it will do some good, instead of using it to shit on other people, or blow up aeroplanes.

Margaret Drabble (1991)[1]

In *The Expression of the Emotions in Man and Animals,* published in 1872, Darwin opened a dialogue among scholars about the dual nature of emotional expression and communication that continues to this day. Darwin wrote about the expression of emotion, which captures the sense of emotion "pressing out" through the face, voice, and body. Expression is an integral part of emotion itself and happens whether we like it or not, whether we are alone or with others. It reveals our genuine or real feelings and gives others a transparent window into our hearts. Expression is founded in our genes and is directly available to others of the same species.

It took over a century for another scholar to write a book called *The Communication of Emotion.* Buck (1984) argued that not only do we express emotion spontaneously, but we also *communicate* emotion to others symbolically and strategically. Communication, as opposed to expression, is separable from the feelings themselves, happens if we intend it to happen, and is sensitive to audiences and situations. Communication can reveal either genuine or false feelings and can be a clear or distorted window into other people's hearts. Communication is founded in individual intention and in society, and communicating emotion is goal-oriented and strategic.

In this chapter, we look at emotion messages both as expression and as communication, blurring the distinction and exploring the vast

---

[1] Quoted in *The Columbia Dictionary of Quotations* (1993) New York: Columbia University Press.

gray area between them. In earlier chapters, we used the metaphor of weaving a fabric for the process of communicating emotion. Social life was the fabric, communication was the act of weaving, and emotions were the colors that enlivened it and created meaning. Following that metaphor in this chapter, we ask whether color is woven into the fabric spontaneously, whether color is chosen strategically to be part of a general pattern, or both. An experienced and knowledgeable weaver cannot make truly spontaneous choices without being influenced by the patterns she has seen, the weavings of others, the dyes available, and the pattern she has in mind, even if only vaguely. At the same time, any pattern designed in advance also comes into being as a product of choices made in the moment.

Managing Emotional Expressions

On the face of it, it seems easy to tell the difference between expressing what we really feel and manipulating our emotional communication for other purposes. You run into someone for whom you feel spontaneous hatred, put on a strategic smile, and say, "Hi, good to see you" as she passes, then you revert back to a spontaneous sneer when she is out of sight. You can even do it well enough to convince people that you are having fun at Cousin Carrie's boring party or grief-stricken at Uncle Louie's funeral.

Managing feelings for the sake of presenting oneself in a particular light or for the sake of the occasion is a well-known fact of social life. Goffman (1959) has documented many examples of how people try to control what cues are "given" and how others try to read beyond them to the uncontrolled cues that are "given off." We may try to present ourselves as fearless, loving, or enraged, depending on the social goals we have in mind (Jones & Pittman, 1982). We try to act loving at family reunions, sad at funerals, joyful at parties, and so on. We follow emotion *display rules* that guide us when we express, suppress, exaggerate, or completely falsify our emotions (Ekman & Friesen, 1975). Most of the time, no one cares to know about real feelings anyway, so long as we express what is appropriate to the occasion.[2]

---

[2] Taylor (1989) argues that positive illusions are needed for mental health and serve to foster persistence, creativity, positive responses to challenges, and ultimately better performance (assuming that the beliefs are not too far out of line with reality). A parallel argument can be made that pleasant and positive sociality, although something of an illusion, fosters cooperation and social bonds and ultimately facilitates group performance, unrealistic though it may be.

In some critical cases, however, it is very important to tell the difference between the felt and the fake. You want to know if the car salesman is really unhappy with his small profit margin or secretly delighted at having found a sucker. You want to know if your date is really having a good time or just pretending. For the sake of yourself and others, you need to know if a criminal truly feels regret or is faking it for the parole board. Hence we all search for the magic formula that will separate the true gold of authentic feelings from the fool's gold of pretense. And as with all magic formulas, we want to keep them to ourselves because their value is lost if everyone has them.

Some expressions are very difficult to control and therefore are good candidates for discriminating felt from faked emotions. Before Darwin, a French anatomist named Duchenne de Boulogne found that the orbicularis oculi muscle, which wrinkles the corner of the eye, is not under conscious control and so contracts only with genuine positive feeling, producing what is now known as the *Duchenne smile*. For its alternative, I might suggest the faked or full-of-*Boulogne smile*, in which the orbicularis oculi's "inertia, in smiling, unmasks a false friend" (Duchenne, 1862, cited in Ekman, Davidson, & Friesen, 1990: 342). In support of the feigned–faked distinction, one study showed that bereaved people who showed more Duchenne smiles and laughter reported more positive and fewer negative feelings, whereas non-Duchenne smiles and laughter were not associated with how they felt (Keltner & Bonanno, 1997). Blushing is another good candidate for a cue to emotion that is not under conscious control and thus gives away embarrassment. Almost everyone has had the experience of being embarrassed, trying to pretend nonchalance, but feeling the face get hot and knowing that everyone else sees the blushing. Pupil dilation is another uncontrollable cue to emotion, although it is a cue to interest, not attraction as many people mistakenly believe. A host of other physiological cues to emotional states are not easily controlled – heart rate, blood pressure, piloerection (hair standing on end), and galvanic skin response (sweating hands) (Frijda, 1986, Chap. 3).

Even these cues are not infallible guides to emotion. First, even though conscious intention cannot produce the cues, many other irrelevant things can. The pupil of the eye responds to an interesting or arousing stimulus, but also to simple light and dark. If you gaze into your date's eyes to see if she is really interested, you had better pay attention to whether you are in sunshine or shade. Perhaps this is why we love candlelight dinners. Second, even if you are sure that the emotion is genuine, you may not be certain about what caused it. The salesman may be smiling genuinely because he finally made a deal with a demanding client (you) or because he landed a sucker (you). Your date's pupils may be dilated because she is interested in you or because she is interested in your eyeglasses. You may blush not because you believe you made a faux pas, but because you were made the center of attention. Third, almost all of the uncontrollable cues are very difficult to observe. How many people are able to monitor other people's orbicularis oculi muscle, pupil dilation, or piloerection? You may be able to detect galvanic skin response from a handshake (but beware of hot days) or heart rate from a hug (but beware of meeting at the top of the stairs). Not even the person experiencing the emotion is aware of her own blood pressure, much less an observer without a blood pressure cuff (even so, watch out for anxiety about the cuff). All told, windows to the heart are not transparent, and the devices we use to see through them are unreliable and unwieldy.

There are additional complications. First, altering the expression of an emotion tends to alter the experience of the emotion as well. When applied to facial expression, this is called the *facial feedback hypothesis*. Asking people to pose a smile tends to make them feel happier, a frown sadder, a snarl angrier, and so on. Theorists argue over issues such as whether facial expressions can initiate an emotion or only intensify one that is already present, whether expressions can change the type of emotion experienced (from sadness to anger, for example), and how much of a change expressions can produce (Camras et al., 1993). Even more controversial are the possible reasons for the facial feedback effect. Two of the more interesting ones (for our purposes) are that we use facial cues as a gauge to our own emotions (if I'm smiling, I must be happy) and that the desire to feel certain emotions produces both the expression and the tendency to experience it (I want to be happy, so I'll act as if I am and believe that I am) (Cappella, 1993; Fridlund, 1994: 173–182). In any case, facial feedback makes it difficult to draw a clear line between a faked and a felt expression, and blurs the distinction between the spontaneous and the strategic.

But more important, the distinction between felt and fake is at best blurry and at worst misleading (as will be argued throughout this chapter). The car salesman may be delighted about making a fortune from you but at the same time unhappy that it wasn't more. Your date may be "letting herself" enjoy your company spontaneously in order to be polite. The criminal may feel genuine regret for his crimes in front of the parole board but delight in getting away with them when out on the street. Your blushing may be felt spontaneously, but at the same time, blushing may have evolved in the human species as a way of strategically signalling to others that you do not want to be the center of attention (Leary, Britt, Cutlip, & Templeton, 1992).

Strategies for Managing Emotions

Clearly, people vary in their ability to control and manage emotional expressions. We see the whole range, from the awkward efforts of small children and bad actors to the brilliant performances of famous actors and infamous imposters. Really good actors have two options for controlling their emotional expressions; they can manage the expressions (what Hochschild, 1979, calls *surface acting*) or they can manage the actual feelings (*deep acting*). Surface acting involves following socially shared "display rules" for emotional expressions. Deep acting involves *feeling rules* that function not just to suppress or elicit emotion, but also to *shape* emotion toward social ends (Hochschild, 1979, 1983). Deep acting introduces a complicated relationship between expressing emotion spontaneously and strategically because it involves *strategically* managing *spontaneously* felt emotions.

Deep acting has several advantages over surface acting, both for yourself and for others. The most obvious advantage is that sometimes you really want to feel the emotions that you are expected to communicate. It would be nice not to have to act cheery on a Monday morning but instead to actually feel cheery. It would be good to avoid flying off the handle at your co-workers but even better not to feel the anger in the first place. In this case, deep acting accomplishes both goals simultaneously – managing communication strategically and feeling what you want to feel spontaneously (Conrad & Witte, 1994; Tice & Baumeister, 1993). A second advantage is that it takes effort and vigilance to manage expressions of feelings. If you can actually feel the right thing, appropriate expressions come naturally, and you don't have to worry about slipping up and getting caught. In addition, you don't feel the strain of being torn between your real feelings and your fake feelings because they are the same. A third advantage is that after a while you start to internalize the feelings of deep acting, and you become the sort of person who fills certain social roles naturally. You may not spontaneously feel paternal love toward the small creature who disturbs your sleep and dirties diapers, but you work on it, and before you know it, you really *do* feel love. Thus deep acting is a tremendous force for emotion socialization, both for children and for adults. Competent adults not only express the emotions they are supposed to express, but they also come to feel the emotions they are supposed to feel. We assist each other in feeling the right feelings, too, by trying to influence individuals directly ("You should feel grateful to Aunt Helen") and through our shared talk and social practices (crying when our friends "pass away" but cheering when our enemies "bite the dust"). Managing emotion itself is so deeply embedded in our psychic and social lives that we take it for granted.

How do people change their feelings? Fortunately for scholars, people are able to describe in some detail how they manage their feelings in a variety of contexts. We know about the strategies that students use to manage test anxiety (Albas & Albas, 1988; Folkman & Lazarus, 1985), that construction workers use to manage fear (Haas, 1978), that medical students use to manage embarrassment, disgust, or lust (Smith & Kleinman, 1989), that flight attendants and Disney-land workers use to manage anger (Hochschild, 1983), that call takers for 911 use to manage anxiety and empathy (Tracy & Tracy, 1998), that bill collectors use to manage anger and compassion (Sutton, 1991), and many others. Emotion management strategies can be used to manage your own emotions, the emotions of others, or both together. Construction workers, for example, manage their own and each other's fear of falling, and flight attendants try to make themselves happy so that they can make passengers happy.

In managing emotion, we alter one or more of the components of emotion (eliciting events, appraisal, physiological changes, action tendencies, expressions), thus regulating the emotion itself, although not quite as neatly or completely as it appears. Typically, people use several strategies simultaneously. Some of the strategies seem to contradict each other (such as gathering information or distracting yourself), but they work in different ways. It is also important to remember that emotion management is not a momentary occurrence but rather is a process that continues over the course of the event (such as the feared exam) and often over the course of a lifetime (such as managing public speaking anxiety).

Managing Eliciting Events. The most direct and obvious way to manage emotion is to deal with the eliciting event or situation that produces the emotion in the first place. Strategies here can range from avoiding the situation ("What I don't know cannot upset me") to taking concrete measures to change it ("Don't just worry – do something!"). This is called *problem-focused coping* and is, of course, the obvious thing to do if you can manage it. Sometimes, however, you have no control over the situation (you cannot confront someone who is not there) or your emotions are interfering with your ability to do the right thing (when you are too angry to confront someone effectively). Then you must manage your emotion instead of or in addition to managing the situation. Certainly, people do a mix of both. Despite the widespread belief that men tend to focus on the problem whereas women tend to focus on the emotion, Goldsmith and Dun (1997) found that college students of both sexes tended to focus on the problem or actions to be taken rather than on the emotion, with variations depending more on the situation (e.g., having to give a speech versus being dumped by a boyfriend) than on the person's gender.

Workers in various professions exert some control over events that upset them emotionally. For example, construction workers whose job is to construct 20-story buildings manage the objective problems of ice and wind by shoveling or melting the ice off of steel beams and by dragging sheets of plywood instead of carrying them in the wind (Haas, 1978). Students manage tests in several ways (Albas & Albas, 1988). Some students prioritize their studying earlier in the semester, and others depend on last-minute cramming. Some students also analyze the difficulties they have with exams and make concrete plans to deal with them, but, of course, others do not. Even in situations that workers cannot control directly, such as being laid off, their employers can refrain from creating more emotionally charged problems by following consistent and fair guidelines and by not raising the chief executive officer's pay when downsizing (Folger & Baron, 1996: 73).

Managing Appraisals. One of the most common emotion management strategies is to change how we think about or appraise emotion-eliciting events. Intuitively, we seem to recognize that thinking about events differently can change our feelings. Thinking is also strongly influenced by talk, both directly and in indirect and subtle ways, so that communication is almost an inextricable part of managing appraisals. Myers (1992: 44–45), for example, notes that *poortalk* – complaining about what we can't afford – is not only insulting to the truly poor but also sours thinking and magnifies discontent. Instead of "I need that," we should say, "I want that"; instead of saying, "I can't afford it," we should say, "I choose to spend my money on other things." As a result, we would be more likely to view ourselves as making choices rather than being victims.

One way to manage feelings is to manage the *attention* that you give to the eliciting event or to the feelings themselves. If you attend to something else and distract yourself, those events will not continue to trigger the emotions. Indeed, emotional experiences can sometimes be so overwhelming that it is necessary to distract yourself from time to time to cope. Distraction is a commonly used strategy and seems to work so long as it is not overdone and does not become long-term avoidance. People manage anger by directing their attention elsewhere by reading, watching television, or seeing movies. Anything that is mentally absorbing works, and preferably it should also be positive, calming, and unrelated to the source of the anger. Wildlife videos are my personal favorite. Students sometimes manage test anxiety by trying to forget about the test, a technique that can backfire if you focus on what you are trying to forget (Wegner, Erber, & Zanakos, 1993). Medical students manage embarrassment, disgust, or sexual arousal by covering body parts that they are not working on, especially genitals and breasts, and hence focusing attention on only the relevant organs (Smith & Kleinman, 1989). Talk among skyscraper construction workers directs attention toward danger (which they can do something about) but away from fear (which is seen as endangering everyone and therefore not to be tolerated). Fear is a taboo topic among co-workers and is seldom discussed even "backstage" in private conversations (Haas, 1978).

Emotions tend to be stronger when the situation is uncertain than when things go as expected, so another way to manage emotions is to gather information and *familiarize* yourself with the situation. Students look over past exams, talk to professors to gather information, or become familiar with the physical environment by looking around the exam room in advance. A roofer told me that she walks around on roofs before beginning every new roofing season to familiarize herself anew with the experience of being on high (M. Crepeau, personal communication).

We feel less strongly about less important things, so emotions can be managed by trying to *minimize the importance* of what is occurring. Students do this by reminding themselves and others that the course is outside their major or by calculating the minimum score they need to pass (which is usually easy to attain) (Albas & Albas, 1988). Jokes about virtually anything make it seem less important unless you think the topic is so important that the joke is offensive.

Yet another strategy is to guide thoughts in the desired direction, usually toward the *positive* but sometimes toward the *negative*. Students studying, for example, engage in wishful thinking, conscious strategies to accentuate the positive, and optimistic thinking. Sometimes, however, they think pessimistically, based on the strategy of expecting the worst and so being pleasantly surprised when it doesn't happen (Albas & Albas, 1988). Medical students accentuate the positive by thinking that performing a potentially embarrassing physical examination is "real medicine," not just book learning (Smith & Kleinman, 1989).

Linguistic strategies such as euphemisms and dysphemisms skew thought processes in subtle ways to emphasize the positive (for euphemisms) or negative (for dysphemisms). Other terms shift blame or deemphasize the importance of situations. Flight attendants are trained not to speak of "obnoxious" or "outrageous" passengers, only of "uncontrolled" or "mishandled" ones. "By linguistically avoiding any attribution of blame, the idea of a right to be angry at the passenger is smuggled out of the discourse" (Hochschild, 1983: 111). By referring to "incidents," not "accidents," both danger and blame are concealed. Students talk about "tests or quizzes" but not "exams," thus making them seem less important (Albas & Albas, 1988: 268). Construction workers on top of buildings talk of "falling in the hole" (thus imagining themselves on level ground and normalizing their work), and they ridicule new workers by saying that they are "cooning it" (crossing beams on all fours), "cradling it" (holding on to beams), or "seagulling it" (holding their arms out for balance) (Haas, 1978). Bill collectors talk about "loafers" and "deadbeats" (Sutton, 1991). Disneyland workers refer to "guests" not customers, "attractions" not rides, "security hosts" not guards, "costumes" not uniforms, and, as with flight attendants, "incidents" not accidents. In private, however, "guests" are "ducks" (Van Maanen & Kunda, 1989).

People also tend to feel better when they have confidence and *control*, even if the control is not real. Students studying for exams report putting on their best clothes to feel more confident. They also engage in compulsive behaviors such as sharpening pencils, tidying up the apartment, and "nesting behavior" (settling into a seat and arranging pencils, erasers, calculators, watches, facial tissues, cough drops, and perhaps a good-luck charm) (Albas & Albas, 1988). Mountain rescue workers often give the injured person (and the potentially more problematic uninjured companion) something to do that makes them feel useful (J. Sparhawk, personal communication). All of these strategies may provide a sense of control, at least over small and manageable things. When conditions are especially dangerous for construction workers, they control whether or not they work, which is both practically and psychologically important (Haas, 1978).

A very common strategy for managing uncomfortable situations is to find *humor* in them. It is almost impossible to laugh and be angry at the same time. Humor tends to make situations seem less important by virtue of their absurdity or our detachment, and humor reframes the situation as less threatening or anxiety producing. As the film and TV show *M*A*S*H* illustrated so clearly, medical workers use a lot of sexual and gallows humor, but it is strictly backstage and reserved for the in-group. Medical students tell "cadaver stories" to beginners, such as the one about medical students dressing up a cadaver and taking it to a homecoming game (Hafferty, 1988: 347). Workers who respond to 911 calls laugh, joke, and tell stories to relieve their own and their co-workers' tension (Tracy & Tracy, 1998). The 911 callers would probably agree with James Thurber's quip that "humor is emotional chaos remembered in tranquillity."

People also manage emotions by using *trained imagination* to conjure up an image of the situation that is more consistent with the desired emotion. This is how Stanislavski or method acting works (or deep acting for Hochschild, 1983). If you want to be sad, imagine losing something precious to you; if you want to be angry, imagine a shocking insult; and so on. In interpersonal situations, some useful techniques are to imagine what the other person must be thinking or feeling, to think of the other as a certain kind of person, or to assume certain motives. For example, people manage anger by trying to imagine how the other person must be viewing the situation. Flight attendants, in particular, are trained to imagine circumstances that would excuse the behavior of troublesome passengers (such as a personal tragedy) or, if they really got out of hand, to think of the passengers as unruly children. Bill collectors, on the other hand, are encouraged to think of their clients as irresponsible malingerers who are only hurting themselves by ruining their credit ratings. Medical students are encouraged to think of their patients as objects (especially as collections of body parts) or as intellectual puzzles.

Managing Physiological Reactions. A third strategy used to manage emotion is to alter your own or others' physical responses through exercise, relaxation, physical work, sleeping, bathing, drugs (including caffeine and alcohol), eating, fasting, smoking, chewing (pencils, nails, or tobacco), or self- or other-oriented touch (such as fiddling with your hair or giving someone a comforting hug). We all know that some of these strategies are healthier than others in the long run (exercising and relaxing being far better than smoking, eating, and taking drugs), although they all seem comforting at the time. Many work in combination with appraisal-based strategies, especially distraction. It is difficult, though not impossible, to carry your anger onto the jogging path, into the bathtub, or into bed, but it is certainly better if you don't.

What makes many physical activities and substances addictive is that they work for a short time and then have a rebound effect, working against you (Thayer, 1996: 157–168). Cigarettes, for example, calm you down for a few minutes, but as their effect wears off, you become more worked up, so that you need another cigarette to calm you down – on to chain smoking. Sugar works in much the same way. You get a momentary rush of energy at the end of the day when you eat that candy bar, but an hour or so later, not only has the sugar high worn off but it has consumed energy, so you are even more exhausted than before. Exercise, on the other hand, is addictive in the benevolent sense. The more you exercise, the more energized you feel (unless taken to extremes). Relaxation training is equally therapeutic.

Managing Expressions and Impressions. As the facial feedback hypothesis suggests, people can manage the emotions they feel by managing what they express. Managing emotional expressions at work is so ubiquitous that some people consider workers who do not smile to be "facial loafers." Hochschild (1983: 127–128) reports the following incident: "A young businessman said to a flight attendant, 'Why aren't you smiling?' She put her tray back on the food cart, looked him in the eye, and said, 'I'll tell you what. You smile first, then I'll smile.' The businessman smiled at her. 'Good,' she replied. 'Now freeze, and hold that for fifteen hours.' "

A slightly different strategy is to express emotions outright, but to redirect them in ways that cannot be seen or heard by others. Workers who take 911 calls "make faces, roll their eyes, stick out their tongues, plug their noses and throw up their hands (or other objects) to express an emotion that they were not supposed to express in their voice" (Tracy & Tracy, 1998: 13). One bill collector dealing with an abusive debtor "hit the 'mute' button and said some words that he would have been fired for saying if the debtor could hear them: 'You asshole, my credit card never looked that bad. I'm not a deadbeat like you.' " Another was seen pounding the desk and cursing "that jerk" or "idiot," but only after the phone conversation was over (Sutton, 1991: 263). Disneyland employees go "backstage" or, more accurately perhaps, "understage" to the honeycombed tunnels beneath Disneyland to yell at little Suzie or kick a garbage can (Van Maanen & Kunda, 1989).

Social and Antisocial Strategies. Emotion is often managed by seeking out other people, avoiding them, or interacting with them in ways that produce the desired emotion. These methods do not seem to line up neatly with components of the emotion process; social situations are typically complex enough to involve several components. For example, people report managing anger by removing themselves from the provoking person or situation, the often used *time-out* strategy. Time-outs may work because of distraction (you think about other things), by providing a chance to consider the other's perspective (when you don't have to think about defending your own), through exercise (if you literally walk away from the situation), by making the situation seem less important (by getting some psychological distance), or all of these. Most likely, however, they work by preventing misguided problem-focused coping in the form of saying something hurtful that you probably didn't really mean.

We may also seek out other people as a way of managing our emotions. Vernon (1941: 460) studied people who continued to live in blitzed British cities during World War II and concluded: "there is no doubt that being with others [during air raids] helps the majority of people, and that those who live alone tend to find raids much more trying." He said that "the influence of a few confident and unconcerned individuals in a group, or the cheerfulness of a warden or shelter marshal, calms those who are inclined to be nervous" (pp. 460–461). Unfortunately, other people do not necessarily act the way we want or expect, so they may not always help us manage emotions the way we would like. If you seek out friends to calm your anger by telling them your account of what happened, they may (quite understandably) fuel your anger by telling you that the situation is indeed awful, unfair, and not to be tolerated (Tice & Baumeister, 1993: 399). If you are feeling unloved, there is always the risk that the person you turn to for love will not respond, making you feel even more unloved.

You can also compare yourself to other people. If you wonder whether you have studied enough for the exam, you can seek out your classmates, and the odds are good that you will find someone who has studied less and someone who has studied more. You can take that to mean that you studied just enough (Albas & Albas, 1988). Seeking out familiar others can be reassuring in its own right. When workers constructing skyscrapers reel from the emotional crisis of seeing one of their co-workers fall to his death, they quit working, go drinking, and reminisce together (Haas, 1978).

Emotion can also be managed socially by trying to create a certain impression or act "as if . . ." in the hope that the role will become the reality. Students try to project an image of being "calm and serious, but not ruthlessly competitive," presumably to convince both themselves and other people (Albas & Albas, 1988: 272). Construction workers walking on the tops of buildings act confidently and are very critical of others who show fear (Haas, 1978). Presumably, if facial feedback from faking a smile makes you feel more positive, faking an entire repertoire of verbal and nonverbal cues has a more powerful effect, especially when others treat you as if you were confident and fearless. You may start to believe it yourself.

Acting and Reacting Emotionally

With all the strategies that are available to manage emotion and with all the practice we get, why do we still find it so difficult? Even though we often think of emotional expression and emotional experience as primitive and simple, they are actually well rehearsed and very skilled activities. As with other skilled activities such as playing a piano or weaving a cloth, any seemingly spontaneous performance is built on years of practice, and even the most carefully followed pattern must be executed one note or one thread at a time. One difference, however, is that there are people who have never touched a piano or a loom, but everyone has practiced emotional expression from birth.

Emotion management is difficult because emotions often do not give you time to think – and for good reason. If you hesitate when confronted by a grizzly bear, you may be dead meat. In fact, emotion theorists have argued that emotion helps creatures survive (including human creatures) by providing for quick action (or inaction in the case of freezing in fear) when contemplation or indecision could be fatal. Darwin gave us the famous example of leaping back from a snake striking at its glass cage (1872/1965: 38). His conscious mind knew that there was no danger, but his automatic reactions did not. Confronting a snake is no time to deliberate.

We can make choices in a flash based on split-second judgments, but scholars debate whether these are true emotions or simpler reactions such as inclinations or urges.[3] Even if they are not emotions in the richest sense, we should not underestimate the importance of instantaneous reactions in social life, especially those associated with approaching and avoiding other people. A large body of research on nonverbal responsiveness indicates that people make adjustments to each other in terms of length of turns at talk, pausing, distance, body lean, and eye gaze, based on simple arousal and valence judgments, in ways that are too subtle and microscopic to be controlled consciously (Argyle & Dean, 1965; Burgoon, 1993; Cappella, 1981; Cappella & Greene, 1982). These emotions or quasi-emotions can have a profound impact on whether we feel comfortable and interact easily with other people.

Even though many ways of adjusting to one another nonverbally are under limited conscious control, we are often quite aware of our emotional reactions and, given a moment or two to get a grip, we can sometimes, if not always, react the way we know we should.[4] Goleman uses the term *emotional hijacking* to refer to the sense that our emotions control us, but we can also learn to control them (disarm the hijackers, if you will). Impulse control skills develop early in life, are extremely valuable, and are critical components for school curricula on "emotional intelligence" (Goleman, 1995). For example, the amount of time (up to 15 minutes) that 4-year-olds could wait for a marshmal-

---

[3] Zajonc (1980, 1984) and Lazarus (1982, 1984) have gone several rounds on this issue. Zajonc claims that emotional responses precede and do not depend on appraisal; Lazarus claims that appraisal processes are necessary for a true emotional reaction.

[4] LeDoux (1994: 272) argues on neurological grounds that "to the extent that the emotional stimulus is one that the species has developed specific response strategies to cope with, the initial reactions will be automatic and involuntary and the secondary reaction will be voluntary." Oatley (1992: 131) cites research indicating that in practice, however, only about 15% of people in fires and floods behaved in an organized way, and only about 15% of soldiers in battle actually fired their weapons. The wiring may be there for voluntary control, but this does not mean that we necessarily use it well.

low or pretzel was positively correlated with their SAT scores 14 years later (Shoda, Mischel, & Peake, 1990). The positive value of controlling more antisocial urges such as the urge to beat your children or to shoot a police officer goes without saying. Skill in emotion control can help you goes to college and avoid going to jail.

Some people are able to stand their ground when the grizzly bear charges or react calmly when the boss yells. Their reactions seem spontaneous, but in fact, preparation and training have probably gone into cultivating the "right" response. Clearly, part of this skill is impulse control, but part of it also involves developing habits of mind (appraisals) that lead to the appropriate emotion. Flight attendants are able to manage their anger by blaming themselves for passengers' bad behavior, so much that it seems to be the natural way of thinking, and being nice is their spontaneous reaction. It takes time, however, to set the new patterns of thinking in place and to override the previously natural reaction of holding the passengers responsible for their own bad behavior. It can be done, but as with learning to weave a complicated pattern easily, it takes commitment and practice.

The danger of managing appraisals in the service of specific emotional situations is that the appraisals may not stay specific to one situation. If you train yourself to feel responsible for passengers' bad behavior, you may start to feel responsible for everyone's bad behavior. If you develop an attitude of "looking on the bright side" in a situation you cannot control, you may not recognize a threatening situation that you need to confront or avoid. Worse yet, if you develop a defiant attitude in order to stand up to a grizzly bear's charge, you might continue to be defiant when attacked, which would be a big mistake. The same might be true if you are attacked verbally by your boss. Similarly, impulse control and behavior control can themselves get out of control such that you are constantly questioning and never acting. Because of the great variety of situations to which we respond emotionally, it is impossible to develop an emotional stance that is always optimal. This is one of the reasons that emotion is often considered to be "irrational" (Oatley, 1992). Perhaps the best we can do is to achieve a stance that is generally helpful and to try to be flexible as new circumstances arise.

"Irrational" automatic reactions are especially likely to come into play when people are stressed (Zillman, 1993). I am reminded of a friend who swore that when her child cried she would never respond with the statement that she hated to hear from her own mother: "If you don't stop crying, I'll give you something to cry about." When her daughter nearly pulled a hot iron over on herself, was pulled away, and started crying, the mother said, "If you don't stop crying, I'll give . . ." and caught herself. Such automatic reactions persist if we never reflect on our reactions, if we believe we cannot or should not control our emotions, or if we are under such stress that emotional control is very difficult. The moral of the story is to be careful about what emotional responses you practice enough to make them automatic; they are always with you. Yet even if certain emotions are difficult to manage in the short run, they may be more tractable in the long run, and that is the basis for most counseling. Deep-seated, maladaptive thinking patterns that lead to dysfunctional emotional reactions are a common focus of therapy, based either in childhood experiences or in present-day patterns. Those that operate below the level of conscious awareness may be especially difficult to understand and to change.

We may also fail to manage our emotions effectively because, let's face it, we do not really want to. For one thing, we cherish them as aspects of our "genuine" and "authentic" selves. And we cling to them because they are deeply familiar and are ways of coping with the world, even if they are not always pleasant or effective. As one therapist wrote about a patient, "to give up his main way of being in the world would be so terrifying that his present misery would seem happiness by contrast" (Bugenthal, 1990, cited in Lazarus & Lazarus, 1994: 30).

For another thing, managing emotions takes effort. It may be easier just to suffer from the unwanted emotion, especially if you are not the one to suffer. Using shame to discipline your children, although potentially harmful to them, may be easier than facing your own shame and trying to change it. You may make efforts to change only when you believe there is something very important at stake – your job, your marriage, your family, your own or others' mental health. The habits of a lifetime are difficult to change, especially when they lie as deep and are as much a part of the self as are emotions.

Finally, emotions may serve as an excuse for behaving as you please (Averill, 1993). I lashed out at my husband because I was angry; the anger made me do it. I beat my wife because of "uncontrollable jealousy" (Gelles & Straus, 1988). To be legitimate excuses, however, emotions must be intense and involve a strong physiological component; no one would accept uncontrolled irritation or unmanageable fondness as excuses. Only powerful emotions are capable of "carrying us away." On the other hand, if we as a culture believed that people should be able to manage their emotions, people would be held responsible for their actions even in the "heat of passion" or the "depths of despair."

In the end, emotion control is always a matter of degree. No one can be under complete emotion control at all times, and no one is completely out of control. Emotional experience and its expression/communication are a rich blend of both automatic and controlled processes. It makes as much sense to ask if emotion is spontaneous or strategic (or, alternatively, whether emotion is expressed or communicated) as it does to ask whether bicycle riding or piano playing is spontaneous or strategic. All three depend on both automatic and controlled processes that work together in complex ways to produce a highly skilled performance that has been practiced so much that it looks instinctive.[5]

Adapting Emotional Messages to Audiences

There is a second sense in which emotion expression/communication is goal directed. If emotion is expressed spontaneously, it is displayed the same way, regardless of whether you are alone or with others. If you feel anger, you express it, period. Emotion that is communicated strategically, however, may change as it is adapted for an audience because some goal other than "letting it out" is operating. If you feel anger in the presence of other people you may express it, but you may also suppress it, exaggerate it, or change it in order to create a certain impression, manage a conflict, or just go about your business.

There is a great deal of evidence that people often *do not* express emotion when they feel it and that they often *do* express emotion when conditions are optimal to reach an audience. Think of the child who hurts herself but cries only when a sympathetic audience appears (Fridlund, 1994: Chaps. 7 and 8; Zeman & Garber, 1996). In fact, we may make those adaptations instantly and automatically, often without even being aware that we are doing so. Imagine that you are

---

[5] Ekman and Davidson (1994a: 281) state that "to the extent that such regulatory strategies become automated over time, there might never be a point where emotion is completely uncontrolled. Rather, it might be more appropriate to consider the degree of regulation that is in effect, not whether such regulation is present."

watching someone with an injured finger move a heavy TV, and he accidentally sets the TV down on his finger. You are likely to wince in pain, mimicking his expression a second later (scholars call this *motor mimicry*). What may surprise you, however, is that you would be more likely to wince if the injured person were facing you, especially at the point when the two of you make the greatest eye contact (Bavelas, Black, Lemery, & Mullett, 1986). Is your wince expressing your vicarious pain or communicating your sympathy? It is probably doing both (Hess, Banse, & Kappas, 1995).

Displays of emotion are also more likely as the situation becomes more fully interactive. Imagine that someone is telling you a story about the time she nearly drowned or was nearly shot by a sniper. You feel for her, so you are likely to grimace or show fear. But you are most likely to grimace when you are talking with her face-to-face, somewhat less likely when talking over the telephone, even less likely when the two of you are separated by a partition, and least likely when she tells the story via a tape recorder (Chovil, 1991). Furthermore, the social nature of the situation need not even be real; it can be imagined. If you know your buddy is in the next room watching the same funny video that you are, you smile about as much as you would if you were in the same room, and more than if you were alone or if your buddy is in another room doing something else (Fridlund, 1991).

These studies demonstrate that emotional displays are ways to communicate connections to other people, not just to express your own feelings, but they also introduce some interesting complexities. First, it seems that we smile when we are happy and we smile when we are social, but more so when we are social. When people were observed in bowling alleys, they smiled more frequently when talking to their friends than they did when they made strikes or spares (Kraut & Johnston, 1979). The presence of strangers has also been found to inhibit expressions of emotion, whereas having friends around tends to facilitate them (Buck, Losow, Murphy, & Constanzo, 1992). But emotion and sociability are not so easily separated (Buck, 1991). We may smile more with friends because they make us happier than even a strike or a spare does, or we may feel another person's pain more intensely when he is facing us than when he is turned away or in another room.

Another interesting implication is that we may never really be separated from others or completely free of social goals if we can conjure up other people in our imaginations. You may continue to be haunted by the specter of what Mom would do if she heard you yelling, what the Little League coach would say if he saw you crying, or how humiliated the family would be if anyone knew that you left the scene of the accident. The *generalized other* (Mead, 1934) is a part of our psyches, so we never really escape social opinion. There is no goal-free, asocial, spontaneous emotional experience that escapes concerns for an audience. Instead, so-called spontaneous expressions have strategic adaptations built into them.

We also manage emotional messages with many specific social purposes in mind. Emotional expressions can come in handy to make the babe at the party think you are a sensitive New Age guy, to intimidate your co-workers into letting you have your way, or to persuade your best friend to quit smoking. Even a genuine emotion expressed spontaneously can also function strategically to advance conscious and unconscious goals, and can be "helped along" when necessary. You can cultivate genuine anger by dwelling on injustice, genuine guilt by dwelling on what could have been done, or genuine sadness by dwelling on your helplessness (Frijda, 1994).

People often get their way by forceful emotional expressions (with adults we call them *outbursts*; with children we call them *tantrums*). Regardless of what else they may accomplish, strong expressions of emotion always do one thing – they get people's attention. Most likely they also convince others (at least for the moment) that the issue is important, although careful reflection may reveal otherwise. And most likely they create an emotional "commotion" or "scene" (as in "Don't make a scene") that must be managed, especially if the outburst continues for any length of time. Ignoring it is always an option, but it is an option that delegitimizes the feeling in a more blatant way than ignoring a fleeting sneer or a subtle smile. You have to IGNORE it rather than just let it pass. Strong expressions of emotion also tend to create emotional contagion. An extremely angry person can galvanize anger in others (for good or for ill). I like the phrase used as the title for a book on this issue: *The Tactical Uses of Passion* (Bailey, 1983). It implies that the passion may be real but is also used for tactical purposes.

At times, we feel exactly as we want to feel and are expected to feel. At other times (and these are the interesting ones!), we are torn between expressing "how we really feel" and going along with "how we are supposed to feel." Some people feel especially torn, and they report having difficulty expressing their true feelings and worrying about the effects on themselves and other people if they do. They are more likely to agree with statements such as "I want to express my emotions honestly, but I am afraid that it may cause me embarrassment or hurt" and "I would like to be more spontaneous in my emotional reactions but I just can't seem to do it" (King & Emmons, 1990). Almost everyone feels this dilemma to some degree, and for good reason. The push to express what we feel can work against the pull to express what we are supposed to feel, and we are caught in the middle.

The Wisdom of Emotion and Risks of Ignoring It

Every day we override the goal of indulging our feelings in the service of other goals. It is a beautiful late summer day in Missoula, Montana, and I am longing to hike in the Rattlesnake Wilderness rather than to sit here in my office writing. It is a complex mental and emotional dilemma, too complicated to be called simply "heart versus head." It involves present emotions (I love the outdoors, but this chapter is fun to write too), future emotions (if I went hiking I would feel guilty for not working, but I'm going to feel guilty if I don't get any exercise), knowledge of long-term goals and conditions that foster or inhibit them (the semester is starting tomorrow, so I had better write, but cold weather is coming soon, so I had better hike), and plans that may take both into account (I'll write now but hike later and gaze out the window in the meantime). I am acting like an older version of the 4-year-old child who delays eating one marshmallow in order to get two later, but who is to say that this is wise? Sometimes we know that emotions are irrational (fear of mice), inappropriate (wanting to wave and yell at someone during a symphony concert), against our long-term interests (having the urge to ram the driver ahead), or otherwise clearly leading us astray. We admire the child who develops the feeling habits that will lead her to higher SAT scores and less immediate gratification, but should we?

Emotion has its own wisdom, and ignoring it entails certain risks to the individual and to the species. Millions of years of evolution can be wrong (because our circumstances are always changing), but they do deserve consideration. Many theorists have speculated about the functions that emotions serve for all humans and probably for other species as well (Darwin, 1872/1965; Ekman & Davidson, 1994b: 99–139; Oatley, 1993). As discussed in Chapter 1, emotion orients us to important concerns, monitors the state of our goals and well-being, mobilizes (or demobilizes) the body, resets action priorities, and makes this state known to others through expression.

Specific emotions also serve specific functions. Some are obviously linked to physical well-being but also generalize to social and spiritual well-being. Fear helps us avoid or escape danger (from lions or public speaking at Lions Clubs). Curiosity helps us learn about the world (where to find food and how to search the Internet). Disgust helps us avoid noxious foods and odors (rotted meat and revolting table manners). Other emotions help us survive socially. Love forms and cements social bonds; loneliness and jealousy foster and protect connections; shame and guilt goad us to conform to social expectations. Still other emotions orient us to more general goals. Boredom may lead us to set goals; anger may push against obstacles to our goals; pride and joy are the rewards for accomplishing goals.

It is more difficult to see the wisdom in negative, seemingly pointless emotions such as regret or grief, but they too have their purposes. Knowing that we may feel regret "can make us think twice in order to avoid doing something we will later regret, or should later regret" (Landman, 1993: 23). Grief is also puzzling. We grieve over what is irretrievably lost, so it seems like an emotion that is too painful too late. Knowing that we will feel grief, like anticipating regret, may motivate us to appreciate what we have, but love and joy do the same thing and are much more pleasant. What good does the suffering do? Is it a necessary evil, like a disease that is painful but from which most people recover? If so, there is no wisdom in grief; it is just part of the human condition, and it is best either to suffer without complaining or to get over it as soon as possible. But another view says that there is wisdom in grief. Grief forces us to withdraw from everyday life and come to terms with the meaning of the loss (of a loved one, a job, or a dream), to face the void, and gradually to rebuild new meanings on new foundations (Cochran & Claspell, 1987). According to this view, we need to respect our emotions, especially the unpleasant ones, rather than trying to "get over," escape, or ignore them. A recent book called *The Care of the Soul* (with chapter titles like "Jealousy and Envy: Healing Poisons" and "Gifts of Depression") sent this message from the top of the *New York Times* best-seller list (Moore, 1992). The message is neither to suppress nor to give in to emotions, but to pay attention to them, respect them, and consider what role they do and should play in your life.

Sometimes that is easier said than done; our emotions can also demand too much. It is not unusual for the agonizing fear that can result from trauma or devastating grief over profound loss never to be resolved with new beginnings (as will be discussed in the next chapter). Emotions may heighten one's sensitivity to dangers that no longer exist and therefore make no sense, such as when combat veterans become panicked at the sound of a car backfiring. Then it makes sense *not* to pay attention to one's emotions, but emotions can be very insistent and require enormous energy just to ignore, much less to manage effectively.

Skills at reading and managing one's own and other people's emotions are key components of emotional intelligence (Saarni, 1990; Salovey & Mayer, 1990). In some cases, however, the most effective way to communicate may be NOT to manage your emotions to create a calm, "presentable" emotional demeanor, but rather to be spontaneous. Konradi (1996: 415–416) reports that one rape survivor she studied initially "sought to achieve an inner calm and to preclude any show of emotion" in court, but after the jury failed to reach a verdict, she "decided to become a 'real' rape victim" ... " 'cause otherwise they weren't gonna believe anything. . . . If they [the jury] wanted somebody hysterical on the stand, they were gonna get one.' "

On a broader social level, it may be difficult to assess how a society as a whole is meeting the emotional needs of its members if prohibitions or constraints on expression are too powerful. How can we know how lonely people are if expressing loneliness is viewed as a sign of weakness or lack of self-reliance? How can we change our orientation to shame if shame is itself too shameful to express? Communicating emotions to others serves a role in society that parallels its role for individuals. It helps us stay in touch with the important concerns and goals of society, helps us monitor deviations from them, and motivates action to change things.[6] Yet at the same time, as individuals and as a society, we must do so judiciously. We cannot jump to meet the needs of emotional "squeaky wheels," nor can we assume that "poisonous" emotions always heal or that depression is always a "gift."

---

[6] Taylor (1995) reports that the planning committee for the National Lesbian Conference in Atlanta in 1991 appointed official "vibes watchers" to "stay alert to the collective emotional climate." In an atmosphere of public emotion control, what is a vibes watcher to do?

The Demands of Emotion Management on the Job

Groups and organizations often have to contend with tensions between the collective emotional goals of the group and the individual emotional goals of its members. It seems that there are always some people who fit into the emotional climate of an organization naturally and without effort, and organizations try to hire them. In the days when airlines wanted passengers to think of themselves as guests in someone's living room, airline "hostesses" were predominantly white, middle-class females who were especially well socialized to be pleasant, sociable, and (above all) deferent. Just the opposite was true for collection agencies, which wanted angry, "fire-in-the-belly" types to serve as bill collectors (Hochschild, 1983).

Often, however, the fit between the spontaneous emotional profiles of employees and the emotional climates that organizations try to achieve is less than perfect, even for those who are otherwise well suited emotionally for their jobs. It takes work to feel happy for 15 hours nonstop, to feel angry toward people who have lost their jobs, or to feel delight at the 10th child who pokes you in the belly. It requires "emotional labor" (Hochschild, 1983) – managing your own emotions in order to produce the intended emotional state in others. In my job as college professor, I am expected to show enthusiasm and excitement for the classes that I teach in order to get the students excited. Sometimes it comes naturally; sometimes it doesn't. If it doesn't, I have to "work up" the appropriate feelings. In many occupations, especially service-oriented ones, expressing your own spontaneously felt emotions is not acceptable. You must show the right feelings or you are not doing your job. If you are a hairdresser and can be "naturally" friendly but not "forced," you are likely to be more successful at your job and receive more tips from customers (Parkinson, 1991).

"Maintaining a difference between feeling and feigning over the long run leads to strain. We try to reduce this strain by pulling the two closer together either by changing what we feel or by changing what we feign," says Hochschild (1983: 90). If you change what you feel, you run the risk of becoming totally identified with your job and experiencing burnout. If you change what you feign, you run the risk of losing your job (if you refuse to adapt altogether) or of feeling cynical and phony (if you refuse to identify at all with the feelings that you feign). Several commentators have noted that the distinction between felt and feigned may be oversimplified and the tension between them overblown (Waldron, 1994; Wouters, 1989), but some degree of "emotional dissonance" seems undeniable (Middleton, 1989).

Novice monks who joined Christ of the Hills Monastery chose the option of changing what they felt and identifying completely with the "job" (Bruder, 1992). They adopted the emotional ideals of the group (unaffected, emotionally composed, tranquil), altered their emotional displays accordingly, and reported achieving genuine calm. All this is good, except that being a monk is not just a job; it is a complete life to which members make a deep commitment. For those who have 9-to-5 jobs, total identification is less appealing and a balance of involvement and detachment seems to work better in the long run. For example, nurses, physicians, psychologists, therapists, and social workers at a psychiatric hospital who reported feeling strong empathic concern for their patients, but who did not get caught up in the feelings of those around them, reported being able to communicate with patients in responsive ways, felt effective on the job, and were at less risk of feeling emotionally callous, exhausted, and burned out in the long run (Miller et al., 1988).

On a more sinister note, Flam (1993) argues that many modern organizations inspire loyalty in workers, not through shared pride or shared enthusiasm, but through shared fear – fear of losing their jobs, material benefits, or life chances. Throughout Terkel's (1972) collection of interviews of working people about their work, Flam reads fear. In Jackal's *Moral Mazes* (1988), Flam sees "an anxiety-laden but enthusiasm-displaying corporate world" where even "corporate managers live with the foreboding sense of organizational contingency and capriciousness" (1993: 70–71). She also argues that Peters and Waterman's (1982) widely read analysis of change-embracing organizations, *In Search of Excellence*, fails to note that what may really distinguish excellent from mediocre organizations is the absence of fear. To the extent that there is a uniform and dominant emotional tone to the group's climate, it may be worthwhile to think of social groups such as corporations as greedy, terrorizing, compassionate, or shaming.

There are also many examples of workers who do emotion work and at the same time engage in rebellion and resistance, some of it overt but much of it covert and subversive. One flight attendant who was outraged that a passenger called her friend a "nigger bitch" "accidentally" tripped and spilled a Bloody Mary on the passenger's white pants suit (Hochschild, 1983: 114). Disneyland workers get revenge with a "seatbelt squeeze" ("cinching up of a required seatbelt such that the passenger is doubled over at the point of departure and left gasping for the duration of a ride") (Van Maanen & Kunda, 1989: 66). One secretary reported "drying her shoes on her boss's elegant cream-colored curtains" (Golding, 1986, cited in Putnam & Mumby, 1993: 47). On a more benign note, if you tire of restaurant servers' forced friendliness, try this tactic. "As soon as the waiter walks up, stick out your hand and say in as cheerful a voice as you can manage, 'Hi, my name's Dave and I'm your customer tonight' " (Unterman & Sesser, 1984, cited in Rafaeli & Sutton, 1987: 29). Such small acts of resistance help individuals to go along with the system and yet retain some personal autonomy when dealing with trying or simply annoying circumstances. Nevertheless, most of the acts of resistance reported in studies of emotional labor are destructive and provide little true empowerment.

If workers are given enough autonomy, however, they can often adjust to the emotional demands of their work environments in more constructive, flexible, and creative ways. Emotion work is most demanding when you have face-to-face or voice-to-voice contact with clients (as in most service professions), when a supervisor monitors you constantly (such as when supervisors listen in on phone calls), when others' feelings always count more than yours (when any "onion letter" can get a flight attendant fired), and when there is no place or time for escape (such as in an airplane) (Hochschild, 1983). As an alternative, workers could be permitted to have breaks from emotion work, need not be required to pull off a perfect performance every time, and could be allowed to use the emotion management strategies that work for them. For example, clerks at convenience stores adjust their emotion work by engaging in pleasantries with customers when business is slow but dropping them when things get busy (Sutton & Rafaeli, 1988).

By contrast, rule inflexibility contributes to the emotional exhaustion of police officers (Gaines & Jermier, 1983), and excessive bureaucracy makes nurses angry and frustrated (Thomas & Droppleman, 1997). Some workers try to manage their emotions under conditions that doom them to fail, as did the floor instructors in a workshop for people with developmental disabilities who could not handle the boredom and the frustration of being held responsible for problems over which they had no control (Copp, 1998). On cruise ships, it was so difficult for workers to know when and where their emotion work ended and their personal time and space began that they never really felt that they were off stage and so were subject to burnout (Tracy, 1998).

Too often the structural conditions that produce emotional strain or limit workers' ability to do effective emotional labor are not recognized as organizational problems with organizational solutions, but rather they are presumed to be personal problems to be dealt with by individuals (as emotional problems so often are). Burnout "may be treated as a personal, private pathology – and therefore one that deeply stigmatizes the incumbent" – yet another case of blaming the victim (Copp, 1998: 322). Often the only short-term solutions available to individuals were occasional mental health days or other brief breaks from work, and the only long-term solutions were to move up (if you're lucky) or out ("no more job, no more pay") (Copp, 1998: 323; Tracy, 1998: 26).

We professors must be "on stage" in the classroom, in meetings, and in consultation with others several hours a day, but we also have the freedom (and it is part of our jobs) to hole up in our offices to do tasks best done alone and without interruption (such as reading, writing, grading, and data analysis). Solitary self-discipline requires another sort of emotion management, but at least we have variety and choice, which are built into the structure of academic work. And we have many strategies up our sleeves for doing emotion work. We know how to make jokes when we are frustrated because students haven't done the reading, to channel public speaking anxiety into enthusiasm, and to use our initially fake enthusiasm and plastered-on smiles as a way of bringing ourselves out of bad moods. Certainly, we are sometimes torn between the felt and the fake, but that doesn't mean that we cannot *necessarily* have it both ways. On the other hand, having to muster the enthusiasm to write a long journal article, to read stacks of technical reports, or to face hundreds of students every day may be many people's idea of hell.

Managing the Emotional Climates of Organizations

Any group of people who spend time together have rules and norms about emotional expression, and work groups are no exception (Heise & O'Brien, 1993). There are norms about how much emotion is acceptable to express, about which emotions are acceptable and which are unacceptable, and about how they are to be controlled. Emotion rules and norms can arise spontaneously from the expressive styles of all the people involved; they can be influenced by the nature of the task; they can be adopted from a larger culture or subculture, they can be actively controlled by people in power, or all of these.

Consider the emotional norms and rules for students in medical school. There is a general norm favoring emotion control more than expressiveness, especially for weak or inappropriate emotions such as embarrassment, sexual desire, disgust, or sadness (Smith & Kleinman, 1989). This norm has probably developed, at least in part, because the task of caring for the sick requires that doctors see people naked (fostering embarrassment or sexual desire), bleeding (fostering disgust), or in pain (fostering sadness). No doctor can do her job if she cannot manage those and other feelings. Western medical practice cultivates a climate of "affective neutrality" and "detached concern" (Lief & Fox, 1963) that is consistent with norms for the professions in general and with Western culture's emphasis on rationality and objectivity. Furthermore, "[b]ecause we associate authority in this society with an unemotional persona, affective neutrality reinforces professionals' power and keeps clients from challenging them" (Smith & Kleinman, 1989: 56). Students are socialized to follow these norms in medical school through techniques such as thinking of the body as a machine, but they also come well prepared to orient to facts rather than feelings from years of formal education and a predominantly middle-class upbringing.

So many forces come together to make emotion control in Western medical settings what it is today that it seems right and even inevitable, but there are other ways to do medicine. At the "Gesundheit!" Institute (German for "good health!"), Dr. Patch Adams and his colleagues have developed a medical counterculture based on devoted rather than detached concern and on humor rather than authority. Dr. Adams often wears a clown nose. They criticize the medical establishment for neglecting the emotional and personal side of healing, and have founded a hospital based on radically different rules and norms (Adams, 1993). Southwest Airlines does the same thing in the airline industry. Whereas most airlines cultivate an atmosphere of "gracious seriousness," Southwest tries to get people to laugh, using lines like "Please pass all the plastic cups to the center aisle so we can wash them out and use them for the next group of passengers" (Sunoo, 1995: 62). They have to deal with the same fearful or angry passengers as other airlines, but their strategy is emotion expression, not control (or at least a different sort of control).

It is not uncommon for organizations to try to manage the spontaneous emotional climate of the group strategically, whether or not they are aware of exactly what they are doing. The bill collectors studied by Sutton (1991) shared an open office where they were surrounded by other intense, slightly irritated people, producing an atmosphere of contagious anger. Rituals such as sales rallies, awards ceremonies, or highly orchestrated retreats are used intentionally to cultivate, reinforce, and celebrate feelings of unrestrained enthusiasm, loyalty to and admiration for chosen role models, or just the right brand of esprit de corps. Van Maanen and Kunda (1989: 46) describe Tupperware assemblies as " 'evangelical in style,' wherein good cheer is virtually mandated." Flam (1993: 70) argues that many modern corporations, especially those with powerful cultures, encourage feelings of anxiety and fear in their employees. Employees "are very likely to feel both entrapped and fearful. They may feel anxious not only about breaking the conduct rules but also about leaving" their jobs. But the open expression of fear is taboo, so we have "an anxiety-laden, but enthusiasm-displaying corporate world."

In general, however, emotion suppression and control are more valued in large, bureaucratic organizations than is emotional spontaneity. There is a deep-seated cultural belief that rationality is goal-oriented, productive, objective, and professional, whereas emotionality is chaotic, distracting, capricious, and personal. Obviously, reason should control emotion; therefore, the rational goals and strategies of the organization should control the emotions of its members as they work, and personal feelings should be left at home (Hummel, 1987; Putnam & Mumby, 1993; Waldron, 1994). Emotion should be excluded from all decisions, paving the way for clear cost-benefit analysis; and workers should be motivated by rational incentives like pay and promotion.

Emotion is seen very differently in alternative organizations such as the social change organization and the theater troupe studied by Glaser (1993). There emotion was seen as a valued resource that aids decision making, motivates action, and helps bind the group together. A member of the theater troupe says this about passion: "I think that it's a catalyst. I think it's the most positive thing that we have in our group. I think that's when things move, when things really get going." In the feminist health clinics studied by Morgen (1995: 244), "much of the day-to-day interaction among staff and many decision-making processes are carried out in an affect-laden vocabulary" and in an "atmosphere of open emotional expression" (see also Morgen, 1983: 212–213). Emotional countercultures like these include members' feelings as an integral part of the work, but they also value the positive role that emotion plays in promoting group cohesiveness, individual and group motivation, and good decisions.

The irony is that we can find organizational discourse promoting the strategic communication of emotion (smiles are part of our jobs) and an alternative discourse promoting spontaneous communication (cry if you need to), but still little discourse about the need to *fuse* spontaneity and strategy. For example, the feminist health clinics mentioned earlier had regular "feelings meetings" alternating with "issues meetings," but how can issues and feelings be separated? In a similar vein, the volunteer activist and theater groups mentioned earlier were able to choose their projects based on the amount of enthusiasm generated among the members. If there wasn't sufficient interest, it wasn't done. But imagine a hospital that chooses its projects based on how much enthusiasm the nurses, doctors, and orderlies are able to generate. Probably many a patient would bleed to death, many a bedpan would overflow, and some of those grouchy old coots would get pretty lonely.

The Body Shop, a cosmetics company that employs thousands of workers in over 40 countries, primarily though not exclusively women, strives to make emotion an integral part of their organization. Their founder states that "business practices would improve immeasurably if they were guided by 'feminine' principles – qualities like love and care and intuition" (Roddick, 1991, cited in Martin, Knopoff, & Beckman, 1998: 447). Researchers who studied the organization heard the employees discussing a wide range of emotional topics and noticed affectionate nonverbal communication (hugs, kisses) and a great deal of emotional understanding and consideration among them, in addition to the strategic emotional work that one would expect with clients (Martin et al., 1998: 448–449). Nevertheless, it was difficult for Body Shop workers to maintain an emotionally satisfying community under the pressures of growth (new employees they didn't know), time and financial pressures (social events taking lower priority), emotional diversity (some employees thought, "Don't get emotional; let's just deal with it"), and stress (long hours leading to emotional exhaustion) (pp. 451–457).

Finding ways to achieve the emotional goals of the organization and its members more constructively is a creative and challenging enterprise. Organizations should recognize that "emotion ... is not simply an adjunct to work; rather, it is the process through which members constitute their work environment by negotiating a shared reality" (Putnam & Mumby, 1993: 36). It is not just a resource to be manipulated (as the term *emotional labor* implies), but a way of relating to the work that is at the heart of the organization and has a wisdom of its own (as the alternative term *work feelings* implies). In addressing resistance to emotional control, Waldron (1994: 400) asks, "what are the more constructive verbal equivalents of these revenge moves?" Conrad and Witte (1994) also argue that we may be better off if we (and especially others) are encouraged to control feelings at work and that emotion rules are "complex, ambiguous, and malleable" enough to be used artfully to escape the dilemma (p. 426).

Some research shows how this can be done better. We can try to optimize people's work experience by structuring jobs to provide the right degree of challenge (neither boring nor overwhelming) so that people remain interested and feel good about developing their job skills (Csikszentmihalyi, 1990). We can make sure that all employees understand the "big picture" of their work so that they can take justifiable pride in their own contributions to the group effort. We might reflect on whether certain jobs really are worthwhile, or whether they could be restructured to be both more satisfying for the worker and more valuable to the organization. We can provide on-site day care, flexible time, and support programs as a way of recognizing that a worried, distracted, or distressed employee is not giving her best to the group.

We can also communicate in ways that fuse reason and emotion rather than continuing the war. In meetings, we can try to express cogently both our feelings and our thoughts on the issues. We can recognize that emotionless employees and highly emotional ones can be equally threatening because the former may be alienated and amoral and the latter may be overwrought and self-righteous (Putnam & Mumby, 1993: 40). We can define emotion and emotional labor as legitimate topics of discussion that can help to share the burden and muster support among coworkers. Occasionally perhaps we can go so far as to cross the employee–client emotion-control barrier to confess forbidden emotions or permit lapses in control. One author gives the example of an airline employee who described her day as an "emotional roller-coaster" and began to cry when explaining that the wife of one of her colleagues had died. She exclaimed, "I know agents are supposed to control their emotions when they are at work." Fortunately, she had met a supportive client who thought it was okay to express feelings (Putnam & Mumby, 1993: 51). Surely we can tolerate a few such lapses.

Perhaps we might even reflect on the emotional demands we make on others. We are the clients that organizations are asking employees to please, so we control the demands that are placed on others in a direct way. I still remember an incident that happened to me several years ago in the Atlanta airport. An obviously very affluent Caucasian woman was trying to get huge boxes of fine porcelain figurines from one plane to the next with the help of the porter, an African American man. When he had difficulty getting the box on the underground train car, she addressed him in a very abusive and condescending way. He, of course, was powerless to respond. To this day, I regret that I did not demand that she treat him with respect, apologize to *him* for *her* behavior, and point out that she, not he, should be embarrassed by the scene that was created. As a bystander (and an airline customer myself), I could have said what needed to be said, whereas if the employee had spoken up, he would have been fired. All of us can take collective responsibility to make sure that no one has to do demeaning emotional labor.

Managing Emotion by Creating Meaning

One of the themes of this chapter has been that the spontaneous expression of emotion for its own sake and the strategic communication of emotion in the service of some other goal are not irreconcilable perspectives, either theoretically or practically. Let's take the concrete case in which you learn that a coworker has taken credit for the work you did on a project over the weekend. You have a nearly overwhelming spontaneous urge to "let her have it" or "give her a piece of your mind." At the same time, you may know very well that what you say will hurt her terribly and perhaps damage your relationship forever. You feel that if you don't tell her off, you will not be true to yourself, she will never "get it," and you will "wimp out." On the other hand, if you tell her, you will have to set aside your very real concern for her feelings, she may not "get it" anyway because she will be so upset, and you will be seen as mean and vindictive. What do you do?

The first step is to recognize that your spontaneous feelings are not really goal-free and coming from your true self any more than your strategic feeling that you should drop it for the sake of peace. Both stances are founded in meanings, just different ones. The first set of meanings is at the very least these: that the incident is important, that you deserve credit you are not getting, that she has done you wrong and should suffer as a result, and that you are strong and capable of standing up for yourself. And that is just for starters. There may be additional meanings tied to believing that your personal life suffers from overcommitment to your job, that it is unfair that your coworker works less than you do but makes more money, that your expertise is often taken for granted, on and on. Because the incident has just happened, it feels overwhelmingly important. You are orienting only to what this means for you, you are viewing the situation from only your own perspective; you are tired after the long weekend and don't have the energy to cope; and right now you need to feel strong. Besides, you take the sheer force of your anger as evidence that you are ABSOLUTELY AND UNEQUIVOCALLY RIGHT!

But there are other ways of interpreting the situation that may be competing for your emotions at the same time and may actually win out in a few minutes (hence the wisdom of counting to 10; Tavris, 1984). You may also later believe that the incident is no big deal, that she may know how you feel but has legitimate reasons for taking the credit (e.g., so that your work group will get credit instead of another work group), that she is prepared to apologize and offer to work next weekend for you, and that you are not weak but rather generous and a team player. Perhaps your nagging hesitation to confront her and a feeling of guilt for upsetting her provide cues that these meanings may also have some legitimacy. Moreover, these two parallel sets just hint at the full range of possible meanings to be created for the situation. You may believe that the incident is important, that it is important for her to understand how you feel *and* for you to understand how she feels, and that you are firm but flexible. You can believe that this incident is the straw that broke the camel's back, that the system has screwed you throughout your life, that you can't take it anymore, and that you're going to shoot her (not unheard of in the late-20th-century United States).

The trick to reconciling your spontaneous and strategic feelings, of course, is to reconcile the belief systems upon which they are based, and this is not always an easy task. The first step is to be aware of your own feelings (in their true complexity) and what meanings underlie them. Then you have to try to work through the meanings by understanding the facts of the case (Did she or did she not really take credit for your work?), how it relates to your concerns (Does the credit really matter to you?), and, perhaps most important, what it means for your identity (Are you weak, strong, generous, flexible?). Identity plays a much bigger role than most people realize, according to some scholars (Clark et al., 1996; Parkinson, 1995). If the situation is an interpersonal one, you also have to understand the other person's feelings and meanings as well. Then you have to settle on the meanings that work for you and act on them (or decide not to act at all). The danger of analyzing deep emotional meanings is analysis paralysis. Doing nothing constitutes a decision about what to do by default, as my failure to speak up in the figurine incident at the airport attests (I am ashamed to say).

None of this is easy. Whole life philosophies may be at stake when your deep-seated meanings (e.g., that others should be treated with respect) come up against meanings that you are asked to adopt for a purpose (getting them to pay their bills). The process is loaded politically because you may find yourself challenging authority or submitting to it. No doubt you will struggle with moral issues. The most unsettling thing of all is that the meanings will keep evolving as your life experience changes, as you talk to other people, and as you take on different perspectives, so there is really no end to the struggle. Nevertheless, simplifying decisions by following your gut feelings puts you at the mercy of the meanings that are salient at that moment, whereas shaping your feelings into whatever the situation requires puts you at the mercy of the meanings of other people that you are trusting by default.

In the next chapter, we consider what is probably the greatest challenge to the process of creating emotional meaning. It is the task of creating (or re-creating) meanings that incorporate the powerful and often overwhelming emotions that often accompany traumas, such as being a victim of violence, natural disasters, or a profound loss.

4. How Is Emotional Meaning Constructed Through Communication?

> What we may need most is a story, one that reconciles us to the past and reopens the doors to the future. The ear that listens to grief or the voice that reminds us of the good in us allows that story to be told.
>
> Calhoun (1992: 122)

When we experience a strong emotion such as overwhelming joy, sadness, or anger, we often feel an urge to "let it out" or communicate it to others. Just the opposite may be the case with shame, regret, or the overwhelming flood of emotions that result from traumas. Then it may be too painful or futile to communicate our feelings with others. The question then arises: Is it better to let it out or to keep it to yourself? Which will make you feel and function better, both in the short run and in the long run? If you do decide to communicate your feelings, what are helpful and unhelpful ways to do it? And even if it is helpful for you to unburden yourself, does it benefit the person who takes on your burden or improve your relationship with each other?

To appeal again to the weaving metaphor used throughout this book, we might ask whether the act of weaving a fabric colored with feelings is in itself therapeutic. Beyond that, does the therapeutic value of weaving an emotional message depend on what is woven, how, and under what conditions? Is it important to construct a coherent pattern or is merely communicating enough? Does the therapeutic value of weaving also depend on how others respond to your weaving and their contributions to the process?

Emotional Meaning Influences Physical Health

One reason we may be inclined to express our emotions is that suppressing them seems to take a physical and psychological toll. There is evidence that people who have not come to terms with trauma and the intense emotions that often accompany it are at risk for physical and mental problems, and conversely, that people who communicate about their emotions reduce that risk. Two programs of research in particular are striking examples.

Dr. David Spiegel works with seriously ill patients through support groups. In one of his studies, women with metastatic breast cancer were randomly assigned either to receive the usual medical treatment or to receive both medical treatment and to attend a support group composed of other women with metastatic breast cancer, led by Dr. Spiegel. The women who participated in support groups coped better with their disease with less anxiety, depression, and pain, but what was striking was that support group members' life expectancy almost doubled (from 2 years to nearly 4 years) compared to women who received only standard medical treatment (Spiegel, 1993; Spiegel, Bloom, Kraemer, & Gottheil, 1989; Wagner, 1993). In another experiment, Spiegel found that men with serious diseases benefited from support groups too, perhaps even more than women, because they may have had fewer opportunities for other supportive interactions (Spiegel, 1995).

The second important program of research is Dr. James Pennebaker's (1997) work with typical college students, Holocaust survivors, people who have lived through earthquakes, and others who have suffered traumas. In his experiments, some of the students were asked to write about their traumas, whereas others were not. The students who wrote experienced emotional discomfort in the short run (triggered by thinking about the trauma) but felt better in the long run. The students who wrote about their traumas visited the student health center significantly less often and showed better immune system functioning than those who suffered traumas but did not write about them.

Spiegel's and Pennebaker's research programs are dramatic and controversial, but there is also a large body of research literature that supports the more cautious conclusion that supportive social interactions tend to facilitate both physical and mental well-being (Albrecht, Burleson, & Goldsmith, 1994). For example, social isolation and lack of support are as strongly linked to the likelihood of death from cardiovascular disease as is smoking a pack of cigarettes a day or being in the upper 20% of the population in weight or cholesterol level (Atkins et al., 1991: esp. Table 2). Studies of battle stress, unemployment, relocation, disruption, and loneliness all point to the need for supportive relationships to buffer people against life's stresses (Hafen, Frandsen, Karren, & Hooker, 1992). People with broad and diverse social networks show greater well-being than those with only a few social connections (Hirsch, 1980). Social support helps in at least two ways: (1) by helping to manage the emotions so that physiological changes do not become marked and prolonged and therefore lead to illness and (2) by encouraging healthy and discouraging unhealthy ways of coping (such as alcohol and drugs or denial and avoidance) (Lazarus, 1991: Chap. 10, esp. 403–406). When social support works, it works very well, but not all types of connections are equally supportive. No one is quite sure, however, exactly why support groups may help – whether it is the social support itself or other factors, such as better mobilizing of resources such as treatment or pain control (Hitch, Fielding, & Llewelyn, 1994).

The old adage "Time heals all wounds" does not work for all emotional wounds any more than it does for all physical wounds. Athletes report thinking about the missed free throw or the narrowly lost race after 10 or even after 70 years (Tait & Silver, 1989). Traumatic events may continue to haunt, coming back as simple regret, recurrent involuntary thoughts, nightmares, or full-blown posttraumatic stress disorders. Consciously suppressing unwanted thoughts and emotions can often produce a *postsuppression rebound* or preoccupation, especially when people have other things to do and cannot concentrate on suppression (Wegner & Lane, 1995; Wegner et al., 1993). Suppressing thoughts and feelings is demanding, complicated, and may have long-term consequences that are insidious (Wegner, 1992: 217–219). People experiencing air raids (Vernon, 1941: 468), earthquakes (Pennebaker, 1993b), or crimes often feel compelled to talk about their experiences. Pennebaker (1997: 5) tells of a bank vice-president who was led to confess to embezzlement by a lie detector test (thus being almost assured of a prison term), who shook the polygrapher's hand, thanked him, and later sent him a chatty Christmas card. The strain of suppressing feelings may also be one of the most important reasons that victims of trauma who do not disclose their feelings tend to fall ill.

They are using energy to distract themselves that could be better spent dealing with the trauma.

Metaphors for Communicating Feelings: Venting, Catharsis, and Weaving Meaning

It seems that we need to pour out our feelings – *to vent* – rather than to bottle them up or keep them in. These terms are so much a part of our everyday vocabulary of emotion that we do not even recognize the metaphor for emotion that lies beneath all of them (examples to follow are from Kövecses, 1990). The metaphor is that the body is a container and emotions are fluids inside it ("she was *filled* with emotion"). Some emotions, such as anger and love, are hot fluids ("he *simmered* with passion"), whereas others, like fear, are cold (a *"spine-chilling"* adventure). As an emotion gets more intense, pressure builds in the container ("she was about to *burst* with excitement") and should be released ("he *vented* his frustration") before it is too late and the container explodes ("she had an emotional *outburst*"). It is difficult to know where the container metaphor originated and how profoundly it affects our thinking. Freud is often given credit for leading us to think in terms of subconscious urges that demand release – urges that, if blocked at one outlet, may burst forth at another or cause uncomfortable pressure and disturbance. In any case, the container metaphor is consistent with the fairly widespread belief that emotions must be released or they will cause damage, either by being held in or by exploding out of control.

Among therapists and emotion researchers, this is known as the *ventilationist* or *catharsis* view. Most believe it is wrong. Unbridled venting of emotion produces temporary relief at best and long-term harm at worst, especially if it is handled badly (Epstein, 1984: 84). Rather than providing a healthy outlet for emotion, uncontrolled expression often provides an opportunity to practice and become expert at negative feelings and action. Various studies have found that angry boys who act aggressively and couples who yell at each other become *more* rather than less angry (Tavris, 1989: 136–137). In addition, an unfortunate by-product of the "explosion" part of the container metaphor is that damage to others is a possible and perhaps unavoidable consequence (if shrapnel hits a bystander). Explosions may provide a convenient excuse for avoiding responsibility for the verbal or physical abuse that so often accompanies emotional outbursts. The social damage caused by expression may more than counterbalance out the physical risks of suppression. As Tavris (1989: 129) puts it, "If your expressed rage causes another person to shoot you, it won't matter that you die with very healthy arteries." Besides, there is also a logical alternative to venting – gradually calming down, cooling off, or "chilling out," as we say these days.

The term *catharsis* is used almost interchangeably in this literature with *venting*, but a closer look gives some hints about how the meaning of the term may have changed over the millennia. Aristotle wrote of the value of tragedies in the theater for producing *katharsis*, which came to be interpreted in the sense of "medical purgation" (a messier form of venting). Nussbaum (1986: 388–391) argues, however, that "the primary, ongoing, and central meaning [of *katharsis*] is roughly one of 'clearing up' or 'clarification' and that they can "give us access to a truer and deeper level of ourselves." The function of catharsis, then, is not to purge ourselves of harmful feelings, but rather to understand ourselves and others through those feelings (see Scheff, 1979: 20–25 on catharsis versus insight).

Not only is the idea of venting misguided, but the larger metaphor in which it is embedded (emotion as fluid in a container) may also have serious limitations.[1] A better metaphor is the one used earlier – the metaphor of weaving a fabric. This metaphor implies that what we need to do is to try to understand our emotions and incorporate them into the fabric of our lives, perhaps even creating beauty from the horrific. We must weave a meaning – not abstract, intellectual meaning, but lived meaning – the kind of meaning that Frankl (1946/ 1984) searched for in Auschwitz, not the kind that you look up in *Webster's*. It would be impossible for Frankl or anyone else to purge the emotional trauma of life in a concentration camp. In fact, it would seem like a travesty to so minimize or disregard it. But it is possible to create a meaning for the experience that guides one's life, that brings the riches of self-knowledge and emotional depth, that lets a person move beyond the emotional experience but also make it a part of the self.

Emotion and thought (both conscious and unconscious) must be

---

[1] Stiles (1987) posits another alternative, the *fever* model of disclosure, in which talking about a trauma is both a sign of disturbance and a restorative process.

woven together into an understanding that makes sense, that is coherent, and that fits with the rest of one's life. Often this meaning is expressed through narrative, or a story that is used to understand the trauma or emotional experience, but it can also be expressed through drama, dance, visual arts, and other media. Regardless of how the meaning is expressed, it is crucial that emotional and intellectual threads are interwoven. Talking about the emotional experience in purely intellectual terms does not help any more than it helps to pour out emotion without trying to understand it (Harber & Pennebaker, 1992: 376; Pennebaker, 1989: 223). This makes sense when you consider how emotions work.

A common view is that emotions occur when expectations are violated, and they alert us to discrepancies between what we expect to happen and what has really happened (e.g., Mandler, 1984). If events in the world are what you expect, emotion is neutral. If they are better than expected, you feel good; if they are worse than expected, you feel bad. Moreover, the emotions move you to take action (the action tendencies noted earlier), so that you can change the world to fit your expectations and advance your goals – jump out of the path of the oncoming car, embrace your loved one, or kick that lawn mower to make it run. This doesn't work, however, when the chance for action is past (as with emotionally traumatic events that are over) or when no action can fix the situation (as with a terminal disease). The discrepancy is still there, however, and the resulting feelings keep up the pressure to reconcile events and expectations (so long as the event and the expectations remain important). The only thing to do is to bring the expectations and the meanings that underlie them in line with the reality of the event (Horowitz, 1991; Oatley, 1992: Chap. 9).

This may seem easy if you think of expectations as abstractions. When someone dies, the reality of the death forces you to update your expectation that that person will be doing something tomorrow. If the person is known only as an abstraction, this is not particularly difficult. Sad as we may be that Picasso will not be painting any new pictures, his death is primarily an abstraction to most of us. If someone close to us dies, however, we may be reminded minute by minute, day by day, year by year that the person is not there. He is not sitting in the chair where you expect; he is not coming home tomorrow; he will not be there to blow out the birthday candles. To the extent that your lives had been intertwined practically and symbolically, your expectations are challenged constantly (Berscheid, 1983). This is the type of lived meaning that is challenged by a trauma or loss and that must be re-created.

Not everyone, however, suffers the loss of meaning with trauma. Some people seem to be able to incorporate great changes into the patterns of meaning that already exist and show little need to "work through" difficult experiences such as the death of a child (Wortman & Silver, 1989). They may have unusual strengths and coping resources, but "the data also suggest that some people may have something in place beforehand – perhaps a religious or philosophical orientation or outlook on life – that enables them to cope with their experience almost immediately" (Silver & Wortman, 1988, cited in Wortman & Silver, 1989: 354).

Many events are traumatic because they challenge not only expectations about day-to-day events, but also expectations founded in basic beliefs about the world and your own place in it. You have woven a certain pattern of meaning as your life, and a trauma rips the fabric so that it starts to unravel. Traumas involving physical harm, of course, can tear apart our expectations about personal security. Traumas such as those suffered by incest survivors can destroy the belief that we can trust others, especially loved ones. Important failures, transgressions, and errors can damage our belief that we are worthy human beings. The death of an innocent can destroy the belief in a just world. The loss of a beloved spouse, the loss of a dream such as going to the Olympics, or the loss of a way of life such as a job or profession can challenge your purpose in life. To re-create meaning after such losses is to weave a new fabric that reattaches the threads that may have come unraveled and creates a new pattern that is your life now.

The process of weaving new emotional meaning (or even working through emotions on a smaller scale) can be painful and tempting to avoid. There is much comfort to be taken in deluding yourself about what has actually happened, distracting yourself by focusing on other things, or anesthetizing yourself with alcohol or drugs. Avoiding may not be entirely bad, especially if done in moderation, but there is always the risk that short-term coping will become a long-term habit. Confronting powerful emotions, on the other hand, is difficult in the short run but becomes less difficult as time goes by and may lay the foundation for better coping in the long run. How important it is to find new emotional meaning may depend more than anything else on whether you will need it in the future, which may be hard to assess. Lazarus (1991) articulates two positions on this issue. Some believe that one always pays a price for distorting reality in order to cope emotionally, but Lazarus believes that "self-deception carries no penalty as long as no effective adaptive action is compromised" (p. 412). In other words, if your delusions catch up with you, you will be in trouble; if they don't, you will be okay.

How Communicating Emotion Helps Coping

How does communicating emotion help this process? The process of encoding an emotional experience into language, even if only for yourself (as in writing a diary), helps to weave together thoughts and feelings (*katharsis* in the ancient Greek sense). Although we do not entirely understand catharsis, a number of writers have suggested some basic processes.

First, it is helpful to achieve an *appropriate distance* from the experience – not too little but also not too much. Returning to the weaving metaphor, we might say that to weave the story, the raw materials must be at a focal distance (Oatley, 1992: 401–402). If the experience is too close, the emotional details will be overwhelming and the larger picture cannot be seen; if the experience is too far away, the details and vividness of the experience may be lost (Scheff, 1977, 1979). In working through a traumatic experience from the past, it is important to conjure up the original emotions without being overwhelmed by them. Even in the middle of emotional trauma, achieving some distance can provide relief, at least temporarily.

How do people do this? The act of putting an experience into words seems to help. The vast majority of people who wrote about trauma in the Pennebaker studies said that writing helped them put their traumas into manageable perspective (Harber & Pennebaker, 1992: 376). Consider what you do when you write about your own experiences. You move back and forth between the role of subject and object. When writing, you are the subject who is constructing the narrative or account, but when you write about your own experience, you are also the object. As one writer put it, [The writing] "helped me to look at myself from the outside" (Harber & Pennebaker, 1992: 376). The act of writing achieves the distance, whereas recalling the experience achieves the closeness. Moving back and forth between these two states seems to achieve the balance that one needs to deal with the trauma effectively.

Other strategies can be used as well. Frankl used humor even in the death camps because, in his words: "humor, more than anything else in the human make-up, can afford an aloofness and an ability to rise above any situation, even if only for a few seconds" (Frankl, 1946/ 1984: 68). He and his fellow prisoners used to joke about future dinner engagements after they were released from the camp when "they might forget themselves when the soup was served and beg the hostess to ladle it 'from the bottom'" (p. 55). Talking to a therapist is another strategy that makes it possible to immerse oneself in the recalled experience with the assurance that someone else can provide perspective and a safety net if the feelings become overwhelming. We also achieve appropriate distance from our emotions through drama and fiction, which provides us a chance to explore feelings in a fictional world that seems real but is not (Scheff, 1979). In Scheff's words (1977: 485): "There is deep emotional resonance, but the person is in control."

Second, communicating emotion verbally weaves the experience into a *coherent and meaningful whole* because that is the nature of messages (Clark, 1993: Grice, 1975). Stories or accounts of events are coherent (one part does not contradict another part) and meaningful (it relates to what we know about the world) because unless these two minimal criteria are met, a message is not sensible or understandable.

The process of constructing a *coherent* message gathers up threads of memory that otherwise may lie loose and weaves them together. The experience can then be confronted as a whole rather than as fragments. If loose ends are not tied in, they can dangle near consciousness and, when defenses are down, assert themselves as intrusive and unwanted thoughts, dreams, or nightmares (Harber & Pennebaker, 1992: 375; Horowitz, 1991; Rachman, 1990: 281). Unwanted thoughts may plague people for years, making it difficult to come to terms with the experience and reconstruct a new life. Bringing these thoughts together into an integrated whole often requires filling in gaps, which may bring to consciousness repressed or forgotten events that further contribute to the overall pattern. Unimportant fragments are discarded, important threads are recognized, general patterns are found, and a coherent meaning eventually emerges as the event is put into words. The important thing in overcoming trauma is not to have a coherent story to start with, but to create a coherent story over the course of writing or talking, a story that weaves together all the threads of one's personal experience.[2]

The process of constructing a *meaningful* message makes connections between the traumatic event and one's knowledge of the world (van Dijk & Kintsch, 1983). Connections are made between what happened and what you know," which is what we mean by *understanding* experience.[3] The process can be as simple as assigning a particular emotion label to an experience – "I felt afraid." In calling upon your knowledge of what it means to be afraid, you may bring to consciousness certain aspects of the experience that were below awareness ("I remember now how fast the water was moving") and solidify an appraisal ("I could have been killed!") (Zammuner & Frijda, 1994: 38). The experience seems more understandable because it can fit into a standard, familiar framework that unifies the experience and relates it to what you know about fear. In this process, finding the right words is an important element. "Simple labeling, which may at first appear trite and uninteresting, ultimately reveals itself to be a rather subtle index of emotional functioning," write Haviland and Goldston (1992: 225). Emotional labeling has been identified as an effective technique for negotiating effectively with traumatized, suicidal, and psychotic individuals because it helps negotiators identify motives and likely actions. For example, a negotiator might say, "You sound so angry over being fired that you want to make your supervisor suffer for what happened." The response might be: "Yes, I'm angry, but I don't want to hurt anyone. I just want my job back" (Noesner & Webster, 1997).

Many traumas or other emotional experiences, however, do not fit neatly into what you know. Experiences such as incest, random violence, or the death of a child challenge beliefs about loving and trusting relationships, about the predictability of life, or about a just world (Tait & Silver, 1989). These kinds of traumas may shake us to the core. To make sense of them, even on an abstract level, it may be necessary

---

[2] For a detailed analysis of the writing samples of trauma victims, and comparisons between those who show improved health and those who do not, see Harber and Pennebaker (1992) and Pennebaker (1993a).

[3] Stated in more technical terms, *understanding* refers to making links between episodic and semantic knowledge (see, for example, in emotion theory, Oatley, 1992; in clinical psychology, Horowitz, 1991; in text and communication theory, Clark, 1985, or van Dijk and Kintsch, 1983).

to find a new pattern for weaving meaning because the old ones don't work. Thinking and writing in causal terms seem especially important. Pennebaker (1993a) found that people whose health improved after writing about their feelings showed an *increase* in the use of words like "understand," "realize," "because," and "reason" and also showed improvement in the organization of their writing from the first to the last day of writing (Pennebaker, Mayne, & Francis, 1997). Their writing often took the form of a story, with a beginning, middle, and end, which provides closure on the experience and forms it into a meaningful whole.

Third, communicating about emotion helps to *unify feelings and thoughts*. It helps to construct a tapestry in which color is an integral part of the pattern. Feelings alone will not do; thoughts alone will not do; the two must be woven together in a "constant interplay between search for meaning and emotional response" (Silver, Boon, & Stones, 1983: 89; see also Bucci, 1995). It is as if thoughts and feelings can exist on two separate planes, where feelings are not understood and thoughts have no emotional force. This is clearly the case for phobics, who can tell you that there is no reason to fear spiders, snakes, or crowds but whose feelings tell them otherwise. Therapies such as systematic desensitization or emotional flooding are strategies for unifying reason and a racing heart by reproducing a mild or even the full emotional experience in a safe, unthreatening context (often with support from a guide). If all goes well, the person learns at a visceral level that the terror is manageable.

Finally, communicating about emotion can help to provide a *sense of control*, which is an important step in overcoming trauma or coming to terms with any emotionally overwhelming experience. Weaving a story or a message of any kind is a constructive process that puts you in the role of the actor, not of the person being acted upon. Arnston and Droge (1987: 161) write that members of support groups were heard to say "Damn it, this is my story" when others tried to modify or interrupt their narratives. To do something about trauma, even verbally, requires confronting the emotional experience and working with it. Some ways of talking are no doubt more helpful than others. Complaining, defending your victimhood, or blaming yourself when it is not warranted are probably among the worst, although self-blame can be associated with taking responsibility for one's troubles and sometimes has helpful effects, especially when combined with making amends (Coates, Wortman, & Abbey, 1979: 31–32; Weinberg, 1995).

Talking about how to behave differently in the future or about the control that you still have may be among the best methods. Even in the worst of circumstances, talking about suffering or dying with dignity can give a sense of choosing one's own course. As Spiegel (1993: 153) learned from his breast cancer patients, "there is a sense of power that comes with an unblinking confrontation with death."

Finding or renewing the meaning of one's life and experience, however, is not an easy task, either cognitively or emotionally. It requires reliving terrifying or otherwise devastating emotions and at the same time searching for meaning. There may be general guidelines and signposts, but ultimately there can be no preset pattern to follow because meaning is embedded in each person's unique life experience. People working through powerful emotions often reject other people's attempts to provide meaning on the grounds that others do not fully understand their experience, at least not in the early stages of meaning-making. Later, however, they may find that others' advice and support are more helpful. Each person must work through the emotions at his or her own pace, and sensitive listeners recognize this (Burleson & Goldsmith, 1998: 270–273). In Cochran and Claspell's (1987: 113) words: "there is a time to just listen, a time to encourage, a time to advise, and a time to explore, among other things, and the art of counseling would involve knowing when to do what to help forward the unfolding story." Ways of finding meaning may also vary widely and may change over time.[4] When an athlete suffers a serious injury, for example, it might seem tragic at first, but might later be interpreted as a sign that the person should have another calling.

Clearly, no way of constructing meaning from emotional experience is value-free because values are an inherent part of meaning (Pennebaker, 1997: 169–184). Any therapy, support group, or other source of meaning is likely to be grounded in a powerful and pervasive worldview that will probably have implications for many aspects of your life. Many people who had lost a loved one in a motor vehicle accident came to see the world as a "hostile place where things can be taken away in a moment. Such an altered world view is likely to be associ-

---

[4] Evidence from Stanton, Danoff-Burg, Cameron, and Ellis (1994) suggests possible sex differences in effective coping, the profile identified here applying more to women than to men. Reardon and Buck (1989) consider the possibility that any number of coping styles may be effective if they are used consistently and supported by others. Kunkel and Burleson (1998) found "virtually no support" for sex differences in preferences or skills involved in comforting.

ated with depression, passivity, and impaired motivation to engage in subsequent coping efforts" (Lehman, Wortman, & Williams, 1987, cited in Wortman & Silver, 1989: 354). In one study, two support groups for people experiencing loss of a spouse were observed as they used different ideologies. One dealt with divorce and was based on Christian principles oriented to a transformation from "I'm a failure" to "God is challenging me" (Francis, 1997: 158). The other dealt with death and was founded on Kübler-Ross's (1969: 161) stages of death and dying (denial/isolation, anger, bargaining, depression, and acceptance). Both groups sought to redefine the identities of the members and lead them to new emotional meanings, but in different ways.

The struggle to find meaning in emotional experience has certain inherent risks. Not everyone feels better, even in the long run, when they confront their emotions, and most people feel worse in the short run (Pennebaker, 1989). If you cannot consolidate fragments of memory, especially memories associated with physical reactions, or if you cannot handle the intense emotions brought up by reliving the experience, there is a great risk of suppressing the emotions even further, resulting in even more powerful physical symptoms. Bucci (1995: 118) describes storytelling as a powerful treatment that has its dangers, especially if intolerable affect is reactivated and the person responds by "attempting to close down access to the emotion system." There is also no guarantee that efforts to find meaning in emotional experiences will be successful; many people struggle for a lifetime. One study found that individuals who had lost a spouse or a child in a motor vehicle crash continued to think and talk about the accident and were unable to accept, resolve, or find any meaning in it even 4 to 7 years later (Lehman, Wortman, & Williams, 1987). One incest survivor apparently summarized the difficulty that many people have in finding meaning in tragedy: "There is no sense to be made. This should not have happened to me or to any child" (Silver, et al., 1983: 89).

Communicating Emotions to Other People

Meaning-making, as discussed so far in this chapter, can be a solitary activity. You can sit in a quiet place alone and write about your emotional experiences, considering no one but yourself and revealing your thoughts and feelings to no one. In fact, there are many advantages to doing exactly that. Why bother, then, to communicate your feelings to other people when a tape recorder or computer screen will do? Even though the risks of confiding in others are great, the potential rewards are great as well. In fact, people do talk with others about emotional events, usually almost immediately and repeatedly, especially if the emotional experience was intense, but they talk about daily events as well (Rimé, 1995; Rimé, Mesquita, Philippot, & Boca, 1991). Talking with others about your emotions, however, will not necessarily improve your well-being, even if your emotions are traumatic and continue to plague you. Just as there are better and worse circumstances and strategies for writing about your feelings, there are better and worse ways of talking with others. Weighing the advantages and disadvantages of confiding in others may produce dilemmas about whether to communicate feelings to others, and if so, to whom and how. Some of these dilemmas parallel the "dilemmas of support" discussed by other researchers (Albrecht et al., 1994: 434–435; Goldsmith, 1994).

One of the most obvious risks is that you will violate a *social norm* against inappropriate emotional self-disclosure. In American and most Western cultures, emotions are considered personal, and strong norms exist that guide the appropriate disclosure of personal information (Derlega & Berg, 1987; Derlega, Metts, Petronio, & Margulis, 1993: 33–37; Dindia, 1994). Nearly everyone knows that it is not appropriate to disclose intense personal feelings to strangers, although the temptation may exist if you believe you will never see the other person again. Many people have experienced the "stranger on the train phenomenon," in which a total stranger reveals intimate secrets or strong personal feelings. The risks involved, however, come out in various humorous anecdotes in which the stranger turns out to be a future father-in-law or new boss.

In addition to the strong norm guiding the disclosure of personal feelings, there are constraints on disclosing negative information or information that shows personal weakness (Scheff, 1984). Joy (which is positive) and anger (which is negative but strong) have been found to be "talkative" emotions, whereas fear and sadness (both negative and weak) tend to be "silent" emotions (Cosnier, Dols, & Fernandez, 1986: 120).[5] Compounding the problem is the strong possibility that some of the negative and weak feelings are shame or embarrassment,

---

[5] Watson, Clark, McIntyre, and Hamaker (1992) note that the association between positive affect and socializing is quite robust and that each probably causes the other.

which tend to make people want to withdraw socially and t~ ~~rtail communication (Izard, 1991: Chap. 15). Ironically, talking through your feelings honestly and openly may be most helpful when you are feeling weak or ashamed. In addition, some people are simply more ambivalent about expressing their emotions and more fearful of intimacy than others, which tends to make them reluctant to seek out social support (Emmons & Colby, 1995).

Given these constraints, how do we choose appropriate confidants, and what considerations do we need to bear in mind in disclosing our feelings to others? In the section that follows, we consider the pros and cons of disclosing personal feelings (especially negative ones) to three types of confidants: intimate partners (such as friends or family members), culturally sanctioned confidants (such as therapists or priests), and support groups of people with similar problems (such as support groups for people coping with serious illnesses or traumas). For each of these audiences, we consider the effects on the self, the confidant, and the relationship between the two. In the process, we will consider how disclosure works and how it can be managed well.

Dilemmas of Constructing Emotional Meaning with Others

Almost any confidant has certain advantages and disadvantages compared to communicating with yourself through writing or tape recording. For most people, it seems more natural to talk to another person than to talk into a tape recorder or to write about feelings. There is a certain stigma attached to people who talk to themselves. Talking to almost any confidant also provides some distance from the feelings and a different perspective, if for no other reason than that your feelings are not theirs. On the other hand, with any confidant there is the risk of being judged negatively, of having private information revealed to others, of having your interpretation of your feelings shaped by their views, of upsetting the other person, and of damaging your relationship. None of these are concerns when communicating only with a piece of paper or a computer screen, but if you do choose to talk to a human being, you will be confronted with dilemmas about whom to choose and how to talk with them.

Communicating with Intimates

By *intimates*, we mean people with whom you have a close relationship, including close friends, spouses, romantic partners, and family members. In these types of relationships, norms for self-disclosure are different from the general rules. Negative information is tolerated more, and close personal information is not only tolerated but even expected. Choosing to talk to an intimate about feelings, however, has its own risks. There is no guarantee that it will make you feel better, and there is the other person to consider.

One consideration is when and how to talk about different types of feelings. Learning from the literature on stress, we can distinguish among the feelings brought on by *major life events* (such as a major loss), *chronic conditions* (such as ongoing conflicts or continued frustration at work), and *daily hassles and disappointments* (such as an argument or missing the bus) (Burleson, 1990). We may be especially likely to turn to counselors or support groups to deal with major life events and some chronic conditions, but we talk to our intimates about all three.

Most of the research literature deals with acute and intense emotions that interfere with everyday activities and have persistent consequences, such as intrusive thoughts. Little is known about when and how to discuss everyday feelings, especially negative ones. Even though they may seem minor compared to trauma, they are the stuff of daily existence and strongly influence the quality of everyday life. Unlike traumas, which (hopefully) occur rarely and have a certain urgency about them, we can be more selective about sharing everyday feelings. You may decide not to spoil a nice dinner by telling your husband about losing an important contract, or you may choose to cheer up your friend by telling him an amusing event that happened to you today. Day in and day out, it seems to be balance and flexibility that matter most. Excessive and intractable cheeriness can be just as oppressive as constant gloom and doom, but unmitigated negativity is a recipe for contagious depression, marital disaster, and broken friendships (Gotlib & Whiffen, 1991; Gottman, 1994: 413). Coyne (1976: 192) taped phone conversations between depressed and normal female students and noted that "listening to the tapes from the study one is impressed by the willingness of the depressed patients to discuss death, marital infidelities, hysterectomies, family strife, and a variety of other intensely personal matters" (and, I might add, negative ones).

It is tempting to talk to intimates about your feelings without giving it serious thought because intimates are so convenient. You see them often; you may live with one or more of them; and it is easy just to turn to them and "unload." You may also know that you can rely on them for physical comfort (such as hugs), practical support (such as watching the kids for a few hours), companionship, and love in ways that are not appropriate or expected in other kinds of relationships.

Friends, family members, and spouses may accept many weaknesses, faults, and transgressions that you might reveal. Perhaps they have already seen you at your weakest, ugliest, meanest, or craziest, so that you feel you have little or nothing to hide. But shame can also be a major impediment to talking about feelings because it makes you want to hide and withdraw from social interaction, perhaps just at the point when you most need to open up. It is also important that you trust your confidant not to tell others your secrets and not to use those secrets against you at a later time. Other people's advice, however well intentioned, helpful, and caring, can be experienced as interfering or criticizing your competence, especially if it is unsolicited advice (Goldsmith & Fitch, 1997: 461–463).

Intimates also make good confidants because they share your emotional issues, one way or another, for good or for ill. They may share them because they are experiencing much the same emotional situation as you (emotional coincidence). For example, you may be experiencing fear of losing your job and, because your lives and finances are intertwined, your wife may share this fear. When you talk with her about your fear, you feel understood, emotionally in tune, and there is a powerful bonding that can come from this experience (Wood, 1986). Phony statements of empathy ("I know *exactly* how you feel"), on the other hand, are not helpful and may be even insulting (Lehman, Ellard, & Wortman, 1986).

There may also be a downside to talking with people who share your feelings because your conversations may reify and reinforce the feelings. Your wife has no more *distance* on the problem than you do; in fact, together you may define the problem as more serious than it really is. If emotional contagion plays a role, the less emotional person may pick up the expressive cues of the more emotional person (e.g., nervousness), thus "catching" fear. To compound the problem even further, your two coping styles may not mesh well. To achieve appropriate distance (not too little, not too much), people often engage the issue, then back away to recover, then reengage, and so on, using a cycle that works for them. If you want to engage when your partner wants to back away or vice versa, you can easily become either overwhelmed or avoidant.

Someone who shares your emotion is also unlikely to be able to provide a fresh perspective on the situation. If you have talked over the problem with your partner at length, new meanings are probably less likely to emerge. In fact, you may be rehearsing and entrenching problems even more deeply (Borkovec, Roemer, & Kinyon, 1995: 64). Intimates are also likely to share your general worldview, either because that is what attracted you to each other or because your time together has made your attitudes and values more similar. If the emotional experience challenges your worldview ("I thought that if I worked hard I would always have a job"), it will probably challenge your partner's as well. Moreover, to the extent that your shared life is based on this shared worldview, any change that you might make to reappraise the emotion could be a threat to what you share. This may be a form of emotional codependence, not because your partner depends on your being afraid directly, but because she may unconsciously rely on the worldview that also sustains your fear. If you deal with your fear of being laid off by rejecting the philosophy that "hard work pays" and adopting a more "carpe diem" perspective, you may feel better, but your wife may feel worse as she puts in her 12-hour days.

Even if your emotional issue is clearly separate, you expect your close friend or spouse to empathize with your feelings and take them on as their own, which can produce exactly the same dilemmas as shared problems. If your friend empathizes too much, he cannot achieve appropriate distance or provide a fresh perspective on the problem. Empathy may also bring on an overwhelming desire to help. If your partner could just make you feel better, he would feel better too. The urge to comfort, understandable and admirable as it is, works against natural therapeutic processes that are not easily rushed. It is possible for a helper to exert so much control and to be so intrusive that the person being helped falls into helplessness, a feeling of failure, or resistance when "saying 'no' to the helper and rejecting opportunities for positive change may be the most self-affirming accomplishment within reach" (Coyne, Wortman, & Lehman, 1988: 318; Notarius & Herrick, 1988).

Your friend may, however, be able to offer valuable suggestions for dealing with the emotional situation. He may help you design a new résumé. He may help you develop your skills so that you will not be so vulnerable. He may help you find other jobs for which you are qualified. Friends tend to be good at such things because they know you well, and they probably have inside information on your problem based on past conversations. What they may not be so good at is realizing how you may have contributed to the problem and telling you in a helpful way. Your friend may not realize that you do not have initiative, he may tell you in a hurtful manner, or he may not tell you at all. Goldsmith and Fitch (1997: 465–468) found that people often feel torn between being supportive by agreeing and giving honest opinions when they disagree.

Intimates (wives, husbands, friends, mothers, brothers, children) may also be part of the problem. You are terrified of losing your job because you feel enormous pressure to support your wife, who wants to stay home with the children. In that case, confronting the problem means confronting your wife as well, which makes her a very bad candidate for the role of confidant. She has a vested interest in how your emotion is handled – you know it, and she knows it. In such a circumstance, it is virtually impossible simply to "talk through your feelings" without having additional agendas, even though you may be unaware of them. Almost inherent in the simple statement "What you said hurt my feelings" is the implication "so you should not say that." Even if blame is not intended, your message may be interpreted as blaming, so it is better to separate the process of understanding your feelings from the process of negotiating the situation with your partner.

The greatest danger in talking to intimates, however, is that the burden may be too great for them. For example, someone in the throes of divorce has almost certainly lost her husband as a confidant, but probably many friends who were "shared" by the couple as well. Given how powerful the feelings surrounding divorce tend to be, it is tempting to fall back on the only remaining intimates in your life – your children. This is a huge mistake for a number of reasons, not the least of which is that children need to devote themselves to growing up and cannot shoulder the additional burden (Wallerstein & Blakeslee, 1989).

Even strong and resilient adults can find the burden of listening to and supporting someone through a prolonged crisis more than they can bear. For certain problems, however, both people are in it for the long haul and need to find ways to support one another. A study of male myocardial infarction patients and their wives 6 months after a heart attack showed that husbands' and wives' distress was highly correlated and that wives' distress was at least as great as their husbands' (Coyne & Smith, 1991). Wives worried about money and impairments, and the younger ones worried about child rearing and employment. In addition, the more wives tried to protect their husbands' feelings by denying or hiding their own anger or giving in more in arguments with their husbands, the more distress they suffered. If helpers become distressed themselves, they may become self-absorbed, may be less able to perform crucial tasks, and may become overprotective or critical and hostile (Coyne, Ellard, & Smith, 1990: 140–141; Coyne et al., 1988).

Coping has a different time course for everyone, but especially so for those who need support compared to those who give it. When you first lose your job, others may be there for you, but you may be in shock, feeling nothing because you have not yet recognized the full emotional force of the change. Later, when the emotional impact is just starting to hit you, others may want to get on with their lives. They want you to get over it, take positive steps, quit blaming yourself, show some courage, and most of all "Cheer up!" But cheering up on command is almost certainly not the best way for you to work through your feelings; you need to find meaning in them, not suppress them. It is not uncommon for people experiencing trauma or loss to feel well supported at the time the event occurred but much less so when they need support later on. Pennebaker (1993b) found that immediately after the 1989 earthquake in the San Francisco Bay Area, people talked about their experiences often; however, 2 to 3 weeks, later people still wanted to talk but did not want to listen to others. Cochran and Claspell (1987: 74) say, "There seems to be a social timetable for grief that requires one to 'snap out of it on time.' There are expectations to take it well, to show character." If people have unrealistically narrow views about normal grief, they may not be very supportive when someone deviates from "normal" (Wortman & Silver, 1989).

In the words of researchers who studied reactions to victims of disease, bereavement, and rape: "victims may be trapped in a complicated dilemma, in which they can maximize their social acceptance only at the expense of their personal adjustment" (Coates et al., 1979: 28). Victims come across as unpleasant, without courage, and irrational. Moreover, "in their darkest moments, victims may find only social isolation and ostracism" (p 48). Intimates may find these darkest moments frightening, especially if they empathize deeply with the victim. It takes extraordinary strength to be able to withstand those feelings without trying to comfort oneself by withdrawing or blaming, and this is a lot to ask of someone you love. Terms like "providing support" or "comforting" may make matters worse because they suggest that a helper might be able to find "a salve applied by a helper to an emotional wound suffered by the victim" that would make the other person feel better and recover quickly (Burleson & Goldsmith, 1998: 258–259). But there seldom is one.

Because our friends and family know us better than anyone else, we may expect them to be more skilled at helping than they really are. For starters, you may expect your wife to know how you are feeling without having to tell her. This is the risk of "mindreading," which generally results in "disappointment, misperception, and escalation of conflict" (Eidelson & Epstein, 1982: 715). She should be able to see through your masquerade of strength to the real helplessness inside. If she "really loved you," she would know how you feel. You can also signal distress indirectly by crying, hinting, complaining, sighing, sulking, or fidgeting (Barbee, Rowatt, & Cunningham, 1998). In general, indirect messages relieve you of the responsibility for owning up to your feelings and expressing yourself directly, but they leave you open to unnecessary disappointment if she does not notice or misinterprets your feelings. Alternatively, you may be overly dramatic, leading her to believe that you are only seeking attention or are not sincere (Albrecht et al., 1994: 437–438). Asking someone, even a loved one, for emotional support is enough of a burden without asking them to mindread (or "heartread") as well.

In support of the "Just ask for it" perspective, Cutrona, Suhr, and MacFarlane (1990: 38) found that married couples who requested emotional support and stated the consequences if they failed to receive it tended to be happier than those who expected support automatically and believed that efforts to support them would be futile anyway. Gulley (1993, cited in Barbee et al., 1998: 85) also found that both direct and indirect requests for support usually brought help, but direct requests did so more reliably. People also tended to use indirect support in response to their partner's avoidance, so it is difficult to know whether the indirect requests led to more avoidance by potential helpers or whether avoidance by helpers led to people making requests for support more indirectly.

Even if your loved ones know that you need support in handling your feelings, they may not know what to do. Few people do. That is why we turn to the research (Dakof & Taylor, 1990; Goldsmith, 1994).

A common mistake is to say something to try to make the bad feelings go away; it is better simply to listen, especially at first. Sometimes it helps to provide information and advice, but not always. Reassurance, encouragement, companionship, and direct expressions of love are generally helpful. It is helpful to express concern, though not too much and not too little. In short, effective helping and social support do not follow a simple formula, but are arts grounded in sensitivity to the other person's needs and the ability to manage one's own emotions while trying to help.

A final consideration in deciding whether to turn to loved ones to discuss feelings, especially traumatic ones, is that you have ongoing relationships with them that will undoubtedly be affected in some way by the disclosure. You are weaving the fabric of your lives together, and the patterns you create are bound to affect theirs. Sometimes disclosures are surprising, often they are negative, and they may test the relationship in new ways. Your partner may understand and accept the information, but he may not. If he does, you may (re)establish faith in your ability to be open and accepting; if not, what previous faith you had may be shattered (Planalp et al., 1988). With strangers it doesn't matter much, but with intimates you may be putting years of closeness on the line.[6]

Your relationship may also be affected by the one-sidedness of the disclosure. Normally, disclosure is reciprocal and balanced. If one person expresses her feelings, the other person tends to respond in kind. This *norm of reciprocity* can lead to problems. First, if one person complains, the other person may feel compelled to complain back instead of addressing the original complaint ("It hurts my feelings when you talk to me like that – Well, I don't like it when you say . . ."). This can lead to a pattern of cross-complaining, which can be deadly for relationships (Gottman, 1979). Second, you can get into the pattern of one-sided emotional expression, whereby one person always discloses and the other person always listens. It can be frustrating if the discloser wants more reciprocal disclosure and tiresome if the listener wants less. Women and men tend to fall into this pattern because girls grow up finding intimacy in talk, whereas boys find it in shared

[6] Although the ideology of the 1960s and 1970s equated openness with intimacy in the popular literature (Kidd, 1975) and in scholarly literature (e.g., Chelune, 1979), significant reservations emerged in the 1980s (e.g., Bochner, 1982; Hatfield, 1984; Parks, 1982) and in the 1990s. Openness came to be seen as a more complex dilemma (Baxter, 1988; Rawlins, 1992).

activities, thus laying the groundwork for mismatched expectations about intimacy in adulthood. Third, imbalance is inevitable if one person has a trauma or powerful feelings to deal with and the other does not. The emotional helper and helpee are natural, but they can congeal into fixed, almost inescapable roles if the pattern continues.

The way to avoid all of these "risks of reciprocity" is to realize that in relationships between people who are together for some period of time, reciprocity in the short run is not as important as reciprocity in the long run. If you listen to your friend's complaints today, she can listen to yours next week. If you feel the need to establish emotional intimacy through talk this week, you can establish it through common activities next week. If your husband needs to talk about his cancer this year, you listen with the implicit promise that he will listen whenever serious problems befall you. That is one of the great blessings of long-term relationships; you can count on the other person to be there for you. In addition, it is helpful to have a network of people to turn to for support so that the burden can be shared.

Research indicates that we do talk to intimates about our feelings, often for good reason. In one study, cancer patients reported that, on balance, intimates provided more helpful than unhelpful support (Dakof & Taylor, 1990: 82), and intimates were more helpful than acquaintances. Another series of studies showed that the overwhelming majority of people who were surveyed reported sharing their feelings with others, very often with intimates, but the amount of sharing was unrelated to the amount of disruption the feelings continued to produce (Rimé et al., 1991). The question may not be how much you talk with intimates, but how well.

Communicating with Counselors

Counselors are people whose job is to listen to others' confessions and to try to help. Typically, they are religious leaders (such as ministers, priests, shamans, and rabbis) or secular counselors of various sorts (psychotherapists, psychologists, or lay therapists). The role of confessor is sanctioned by the larger society (usually requiring special training and some form of certification), so special norms govern interactions between counselors and clients. Counselors also serve an important function in interpreting and applying cultural beliefs and expectations in the process of understanding and managing the other person's feelings. In essence, they draw on established patterns of meaning that have been developed as resources for their professions.

Counselors are not as easily available as intimates are; usually you need to make an appointment, go to a special place, and pay at least your respects, if not your money. You are not likely to talk to counselors about everyday feelings unless these become persistent problems. For persistent emotional problems or major traumas, however, there is an advantage to going regularly to a place removed from everyday life where you can immerse yourself in the task of dealing with feelings without everyday distractions (Pennebaker, 1997). You can escape everyday life to deal with feelings, then escape the feelings by returning to everyday life in a way that helps to achieve optimum distance from the feelings.

For many people there is a social stigma attached to having emotional problems important enough to require a counselor, especially a psychologist or psychiatrist (Fisher, Goff, Nadler, & Chinsky, 1988: 270). For example, people with phobias may deny their fears even to themselves. The norm may be to "tough it out," and only the very weak or truly crazy would talk to a counselor. If so, the shame of needing help can be compounded by the shame of seeking help, making it difficult indeed to walk into the office of an authority figure and start speaking from the heart.

Once you are in the counselor's office, the risks of disclosure are minimized by professional codes of ethics that regulate interaction between clients and counselors. Counselors are expected to keep disclosures confidential, and their privileged communication with clients cannot even be subpoenaed in court. Often the counselor does not know the client outside of the counseling situation, so there is no question of intruding on his or her privacy. Abuses such as sexual involvement or blackmail are heavily sanctioned. Counselors are usually trained to listen in a nonjudgmental and accepting way in order to encourage people to speak honestly and openly.

In addition, counselors are not part of the problem in the same way that intimates are. Good counselors understand and empathize with your problem, but they are also trained to have appropriate distance. Clients need not be concerned about being an excessive burden on counselors, because that is their job. Nevertheless, as everyone knows, active and continuous empathy *is* very demanding emotionally and often results in burnout unless regular support is given to the supporters. Another advantage is that the client's relationship with the counselor is primarily professional, so that the client is not as dependent on the counselor as on intimates. It is much easier to find another therapist or rabbi than it is to find another husband, mother, or close friend.

Oddly, one of the major advantages of talking to a counselor is that he probably knows nothing or very little about your personal situation, so you have to describe it. You have to explain how you feel, what you are thinking, what has happened, what it means to you, how you are behaving, and so on. You are forced to pull together fragments, search for explanations, make facts and observations consistent, and get some distance on the problem. In short, you need to construct a coherent, meaningful narrative, not just for the counselor but for yourself. Creating the story may be half the battle.

The great advantage of counselors, however, is that they usually have much greater skill at dealing with emotional issues than do most friends or family members (although there are exceptions, of course). They have special training, experience, or both; that is why we often turn to them for help with problems that are intractable otherwise. A good example is an unmanageable fear such as agoraphobia (fear of public places), which counselors treat using techniques such as systematic desensitization (learning to manage a slightly scary situation, then moving toward progressively more frightening ones) and emotional flooding (jumping headlong into the great fear) (Rachman, 1990). Even though they work in opposite ways, both seem to help when handled correctly.

What all therapies provide is a fresh perspective on the trauma or emotional difficulty, and it is unlikely that one type of therapy is best for all problems and all situations (Greenberg & Safran, 1987). *Psychotherapies* focus on the individual psyche as a locus of insight. The least intrusive of these is client-centered or Rogerian therapy, in which the client is encouraged to talk freely enough to achieve new insights herself. Classic Freudian psychoanalysis encourages people to talk about and probe the childhood roots of adult difficulties. Cognitive therapies encourage people to investigate the recurrent everyday thought patterns that underlie troubling feelings. Emotion-focused therapies encourage people to view emotions as clues to problems in their lives, to acknowledge even unacceptable feelings, and to struggle for new meanings that are strongly felt emotionally. Drug therapy has become increasingly popular, but it seldom works well unless it is combined with another type of therapy based on new insights.

Spiritual or religious orientations to confession turn people not inward but upward, so to speak, toward god(s) or other spiritual entities that transcend the self. Consultation with a rabbi, shaman, lama, guru, or other type of religious leader leads you to construct emotional meaning through religious beliefs and practices. You may come to understand that you are simply at the mercy of the ancient Greek gods, that you are being asked to suffer for your faith like Jonah and Jesus, that your suffering is inherent in existence as was that of the Buddha, or that your experiences have meanings and purposes that are simply beyond human understanding. These approaches have the advantage of breaking self-absorption and orienting you to transcendent concerns (Myers, 1992: 183–204).

Since feelings of guilt and shame often arise from violating religious commandments or codes, confession and redemption are common ways of dealing with them in religious practice. Admitting to and even repenting the transgression is the first step, but often that is not enough. You must also set things right through suffering, restorative action, or both. Physical punishment, acts of self-denial (such as dietary restrictions), and acts of restitution (such as service to the church or to the victim) come to mind, ranging in severity from self-immolation to a few hail Marys. A final step that may be needed to complete the cycle is to receive forgiveness and absolution from the appropriate authority, thus affirming that religious principles have been served and the individual is to be readmitted as a genuine believer in action, word, and feeling. As Lewis (1992: 133–134) writes: "Within the formal structure of religion, such as Catholicism, the priest, through his special relationship to God, is given such powers [granting forgiveness and love]. The degree to which the individual believes that the priest possesses these powers is the degree to which confession is a successful medium for reducing shame."

A third form of confession, which might be called *sociotherapy*, is oriented to finding meaning in others and in society. Sociotherapy turns attention outward to others rather than inward to oneself or upward to God. Public confession seems odd in a highly individualistic culture such as ours, where talk about emotion is considered a private matter. In other cultures, however, confessions are made publicly to the group and are used for "transforming ill-feeling into well-wishing, for restructuring relationships to restore social harmony, and for reintegrating the sick person into the social group" (Georges, 1995: 17). For example, two particularly helpful ways of finding meaning in traumatic experience are to turn outrage, fear, or guilt into helping others (called the *helper therapy principle*) and to tackle social problems, such as trying to change legislation (the Brady bill regulating handguns) or social practices (Mothers Against Drunk Driving).

With all these therapeutic options, it ought to be easy enough to construct a coherent and meaningful account of your emotional experience. Your old beliefs have failed, and you are searching for a new perspective that helps explain what you are experiencing now. It is no accident that you are especially open (or vulnerable, depending on your point of view) to new perspectives when you are in emotional turmoil. But there is a catch. For any of these approaches to work, you must *believe* the ideology on which it is based, and believe it sincerely (in your heart, so to speak). You will not find comfort in overnight Buddhism or a forced march through Freudian analysis. It must be a plausible new perspective, one that fits with your lived experience.

Communicating in Support Groups

Support groups are made up of people with common emotional problems (such as those that result from serious illnesses, trauma, or substance abuse) who come together for therapeutic reasons – to help each other weave meaning from their experiences. The group is typically led by one or more therapists or trained leaders, and close relationships often develop among group members. In some ways, support groups work as a combination of intimates and confessors, but they have their own unique properties. What makes support groups different from either friends or confessors is the group process combined with a shared emotional experience.

Support groups are not especially convenient, but they tend to be less expensive than one-on-one therapy, and they are becoming increasingly available to those who experience traumas that are unfortunately all too common – serious illness, rape, incest, the loss of a loved one, and many others. Their power lies in shared experience. When people share the same problem or feelings, there is less shame in confronting and talking about them. You don't feel so weird, so isolated, or so weak. You have a vivid sense that others have similar experiences, that they are trying to cope too, and that you will all get through it together. There is always the possibility that one person's talk will trigger a strong and unexpected emotional reaction from other members of the group, which can be a curse or a blessing. It can produce contagious fear, anger, or guilt, but it also encourages everyone to deal with the experience on a deeper emotional level. In a group context, it is especially important to respect the coping styles and limitations of everyone so that each person retains some degree of control. Support groups can be harmful when members are expected to conform in order to belong (Hitch et al., 1994).

In support groups as in individual therapy, the rules of self-disclosure are suspended and confidentiality is assumed (Lee, 1988: 161). Guidelines for group discussion are set by the counselor who leads the session, and they typically include honesty, openness, direct confrontation of feelings and issues, and mutual respect (including respect for privacy). Group interactions are difficult to manage, however, and members can become dissatisfied with groups that are too large, topics that are too narrow, too much discussion of feelings, one member dominating the discussion, or someone being pessimistic, to give some common reasons (Taylor, Falke, Mazel, & Hilsberg, 1988: 197–198). People may compare themselves unfavorably to others who are doing well, they may not find open and honest talk comforting if they have not accepted their own trauma or, in some cases, impending death (Wortman & Dunkel-Schetter, 1979), or they may be forced to disclose personal information without adequate support and reassurance (Hitch et al., 1994).

A certain degree of understanding and empathy can be assumed in the group because of the common problem group members share. While no two people's problems and feelings are exactly the same, people whose experiences are similar are able to imagine the other's position better than most others. Group members generally are strangers when they begin, so they have no past relationship to protect, no unhealthy patterns to break, and no blame to assign. At the same time, support groups may provide almost ideal situations for friendships to emerge because of mutual sharing and an atmosphere of open disclosure. Struggling to weave a difficult pattern tends to draw people together.

Members of support groups tackle their common problem in all its complexity and in individual manifestations. Alcoholics Anonymous was one of the first, but hundreds of others have followed, dealing with many types of traumas and illnesses. Members of support groups provide practical tips (what drugstores are open late), information and sources of information (the Health Center has information on cure rates), concrete advice (ask the kids to help with laundry), strategies for coping (go off by yourself and cry if you need to), sounding boards for decisions (yes, go ahead and confront your doctor), moral support (you may feel bad after the chemotherapy, but you'll make it), and other benefits (Dakof & Taylor, 1990). All this is supplemented by the professional advice of the counselor as well.

Hearing the stories of other members of the group and getting their reactions to yours also makes it possible to see your problem at least partly through their eyes. You get some distance on your problem, yet it is never too far away because it is so similar. At the same time, you may get new and highly relevant perspectives on your own problem by learning what each member's perspective is on hers. Together you can search for one way or, more likely, many different ways of finding meaning in experiences. A group can also bring out interpersonal feelings and behaviors that would not even occur in isolation (excessive shyness or hostility) and can be confronted as they arise. Other group members also serve as role models, both positive and negative, but the advantage of being in the group is that you can choose the positive ones. No one else is in quite the same position to do this as a fellow cancer patient, a fellow incest survivor, or a fellow mother of a child killed by a drunk driver (Dakof & Taylor, 1990: Tables 3 and 4). As you see someone else functioning well and you understand how she does it, you can adopt the beliefs, strategies, and techniques that work for you and ignore the ones that do not. Positive role models can also be inspiring. You see in one vivid example that all is not futile and hopeless. On the other hand, they may make you feel deficient for not coping as well (Hitch et al., 1994).

Participating in a support group can also do wonders for your own sense of control. Not only do you see other people coping, but you may also be able to *help* others cope, and that is a very positive and powerful feeling. Studies of fear reactions in London during the air raids of World War II found that very few people who performed essential services (such as police officers, medical staff, firefighters, and evacuation organizers) were vulnerable to fear and poor mental health. Moreover, some people who did suffer mental health problems improved after taking up some socially necessary work (Vernon, 1941; Wilson, 1942, cited in Rachman, 1990: 24–25). Part of the benefit of support groups is giving as well as getting help.

One final advantage of support groups is that each member belongs. With many intense emotional difficulties, people report being socially and emotionally isolated from their friends and family members (Dakof & Taylor, 1990). It may be easier not to call, not to get together, not to talk about it, and to grow apart. Concerns and priorities often change with powerful emotional experiences, so that it may be difficult to feel fully a part of everyday life, especially during the time the trauma is being dealt with most actively. Finally, trauma often results from or results in changes in social identities that can be alienating for friends and family. For example, divorce changes one's role from spouse to single. Support group members are able to support these new roles in ways that are difficult or impossible for friends and family members who were used to the old roles (Hirsch, 1980).

Weaving Meaning Together in Everyday Life

The process of weaving emotional meaning is so challenging that it is too much to ask individuals to do it alone, and the fact of the matter is, we seldom try (Rimé et al., 1991). People turn to others in times of trauma not only for a shoulder to cry on, but also for what may be one of the greatest challenges of their lives – constructing new meanings from trauma or loss. By talking to others, each person may gain access to the resources of traditional wisdom and healing, modern psychiatry and psychology, and the everyday homespun insights of the people who surround them.

We also turn to each other on a daily basis to understand our own and each other's feelings in ways which we are probably seldom aware of. You don't only tell your partner or your roommate about BIG emotional events that happen to you; you also tell them about your smaller, everyday joys and sorrows. You may tell the joke that made you laugh or talk about how much you are dreading doing your paperwork. We may feel compelled to talk about trauma, but we do more triage on the trivial. After all, we can't run off to a counselor for every bad day, but the basic framework works just the same. Talking about feelings with others helps us to negotiate meanings for emotional experience that are both personal and shared.

5. How Is Emotional Meaning Both Personal and Social?

> No matter how deeply personal an emotion seems, we embark on a timeless drama not of our own making.
>
> Cochran and Claspell (1987: 157)

The mere fact that we communicate emotion implies that emotion itself is both personal and social. If our feelings were *entirely personal*, with no shared meaning and no implications for others, there would be no need to communicate them. Emotions might help us as individuals to orient to important concerns and guide our actions, but they would not interest anybody else. At the opposite extreme, there would also be no need to communicate emotions if they were *entirely social*. If members of a community felt in unison, emotions would serve to orient the group to common concerns and to coordinate behavior, but there would be no individual variation from one member to another. But emotions are neither purely personal nor purely social; they are *both*. Through communication, our personal emotional experiences are made available to others in society, and at the same time, social expectations about emotion are made known to us as individuals. Communication is a way of bridging the gap between the personal and the social sides of emotion.[1]

The process of communicating emotions is deeply *personal* in several senses of the word. It is personal in the sense that the emotions define us as individuals with configurations of feelings that are unique – like fingerprints. Emotional communication is also commonly ex-

---

[1] Peters (1989:387) states that "*Communication* appeals to us because of the way the concept seems to put Humpty Dumpty back together again. Communication seems a description of the flowering of the private into the public, the overcoming of divisions of subject/object and self/other."

pressed physically and thus is closely linked to the body, the ultimate locus of the personal self. Emotion is also personal in the sense of being private. Often our feelings are difficult, if not impossible, to communicate fully and may be too sensitive to expose to anyone else. And emotional communication is personal in the sense that revealing our deepest feelings to others is considered an intimate act.

Yet at the same time, emotional communication is *social* in several senses of that word. Most of our feelings are directly connected to situations involving other people, and so we communicate emotion about and with other people. Many of our emotions promote and regulate social and communicative connections (Metts & Bowers, 1994). Loneliness moves people to initiate and continue contact, love produces durable bonds, and shame and guilt bring us into line with social expectations. What is more difficult for people from highly individualistic cultures to grasp is that our emotions themselves are shaped and defined socially. Certainly we feel our own personal feelings, but those feelings are socialized to be appropriate for our gender, ethnicity, class, and occupation. They are shaped early in life by care-givers who may have tolerated one emotion but discouraged another, and later by partners in close relationship with whom we try to achieve emotional harmony. We also live in a sea of messages about what emotions mean, how they are to be communicated (or not communicated) to others, how they are to be managed, and what implications they have for other parts of our lives.

Consider love or, more specifically, romantic love. There is no question that romantic love is a personal emotion that is felt and expressed uniquely by one lover with another. No one else's love is quite like another's, and each of us expresses it at a deeply personal level. Yet romantic love also takes (and has taken) a wide variety of forms, and the love each of us feels seems to fit, more or less, the expectations of the dominant culture. Somehow most people "fall in love" with someone of the appropriate sex, age, social class, and marital status; exceptions are unusual, frowned upon, or viewed as decidedly immoral. We are engulfed in messages about love – love songs on the radio, talk about love with friends, lectures about love from parents, TV sitcoms, magazines, romance novels, love stories at the movies (Cancian, 1987; Illouz, 1991). All these messages shape our own unique love, and, in turn, our collective experience and expression of love shape the emotional communication milieu in which we live (Dion & Dion, 1996).

In previous chapters, I used the metaphor of weaving a tapestry to illustrate some of the dualities inherent in emotional communication. In a sense, when we weave an emotional tapestry, we are weaving it in a way that no other person can. Each contribution is uniquely our own and a result of our own personal life experiences. On the other hand, we weave threads that are designed to fit and bond with other threads that together create the tapestry of social life. We contribute to a tapestry that was begun long before we were born and will continue after we are gone. It nurtures, shapes, and constrains our contributions and, at the same time, our contributions make it what it is. The threads define the tapestry, and the tapestry defines the threads.

Individual and Interactional Perspectives

The personal–social duality is known in academic circles as *individual* and *interactional* perspectives on emotion. The individual perspective, in particular, the psychological perspective, has dominated both everyday and scholarly views of emotion so thoroughly that we tend to think of emotion as an inherently psychological phenomenon. And it is, but emotion is also sociological, linguistic, communicative, philosophical, historical, and cultural.[2] A wide variety of academic disciplines now address issues of emotion, and together they give us a perspective that is multifaceted and diverse. In particular, emotion has moved outside individuals' bodies and heads, and into the world of talk, relationships, social roles, and social structures.

In a sense, it is misleading to talk about any separation between the individual and society. Society is, after all, made up of individuals, but it is not just a collection of individuals. It is rather a complex arrangement of individuals' goals, abilities, actions, and social roles that are coordinated to serve collective functions. What makes individuals stick together as a society? In part, it is because they have emotions that encourage sociability and discourage isolation (what are often called the *social* emotions). In addition, emotional communication is an important means of producing, maintaining, and negotiating the relationship between individuals and the societies in which they live.

---

[2] The *Handbook of Emotions* (Lewis & Haviland, 1993) begins with Section 1: Interdisciplinary Foundations, including chapters by a philosopher, a historian, an anthropologist, and a sociologist, in addition to a psychologist and a neuropsychologist.

As individuals we do not need to build connections with society because we come into the world via social relationships, and most people spend their lives in society with others (except for a few hermits). Nevertheless, babies are not born Masai or Huaorani or Japanese; they are born more or less generic babies, who are socialized into their home cultures from birth. They must be taught to feel what a Huaorani feels and express their feelings the way the Huaorani do. Babies are born girls or boys, but they are not born with emotions that are feminine or masculine according to the standards of the culture; those must be learned. Babies may be born into the aristocracy, into the untouchable class, or into relatively egalitarian societies, but they must be socialized to feel and display the emotions that are appropriate. In this section, we turn to the role that emotions play as social glue. Later, we consider how individuals are socialized to feel and express the emotions that fit their station in life.

Social Emotions and Sharing

It is important to recognize that society is not just a social overlay on a biological foundation; the social nature of emotion seems to be built into our genes. Scholars have long assumed that emotions are adaptations to a physical environment that may threaten physical safety (fear), may foster or impede goals (joy or anger), and produces inevitable losses (sadness). But the social environment may be even more important. Individuals could not survive (much less reproduce and successfully raise offspring) without being part of the group, and the group's survival depends on its members sharing food, goods, assistance, sex, and probably other more abstract things such as information, rituals and religion. Therefore, as humans were evolving, there must have been a great deal at stake in establishing, maintaining, and protecting social connections, and we can see today how those forces have shaped our emotional makeup.

Baumeister and Leary (1995: 497) have argued for the need to belong, defined as the fundamental human "need for frequent, affectively pleasant interactions with a few other people in the context of a temporally stable and enduring framework of affective concern for each other's welfare." Evidence for their claim comes from the strong link between emotional well-being and social relationships. Love accompanies the formation of new and desired social bonds (e.g., marriage and parenting). Threats to social attachments produce powerful negative emotions such as jealousy that move us to try to protect those connections. Actual losses produce grief and loneliness, emotions that lead us to come to terms with the loss and eventually to establish new connections. Hurting or neglecting another person, especially someone with whom one shares a strong personal connection, often produces guilt, an emotion that leads one to make amends and try to repair the damage and the relationship. After reviewing the evidence, Baumeister and Leary conclude that "many of the strongest emotions people experience, both positive and negative, are linked to belongingness" and that "one of the basic functions of emotion is to regulate behavior so as to form and maintain social bonds" (p. 508).

Social emotions may provide the motivation to form and maintain social bonds, but communicating those feelings enables individuals to reach beyond their private feelings to make social contact. Emotion accomplishes very little in the social world unless it is communicated. Unexpressed love is probably unrequited love, which does nobody any good. Fear and loneliness experienced privately just make you miserable, but screaming is likely to bring Mom running. In fact, if screaming does not bring Mom running, emotions may become more intense and the motivation to make contact more pressing. The original research that served as the basis for attachment theory showed that when infants first lost contact with their caregivers (most often when mothers left for an extended period of time), crying and wailing intensified, but if those efforts continued to be unsuccessful, the motivation eventually disappeared, resulting first in hostility and then in apathy toward the attachment figure (Bowlby, 1969a, 1969b). The lack of communication may itself become an added source of emotional distress, up to the point where the infant eventually gives up. Even infants cannot sustain unrequited love.

Communicating emotion, especially positive emotion, is also a common and effective way to establish social connections. Happy people are likeable (Clark, et al., 1996: 25), and simply talking with another person increases the chances that the other person will like you (Sunnafrank, 1984). Better yet, if you express liking for the other person, the odds are good that he will like you in return, and perhaps you will become friends (Backman & Secord, 1959). If you go on a date with someone, positive emotional expressions will be more socially acceptable than negative ones (although early on in a dating relationship even positive emotion should be expressed with some caution, presumably so as not to appear *too* interested) (Aune, Buller, & Aune, 1996). Sharing emotions (either positive or negative) also serves an important function in galvanizing or "crystallizing" small groups and in generating the feeling of solidarity that makes members feel that they belong (Moreland, 1987). Ritual interactions such as family reunions, awards banquets, or religious ceremonies provide the chance to get caught up in each other's emotions, feel in tune with one another, and share a common mood. "One gets pumped up with emotional strength from participating in the group's interaction" (Collins, 1990: 32).

Not only does the individual benefit from feeling social emotions and communicating them to others, but the group also benefits from the individual's experience if it is communicated effectively. If one person runs into danger, expresses fear, and alerts everyone else, the whole group benefits. If his story is lucid and compelling (as accounts of trauma often are), it will have all the more impact on others. If he feels compelled to tell the story over and over again (as victims of trauma often do), he may function as a "human broadcaster" who alerts the whole community to the danger (Harber & Pennebaker, 1992: 382). If others tell his story in the very common process of *secondary social sharing* the word will spread even more widely (Christophe & Rimé, 1997). Finally, if he confesses his trauma to a priest, shaman, or other authority figure, useful information is passed on to someone who is in an especially strong position to do something about it. The Kogi are a tribe in Colombia whose society has barely been touched by the European invasion 500 years ago, and they want to keep it that way. When members make contact with the outside world and return, they tell everything to their spiritual leaders. In this way, the leaders acquire extended eyes and ears and get the information they need to make decisions about how to deal with the outside world without risking physical harm or spiritual corruption to themselves (Ereira, 1992).

The Socialization of Emotion

By the socialization of emotion, we mean "how people come to feel as they do as a result of their relationships over time with others" (Saarni, 1993: 435). Emotional messages are both *what* are being socialized (for example, trying to teach a child not to scream when he is angry) and the *medium* through which we do the socializing ("Stop that temper tantrum now!" said in an angry voice). In order to appreciate how emotion messages function in socialization, we need to look at emotion messages from both points of view. What is surprising is just how early emotional socialization begins, how deeply emotional communication is socialized, and in how many different ways.[3]

Emotional Communication as What Is Socialized

There is some evidence that our emotions do not become *less* personal and *more* social as we get older, but just the opposite; they become *more* personal and *less* social as we develop separate personal identities. Newborns have been observed crying in response to the distress cries of other newborns in what appears to be a rudimentary form of emotional contagion (Thompson, 1987). At 3 months of age, babies of depressed mothers already showed more signs of anger and sadness in their faces than did babies of nondepressed mothers (Pickens & Field, 1993).

The capacity for true empathy starts to develop during the second year of life, when toddlers first recognize other people's distress as separate from their own. It takes a bit longer for children to develop effective comforting skills, starting with physically comforting acts such as patting or touching when they are young, and progressing to verbal reassurances, sharing, and other practical help as they get older (Thompson, 1987). The socialization of responses is antisocial when abused children learn to treat others as they have been treated – first with attempts to console, but if that fails, with expressions of anger and then physical violence (Klimes-Dougan & Kistner, 1990).

Young infants seem to be tuned to emotional messages from others as a source of information about how they should behave (and perhaps about how they should feel). Scholars call this *social referencing* (Walden, 1991). In one study, 1-year-old infants were confronted with a visual cliff (a clear Plexiglas platform that looks like a drop-off). They were unsure about whether to cross it or not, so they looked to their mothers for signs of what to do. When their mothers looked happy or interested, most of the infants crossed (25 of 34); when their mothers looked fearful or angry, very few did (2 of 35) (Sorce, Emde, Campos, & Klinnert, 1985). This is dramatic testimony to the ability of

---

[3] For excellent recent reviews, see Halberstadt (1991), Manstead (1991), Manstead and Edwards (1992), Saarni (1993), Harris (1989), Lewis and Michalson (1983), Saarni and Harris (1989), and Blechman (1990), to name a few.

even young infants to use emotion cues from others as guides to their own choices.

From birth babies elicit aid and comfort by screaming and crying. This is not a particularly subtle form of communication, but it is effective. In a few months, infants begin to adapt their messages to others, as Dunn and Brown (1991) note. Experimenters studied how infants' expressive skills develop over time by restraining the arms of 1-, 4-, and 7-month-olds. The 1-month-old infants showed vaguely negative emotions, the 4-month-olds looked at the restraining hands with angry expressions, but the 7-month-old infants directed their angry facial and vocal expressions toward their mothers or toward the person restraining them (Stenberg & Campos, 1990: 275). The 7-month-olds had already learned that communicating emotion can mobilize social resources; later they learn that *how* they communicate makes a difference in their chances of being successful. If they express their own feelings in socially acceptable ways, others are more likely to respond positively. Second and fifth graders reported communicating sadness as a way of getting support but controlling anger because there might be negative consequences (Zeman & Shipman, 1996).

Children learn surprisingly early what emotion messages are appropriate to express to whom (strangers, friends, family members) and why (that is, what social consequences are likely). Children "tell us that there are social situations where it is important to dissemble one's genuine feelings, but they are also adamant that there are situations where it is similarly important to express one's real feelings, as in friendships or with one's parents" (Saarni, 1990: 64). As early as age 6, children knew that they should refrain from expressing honest feelings when someone else was likely to be hurt as a result, and they anticipated that their parents would react negatively if they did not show the socially appropriate expression (and correctly so). At the same time, children as young as 6 also thought that a child who almost never expressed his or her real feelings to others would not fare well and would be disliked (even though he or she might be able to avoid getting into trouble). The children viewed either complete expression or complete suppression as problematic (pp. 66–68).

Choosing to express personal feelings or to adapt to the social situation also depends on children's relationships with other people and how they react. Elementary school children reported controlling emotional expressions more when they were with peers than when they were with parents or alone, primarily because they expected negative interpersonal consequences if they disclosed their true feelings to peers (Zeman & Garber, 1996). Adolescents reported confiding their feelings to both peers and parents, but parents' reactions were not always supportive and did not always encourage disclosure. "If parents respond by criticizing or blaming the adolescent; ordering or commanding him/her to do something; denying the existence of the problem; or lecturing the teenager about how they should have done things differently, then subsequently the adolescent is likely to take problems elsewhere" (Wills, 1990: 83).

Emotional Communication as a Way of Socializing Emotions

How families respond to a child's emotional messages makes an especially critical difference in the skills that he or she develops to cope with the dilemmas of emotional communication in everyday life. Scholars have identified four primary means of emotional socialization that involve communication – modeling, reinforcement, coaching, and labeling (Halberstadt, 1991; Saarni & Crowley, 1990). *Modeling* of other people's emotional communication occurs when infants, children, or adults observe how others communicate emotion and imitate them. Emotional expressions may be modeled because they are seen as normal, as admirable, or simply because they are the only way to communicate that is ever observed. *Reinforcement* comes into play when other people indicate through their messages that a certain pattern of expression is good or bad. Reinforcement does not need to be verbal, of course; a discouraging glance or tone of voice can work just as well. Some verbal *coaching* might be done ("Just stand up straight, take a deep breath, and say your poem"). Emotional styles may also be socialized by *labeling* one child as "sweet and loving" or another as "quiet and shy," producing expectations that children may internalize and enact.

Emotions are also socialized through the use of emotion *terms* and other kinds of *emotion talk*.[4] Assigning an emotion word to a feeling

---

[4] Oatley and Jenkins (1996: 181) describe this process as follows: Children can talk about a feeling, give their version of its cause, refer back to emotions, and alter their understanding of them. And crucially, instead of a model based only on the child's experience, parents can offer their understanding to be put together with that of the child. Similarly, parents can understand an event from their child's perspective. The shared meanings that are created become part of that relationship and its shared history.

can have an especially strong influence in shaping young children's emotions because the emotions of small children are more general and undifferentiated (although also more powerful) than those of older children and adults. The process may work somewhat like this (Oatley & Jenkins, 1996: 181; Saarni & Crowley, 1990: 60–61). Little Amanda starts crying at the end of the day when her friend Alex leaves. Dad may say, "Do you feel sad that Alex had to go home?" Like many of us, Amanda may not have known why she was crying, and there were a lot of possibilities (not that she is necessarily aware of them) – she was tired or hungry, she just fell down, Alex took her toy, and then he left. What she does learn, however, is that Dad expects her to feel sad when Alex leaves, and so she surmises that those vague feelings may be what Dad calls sadness. As she gets older, she may realize that, in general, people feel sad when they lose something they want, and that she has just lost her playmate, so she *ought to* feel sad. It is easy to see how Ifaluk children could be socialized in similar ways to feel and label their feelings as *metagu* (fear/anxiety in Ifaluk) when they have to walk past a seated group of elders (Lutz, 1986: 272).

Appropriate feelings are also negotiated through emotion terminology among older children and adults, though adults may be less malleable and on to each other's tricks than are children (Bellelli, 1995; Zammuner & Frijda, 1994). A teenager says, "You're angry at me for denting the fender," to which a parent says, "I'm not angry, I'm just disappointed." Students laugh when they hear this example because they read into it the following subtext: "Let's not define this as you standing in the way of my goal; let's define this as you failing to live up to appropriate standards. It's not my problem; it's yours. It's not a situation you can correct; you've already blown it." "You should feel ashamed." Examples go on and on, and there can be a great deal at stake. "I love my boyfriend" – "That's not love, that's just infatuation."

The orientations that families have toward feeling, managing, and talking about emotion vary widely. Some families consider emotion to be unacceptable ("from the devil") or appropriate only for major issues ("I can't afford to be sad" or "What does a kid have to be sad about?") (Dunn, Brown, & Beardsall, 1991; Gottman, Katz, & Hooven, 1997; Hooven, Gottman, & Katz, 1995: 230). Other families are more likely to be aware of emotions, accept them, talk about them, and teach their children how to manage them. Children who grow up in more emotionally reflective families tend to be able to recognize and manage their own emotions better and tend to function better in their close relationships. In particular, there seems to be a benevolent cycle in which children with good emotional communication skills become more popular, their popularity enhances their emotion skills, which makes them more popular, and so on. Unfortunately, there is also a parallel vicious cycle that occurs when children with poor emotional communication skills become relatively unpopular, which hurts their emotion skills, which makes them less popular, and so on (Manstead & Edwards, 1992; Saarni, 1993: 243). In an effort to break vicious cycles and start benevolent ones, schools are starting to develop programs aimed at emotional awareness, impulse control, empathy, and effective communication (Goleman, 1995: Chap. 16).

Most of us learn the basic skills that we need to communicate emotionally when we are children, but even then our work is not over. As adults, we adapt our emotional communication to the different people with whom we have close relationships, to the different social roles we play, and to the different social situations in which we find ourselves. Emotional socialization never ends, which is to our advantage because it creates a fluid, dynamic relationship between the personal emotional communication patterns that an individual brings to the situation and what is expected by society or the many subsets of society in which each of us lives.

Emotion Messages and Close Relationships

As adults, our emotional messages are adapted most to the people with whom we coordinate most strongly and most often – our intimate partners. Nothing is quite so thrilling as lovers being on the same positive emotional wavelength, and nothing is quite as devastating as unrequited love (Baumeister & Wotman, 1992). Even when emotions are negative, they are difficult NOT to share – anger often provokes anger, and fear provokes fear. In a very real sense, the emotions that you feel in close relationships are only partially your own. Because they are also so strongly influenced by the feelings of your partner, they are also joint, shared feelings. Only in isolation can individuals lay claim to their own feelings, and probably not even then.

In Chapter 2, we considered the many ways in which people share emotions with one another. Responding to the same event can produce *emotional coincidence,* such as when both parents are thrilled when their child's musical recital goes well or angry when they find out that he skipped school. Most likely they will also talk about the situation, thus negotiating or reinforcing a shared view of it and probably shared feelings as well. In relationships that are based on highly coordinated lives, opportunities for emotional coincidence are plentiful, and to the extent that partners talk with one another, their feelings will be highly intertwined.

People also share feelings because one person picks up the feelings of the other through *emotional contagion*. Infants and caregivers cannot help but affect one another. Infants pick up on their fathers' sadness, and fathers pick up on their infants' joy. There is also an ongoing process of mutual adjustment in which "each person copes with, and attempts to influence, the behavior of the other so that the emotional dialogue will be more mutually satisfying" (Malatesta-Magai, 1991: 65). Adults show similar sensitivity to one another. You may become excited when your roommate is talking fast and running around or depressed when your partner is slumped over in a chair and uncommunicative. If you spend a lot of time in each other's presence, emotional contagion is bound to bind you together. At a still more sophisticated level, if you know your partner well and understand her situation, you are able to image her situation and feel what she is feeling – you *empathize*.

Researchers have documented the degree of emotional coordination (probably at all of these levels) that often exists between married couples. In a series of studies, couples were invited to come into a lab and talk while their physiological reactions were being recorded (Gottman, 1994). Interestingly, the *dissatisfied* couples showed a strong pattern of physiological coordination when they tried to resolve a major source of disagreement, whereas the satisfied couples did not. That is, in dissatisfied marriages, when one partner became physiologically aroused while engaging in conflict, the other partner did too. The researchers linked the couple's negative entanglement to what they call the *Four Horsemen of the Apocalypse* (Gottman, 1994: 414): complaining/criticizing, showing contempt, being defensive, and stonewalling. In other words, it was not just the negative emotion, but also *how* it was communicated, that locked the couple into a cycle of bad feelings. It would be interesting to know if more satisfied couples not only are able to escape these vicious emotional communicative cycles, but also if they are able to set up positive cycles grounded in complimenting, mutual respect, and mutual responsiveness.

Society is made up not just of individuals, couples, and families, but also of more elaborate hierarchies (such as supervisory ranks), task groups (such as committees), and even very elaborate organizations (such as hospitals or government agencies). Our emotional messages are influenced by our roles and positions in those structures; a male, lower-class auto worker, Scout troop leader, and political activist has a different emotional life than a female, upper-class advertising executive who participates in an infertility support group.

Emotional Communication and Social Roles

One of the great contributions that sociologists have made in turning their attention to the study of emotion was to help us realize that emotion is not just a personal experience, but also an enactment of social structure. Emotional communication reflects, enacts, supports, challenges, and repairs the social structure. Think about traditional Western parenting roles, in which mothers nurtured and supported the children emotionally and fathers supported the children materially and disciplined them. Mothers inspired love; fathers inspired fear. Parental divisions of labor were accompanied by emotional divisions of labor. Whenever Mom comforted a hurt child, she was doing what mothers were expected to do (reflecting and enacting her understanding of the social role), and she was perpetuating that expectation through her own actions. Whenever Dad yelled at a child who misbehaved, he was reflecting, enacting, and supporting the traditional "Dad" role by communicating emotion as dads do.

Nowadays, the roles are all mixed up, and so are the patterns of emotional communication. Mothers who yell at their kids and dads who try to protect the poor things from the wrath of Mom challenge the purity of the traditional roles (and, of course, those roles never were all *that* pure anyway). Children who pull Dad aside when they really need to talk or who hide their tears from Mom because she won't tolerate them are doing the same thing. That is, social roles guide our emotional communication, and at the same time emotional communication shapes our social roles. Perhaps more important, there is a fluid, dynamic relationship between the personal emotional communication patterns that an individual brings to the situation and what is expected by society.

Enacting Social Structure Through Emotional Communication

We can see the influence of social structure on our emotions more easily by contrasting situations that are strange to us with those that are more familiar. For example, in ancient Rome, fathers had absolute power over their sons (not to mention their wives, daughters, and slaves), including the right to condemn them to death. Not surprisingly, sons often hated and feared their fathers (Gordon, 1990: 147). This seems strange to those of us who are used to a more equal balance of power within families and to the feeling of love that binds them together. Of course, there are sons who hate their fathers even though they may have no real power over them, and no doubt there were Roman sons who loved their fathers despite their power. The point, however, is that feelings and their expression are at least partly determined by social structure and also serve as cues to social structure. Clark (1997: 233–234) says, "I believe that it is often an emotion cue – a surge of smugness, a little anxiety, a feeling of hurt, or even a pang of guilt – that tells a social actor what his or her place is, or how it has changed, often before other kinds of cues come to awareness." The hostility and resentment felt by many teenagers, for example, may be a sign that they are getting to a position of challenging their parents and becoming independent.

Power and status are especially important and may be the real forces underlying emotional expectations based on sex, age, race, and occupation. In general, greater power and higher status tend to give people more emotional freedom, whereas less power and lower status require more emotional restraint and more monitoring of the status superior's emotional messages. For example, students were more willing to express feelings openly when they thought interviewers were other students (status equals) than when they thought they were professors (with greater status) (Thimm & Kruse, 1993). One interesting explanation that has been offered for the intriguing finding that women (compared to men) and African Americans (compared to European Americans) tend to be better judges of emotion is that relatively low status leads people to be especially sensitive to the emotional messages of their status superiors (called the *oppression hypothesis*) (Gitter, Black, & Mostofsky, 1972). Powerless people are also more vulnerable to emotional contagion from the powerful than vice versa. On the other side of the coin, male flight attendants seemed to be protected by a "status shield" that led passengers to respect their feelings more than those of their female (lower-status) counterparts (Hochschild, 1983: Chap 8). A good litmus test of power and status is to consider who is permitted to express feelings and who is not. Often the boss can yell and scream at employees, but usually not the reverse. European upper-class ladies in the 19th century might have fainted at a shocking scene, but their maids could not afford that luxury (Gordon, 1990: 157).

In addition to status, a second major dimension of social life that is enacted through emotional communication is connection. People enact, enhance, affirm, and deny their connections with other people by communicating emotion. Husbands and wives, parents and children, and close friends communicate their love for one another in many ways, including verbal expressions of love, physical affection, and emotional support in everyday interaction, and they reaffirm their bonds by special rituals such as anniversary celebrations, Mother's Day phone calls, and holiday gifts. Socially illegitimate relationships such as extramarital liaisons are not permitted such displays in public, and others would be scandalized if they were. Of course, connections are not always positive. Adversaries or enemies may communicate their relationship by real or ritualistic challenges, threats, or insults or by refusing to communicate altogether. Only when the game or the war is over are new possibilities for positive connections proposed in the form of handshakes or treaties.

We also use emotional communication to define our own status relative to that of other people in a variety of ways (Clark, 1990, 1997). We may express contempt in order to put someone else down ("what a ridiculous idea!") or admiration to flatter him ("Great idea!"). We may enhance our status by trying to make others feel obligated by giving emotional gifts that make them feel inferior ("Let me help you, you poor thing"). We may express anger in order to demonstrate our power and appear intimidating, or we may express sadness in order to appear helpless and dependent (Clark et al., 1996). Similarly, we reach out for connection by communicating in ways that are open, pleasant, and accepting, and we put people off by being unavailable or unpleasant. Chronically lonely people seem almost to invite rebuff by communicating in ways that might be described as self-centered, judgmental, and rejecting (Jones et al., 1982). Making others feel obligated through appeals to guilt can work to reinforce connection even if the other person is not entirely willing (Vangelisti, Daly, & Rudnick, 1991).

Relations of status and connection are so important to emotion messages that they are written into the very vocabulary of emotions. Friends love one another; enemies hate one another. The weak fear the strong; the strong get angry at the weak. The strong have nothing to fear from the weak, and the weak cannot do much to prevent the strong from obstructing their goals, so there is not much point in feeling anger. Resignation and depression make more sense. We respect superiors but feel contempt for inferiors. In fact, saying that we feel contempt for our social superiors (such as high-ranking public officials) really implies that we have negative connections with them and consider them in some other way to be our inferiors (for example, immoral or untrustworthy). Similarly, saying that we respect our social inferiors (such as our employees) implies that we have positive connections and that they are somehow superior (for example, hardworking or humble).

When we communicate emotion, we are guided in part by social roles; and yet, each of us enacts those roles differently, depending on our temperaments, our family backgrounds, the constraints of our lives, our social skills and sensitivities, and even our personal feelings at the moment. This gives the social structure a certain amount of flexibility that permits it to bend without breaking, and it gives the individual some leeway in enacting social roles in ways that fit personal circumstances. Over the centuries, parent–child relations have come to be based less on fear and more on affection through gradual changes from one generation to the next (Shorter, 1977: Chap. 5; Stearns & Stearns, 1986).

On the other hand, one person's refusal to enact her appropriate emotional role can cause a firestorm of emotional reactions, lining up supporters and opponents on both sides and setting off dramatic and unforeseen consequences. No one knows what Rosa Parks was feeling the day she refused to give up her seat on the bus to a white man, but she did not communicate the timidity and resignation expected of a black woman in Alabama in 1955. People seem to be especially likely to break out of their emotional constraints when role expectations are contradictory, changing, or oppressive (Thoits, 1990). The pre–World War II feminine role did not fit the emotional demands of the wartime economy, leading to the less demure and more courageous female role personified in Rosie the Riveter. Once the change was underway, it was easier for the next generation of women to alter their emotional roles, and later for articulate spokespersons to draw attention to the nature of those role constraints, leading still other women to break out of them more purposefully.

Changing Social Roles Through Emotional Communication

When the social fabric is torn, it becomes apparent when emotional threads are hanging loose. Emotion is an important signal that the existing social structures are not serving the interests of individuals, and it goads people to take action to change things. Loneliness moves people to seek out others, to communicate with them, and to try to establish close bonds. Jealousy moves us to protect the bonds that we think are threatened. But above all, anger, especially anger that is communicated to others, moves us to reassess whether the ways we function in our social roles are best for ourselves, for our partners, and for society as a whole.

There are plenty of things to be angry about these days, and one is the division of labor between husbands and wives. In U.S. households where wives work outside the home, they do more housework than their husbands, clocking in what has been estimated as an average of an extra month of 24-hour days per year of housework (Hochschild, 1989b: 3). Whether couples thought this situation was unfair depended on how they defined their social roles, and their emotions differed as a result. Some couples were content in their traditional roles, agreeing that the wife had no right to feel angry if her husband did not help with housework because housework was women's work, but she did have a right to resent having to contribute financially because that was her husband's job. Husbands had no responsibility to do housework, deserved their wives' gratitude when they did any housework, and had no reason to feel guilty if they did not. Some wives did not agree and staged "sharing showdowns" for which they prepared emotionally (Hochschild, 1990: 130–135). "[T]hey had to rivet their attention on the injustice of the unfair load they carried and dwell on its importance to them. They distanced themselves from all they would otherwise feel for their husband and suspended their empathy for his situation. They steeled themselves against his resistance." In some cases, conflict over roles pushed couples' relationships to the breaking point, which often meant choosing between anger and love. As Hochschild explains, personal emotion work picks up where social transformation leaves off.

As this recent example illustrates, emotional communication serves as an impetus for change, as a way of negotiating it, and as a way of managing the results, but it is by no means the only example. Any change in social structure, whether on a grand scale or within a family, may set similar emotional communication processes in motion. The birth of a child can set in motion new forms of love and jealousy that may strain roles. When that child reaches adolescence, his struggle to attain independence from his parents can produce new dynamics of anger, guilt, anxiety, hostility, and so on. Someone who moves up the social ladder may feel a mixture of pride (at her accomplishments), shame (at her humble beginnings), guilt (at leaving others behind), and pity or contempt (for those who are still lowly). Even whole societies may suffer from shame when their national stature is degraded, as Germany's was in the Treaty of Versailles at the end of World War I; then they are highly susceptible to a leader like Hitler who offers pride and self-confidence in the place of shame (Scheff & Retzinger, 1991: Chap. 8). Feelings of gratitude, guilt, shame, anger, and many others are important indicators of where one stands, wants to stand, or believes one should stand in the social structure.

Communicating Emotion to Manage Social Situations

Emotions are one way to manage social problems. You forget your friend's birthday, and later you apologize – you say that you feel bad and that you are sorry. As a result, he is less angry or disappointed. Your colleague does some extra work for you, and you express gratitude. She feels treated more fairly. You tell someone at a party about what a slimy so-and-so your landlord is; then she introduces herself as his wife. You feel embarrassed, and your embarrassment pacifies her a bit. The social situation has been disrupted (for good or for ill), and you attempt to put things straight by communicating the right emotions. Or perhaps it would be more accurate to say that your emotions function to try to repair relations, whether you communicate them intentionally or not (Baumeister et al., 1994; Frijda, 1993).

Are these, in fact, your emotions? Perhaps they are, perhaps they aren't, but you would communicate them anyway because the situation requires it. In fact, it is probably more important that you *express* the right feelings than that you actually *feel* them, although relational harmony is more likely to be restored if the apology is reinforced by nonverbal expressions (acting guilty and ashamed) (Metts, 1994). Three types of emotional communication are especially strongly tied to situations in which the social fabric is torn and messages are used to repair it and reinforce social ties. These are apologies, expressions of gratitude, and displays of embarrassment.

Apologizing

The basic pattern to an apology is that "something is said or done that is interpreted and judged offensive, improper, or harmful. An apology is called for, someone apologizes, the apology (let us assume) is accepted, the offender is forgiven, and life goes on *as if* nothing had happened . . . for all practical purposes, the slate is wiped clean" (Tavuchis, 1991: 4). Apology is a three-act play of transgression, confession, and redemption. In the first act, a social norm or rule is violated, usually by an individual but possibly by a group. Violations can range from the trivial (interrupting someone), through the troubling (defaming someone's character), to the tragic (the Tuskegee Alabama syphilis experiments). A crucial feature of the apology is that the transgressor admits fault, and in so doing she recognizes the legitimacy of the rule or norm that has been broken and owns up to having broken it. This is why legal counsel often discourages apologies; they constitute an admission of fault. It is also important that the transgression be identified precisely. President Nixon's apology for Watergate, for example, was not satisfying because he apologized for the pain he had caused the nation but never admitted to the betrayal of public trust, which was the real offense in most people's eyes (Tavuchis, 1991: 54–58). Conversely, in 1986 the United Church of Canada officially apologized to Canadian native people as follows: "In our zeal to tell you about Jesus Christ, we were blind to your spirituality. We imposed our civilization on you as a condition for accepting our gospel. . . . As a result, we are both poorer. We are not what God meant us to be." This apology was accepted as sincere and appropriate by the native people who were present and who responded with "almost unbelievable happiness." They accepted the apology publicly with a standing ovation (Tavuchis, 1991: 109–112).

Apologies count as apologies only if they are communicated, and often only a public apology will do. It is meant to go on record as a commitment to avoid the transgression in the future, to try to heal wounds, and to reestablish relationships that may have been damaged as a result. The offended person has the option of refusing the apology – refusing to forgive, refusing to forget, or refusing to reestablish the relationship. Apology is a type of social exchange, as is apparent when we talk about "owing, giving, offering, receiving, and accepting an apology" (Tavuchis, 1991: 33).

We wonder about people who apologize for everything because they seem to be communicating that they feel responsible for all social ruptures and are socially unworthy. But people who refuse to apologize are doubly deviant – unwilling to follow social norms and unwilling to apologize on top of it. Such people communicate either that they do not take responsibility for the offense or that they believe the relationship is strong enough to withstand offense without needing repair, or both. Judith Martin (aka Miss Manners) has an opinion: "People who boast that they 'never apologize, never explain,' or who claim that 'love is never having to say you're sorry' ought to be ashamed of themselves and admit it and ask forgiveness" (Tavuchis, 1991: 29). We also wonder about people who accept apologies too easily; they seem to gloss over the seriousness of the offense or they seem not to care much about sincerity. At the same time, we wonder about people who cannot accept apologies because they seem to prefer their own feeling of self-righteousness over renewed social bonds.

Apologies must be offered correctly, and others have a vested interest in monitoring apologies because they are not just private matters, but also social institutions. Observers make judgments about whether the circumstances require an apology ("She owes you an apology for that"), whether the apology has been performed correctly ("He was too quick to apologize. He didn't really mean it."), and whether it should be accepted or rejected ("He apologized, so forget it!"). Children, especially, must be taught the rules for apologizing and must be made to practice until they get it right, with expectations rising as a child gets older. In some cases, apology is a matter of public controversy. Watergate was one example. Other interesting cases are when private transgressions reflect on a public persona, such as Bill Clinton's affair with Monica Lewinsky. Is this a private matter or did it call for a public apology? Was the apology sincere and appropriate? Should the public accept the apology, forgive, and (more important) trust him in the future? And what about the next time?[5]

Expressing Gratitude

Normally, we do not think of social disruptions as producing positive results, but sometimes they do. One of the basic principles of social living is the norm of reciprocity – if someone does something for you, you do something for her in return (Hochschild, 1989a; McConnell, 1993). Some theorists argue that this is the very foundation of social life, but even if it is not, it is easy to see that if you only gave and never received, you would sooner or later deplete your resources, and if you only received and never gave, you would sooner or later lose

---

[5] Tavuchis (1991: 74–83) analyzes a similar case involving a baseball player's sexual indiscretion.

all your friends. In any case, when you receive something and cannot reciprocate immediately, you express gratitude (and, ideally, you should feel it as well). In fact, any circumstance that leads to getting more than you deserve calls for expressions of gratitude. What are you accomplishing by saying "thanks"?

There are three important ingredients to gratitude, as with apologies (following Tavuchis, 1991). First, by saying "thanks," you show others that you know that the social contract has been violated, at least temporarily. You *know* that you are getting more than you deserve; you were not born in a barn. Even during holiday gift exchanges when everyone gives to everyone else, we thank each other because we know (or at least we *should* know) that we have done nothing to deserve the gift, much less a gift as wonderful as that stunning necktie! If you do some extra work for a coworker and he does not thank you, you wonder if he thinks that you (not he) should have done it all along and if he will expect you to do it again next time. This could be cause for alarm. On the other hand, if someone thanks you for doing something that was your duty, you may reject the thanks ("Just doing my job, ma'am!"). Gratitude also functions as a promissory note on future responsibilities, and it is especially powerful if it is truly heartfelt. Not only does the person receiving the favor *know* he should repay it when circumstances permit, but he *feels* that he should, and the feeling puts additional force behind the commitment (Frank, 1988).

Second, feeling gratitude is important, but expressing gratitude may be even more important. Keeping it to yourself does not have the same effect because the other person has not been reassured that you recognize social imbalance and you have made no public commitment to rectify it. Even more important, you have done nothing to validate the relationship between you and the giver. Expressing gratitude is a social ritual that validates relationships as much as it promises to balance the books. We can never repay our parents for all they have done for us, but that is okay because we have a relationship in which each looks out for the other's welfare, not one in which we expect payback. We do, however, expect thanks as a sign that the gifts and the relationship are recognized. This is one reason that gifts are not always welcome (think of jewelry from an unwanted suitor). If we want to reject the relationship, we are almost forced to reject the gift (unless, of course, we believe we deserve it; then it is not a gift).

Finally, expressions of gratitude are not just a private matter between the giver and the receiver, as anyone who has been forced by parents to write thank-you notes knows very well. They are signs of social courtesy, of being civilized, or of being a responsible and sensitive human being. There is more at stake than just the relationship between two people. The larger social contract is being enacted, and that is not a matter that can be left to children. Children who do not feel gratitude for gifts may believe that they deserve them, or they may not recognize the sacrifice made by the gift giver. Either emotional stance can be dangerous to society because it indicates greed or the failure to recognize others' efforts.

Showing Embarrassment

Like apologies and expressions of gratitude, displays of embarrassment are signs that something has gone wrong socially, that we know it, and we show it (Edelmann, 1987). Embarrassment occurs primarily in public, (about 98% of the time; Miller, 1996: 39), and usually we do something that projects the wrong social image to others – most often we feel foolish. Examples abound: falling off a chair in class, getting a singing telegram, throwing up on your date, losing your bikini top on an amusement park ride, or having your car stall at a busy intersection (Miller, 1996: 46–69).

In addition, embarrassment usually occurs because there is a social predicament. You don't know what to do or say, and you are afraid that you may handle the situation badly, resulting in further embarrassment. There is no way to truly repair the situation, as there is with an apology or an expression of gratitude. What do you say when you come walking naked out of the shower singing "Tomorrow" just as a real estate agent is showing a prospective buyer your house? It is a social predicament with no easy solution, certainly not a socially sanctioned and ritualized one like an apology. You have to make it up as you go along, but people tend to do certain things, like apologizing, giving excuses, avoiding or escaping, making jokes, or becoming aggressive. If you pull it off well, you recover quickly, regain your poise, and try to minimize the harm done (Cupach & Metts, 1990).

Finally, embarrassment is contagious, and people tend to feel some collective responsibility to smooth things over. Besides, bystanders and onlookers often get embarrassed too. How would you like to be the people looking at the house when someone walks out of the shower naked singing "Tomorrow"? Other people involved in the embarrassing incident tend to use many of the same remedial strategies that the principal parties use, but in addition they may pretend they didn't notice ("What naked man?"), provide a diversion ("I've forgotten to show you the den!"), or offer support or empathy ("I know how embarrassing this must be for you, but don't worry about it."). Sometimes others make the person even more embarrassed, either intentionally in order to teach a lesson or to gain power and impress others, or unintentionally such as when a joke backfires (Bradford & Petronio, 1998). Oddly, a predicament seems less embarrassing when everyone else is embarrassed, perhaps because shared embarrassment indicates that no one wants to make an issue of it and everyone is ready to restore the social order (Metts, Cupach, & Hazleton, 1986, cited in Cupach & Metts, 1990).

In summary, when people apologize, express gratitude, or display embarrassment, they are not just expressing their personal feelings. They are also enacting socially prompted, socially defined, and socially sanctioned rituals for repairing social gaffes. Insincere expressions of gratitude, remorse, or embarrassment do not cut it, but neither do private feelings kept to oneself. The purpose of the apology, thanks, or embarrassment episode is to bring the individual in line with social expectations, and the individual's responsibility is to demonstrate to others that he deserves to be readmitted to polite society. Of course, it does not always work that way if either or both parties do not believe there is a problem or do not want it to be repaired. This is especially likely when one party feels harmed and the other party either doesn't care, doesn't feel responsible, doesn't think harm was done, or thinks the injured party deserved it ("*You* smashed my car" – "But *you* were in my way").

Solidified Social Routines and Rituals

An apology is a good example of a fairly simple social ritual that has evolved as a solution to shared emotional predicaments. Unlike our fumbling and awkward responses to embarrassment, we can turn to the relatively clearly defined and widely accepted ritual called *apology* to set things right. Major changes in social status can be even more disruptive and require even more elaborate rituals to deal with them in ways that minimize or control the disruption and the volatile feelings that may result. One of the most mundane and yet most intriguing examples of such rituals is the marriage ceremony. At marriage, a woman and a man make the social transition from daughter/son to wife/husband (that is, their primary loyalties and responsibilities have shifted), from eligible maid/bachelor to wife/husband (that is, their relationship becomes exclusive), from a courting couple trying out togetherness to an enduring social tie on which others may be built (that is, wife/husband may lead to mother/father). To the uninformed and iconoclastic, the rituals of romance and marriage may seem a little silly, but they can be seen as symbolic ways of managing social roles, transitions between them, and the emotions that go along (Gillis, 1988). The father "giving away" the bride marks a role transition for him and for her, and bridesmaid/bachelor parties call attention to changing primary loyalties from same-sex friends to husband or wife.

Rituals and ceremonies often accompany elevations in status, such as when priests are ordained, students graduate, or royalty are crowned. Not only are their accomplishments celebrated, but ceremonial oratory and symbols (such as robes or vestments) promote feelings of pride in the recipients and respect or even awe in onlookers. Status elevation ceremonies have their counterpart in "status degradation ceremonies," which change status downward from loyal subject to traitor, from law-abiding citizen to criminal, or from high school graduate to college freshman/fraternity initiate (Garfinkel, 1956). If effective, these ceremonies induce shame in the person denounced and contempt or even disgust in onlookers. During ceremonies, individuals are reminded of what values the group sanctions, how they are to orient emotionally to those values, and what the consequences will be if they are violated. Moreover, not just anybody can crown the queen or deliver a verdict of "guilty"; only legitimate representatives of the group (bishops or judges) have that authority. Everyone involved in a ceremony, including onlookers, participates in the affirmation of group values when they engage in the ritual and feel the appropriate feelings (Collins, 1990).

The most important function of rituals, however, may not be to manage the disparate and often socially unacceptable emotions of individuals or even to put emotional force behind common values, but rather to foster a collective spirit that helps people transcend their individual selves to become unified as a group. Durkheim (1912/1975: 128) describes the phenomenon like this: "When we find ourselves at the heart of an assembly animated by a common passion, we become capable of sentiments and actions of which we are not capable when we are reduced to our own efforts; and when the assembly breaks up, when we are once more on our own and return to our normal level, we can measure the extent to which we were lifted above ourselves." A charismatic orator is capable of inspiring, focusing, and magnifying group feelings in a process again described best by Durkheim: "The feelings stirred up by his words rebound towards him, magnified and amplified, so intensify his own feeling. The passionate energy he arouses reverberates within him and increases his vitality. It is no longer a single individual speaking, rather it is a group incarnate and personified" (p. 129). At such moments personal feelings and group feelings are one (Wasielewski, 1985).

Public ceremonies held to commemorate events that are emotionally significant for individuals and for groups, such as the end of a war or a natural disaster that claimed many lives, play important roles in both individual and collective grieving and in binding individuals to groups (Frijda, 1997). Remembering such events in common (the literal meaning of commemorating) activates emotions that range from the powerful anguish of the survivors or the bereaved to the ritualized respect of onlookers. Through ceremonial speeches and symbolic actions, however, people come together to mark the event as worthy of memory (often on anniversaries), to create unique and shared meanings (struggling with the questions "how could this happen?" or "how has life changed as a result?"), and to feel the presence of those who were lost (Frijda, 1997). Grieving together may help people find deeper emotional meanings than they could achieve alone because their private experiences are understood as parts of momentous events, sacred values, and revered connections that transcend their individual experiences.

The Issue of Responsibility

The question of whether emotions are personal or social is not just an academic one, it also has important implications for decisions that we make in everyday life. When someone flies into a fit of rage and murders another, who is to blame – the murderer or society? At a certain level, the answer is pedestrian; of course, not everyone murders when they are enraged, so the murderer should be held accountable. And indeed he should. But holding the individual responsible for his own emotion-guided actions does not rule out the possibility that society as a whole *also* bears some responsibility, though not in the legal sense. We all may have contributed to producing the conditions that fostered the rage, to making violence seem a natural response to rage, and to perpetuating the belief that rage may produce an "irresistible urge" to kill (Baumeister, 1997: 274). In this way, the frequency of school shootings by children in the United States in the late 1990s reveals something deeply disturbing – not just about the children who pulled the trigger but also about the larger culture of violence.

On a more positive note, when children raise pennies for muscular dystrophy or when rescue teams risk their lives for others, do we all deserve a little bit of credit for building a society that cultivates generosity and caring? It doesn't come easy for highly individualistic Westerners (especially Americans) to reflect on the ways in which collective messages about emotion cultivate certain emotions and shape the kinds of actions that should and do follow from them, but it is important that we do. We know that personal feelings do not arise in a social vacuum. They are refined in the cauldron of our collective experiences and emotional messages to be at once uniquely our own and shared by all.

Another sense in which our feelings are both personal and collective is that they define and guide the moral stances by which we live with one another in society. Emotional messages are a story not just about what people and society are, but also about what they *should be*. Feelings serve as a touchstone for moral behavior or moral violations in ways that we examine in the next chapter.

6. How Do Emotion Messages Communicate Moral Meaning?

In emotion, we see values as virtual facts of the world.
Cochran and Claspell (1987: 159)

One of the most emotionally powerful photographs in recent years is of a firefighter carrying the bleeding body of a toddler from the wreckage of the bombed federal building in Oklahoma City. Through the photo, we felt the anguish and despair of the people who loved that child, of the firefighter and other rescue workers who were carrying out the victims, and of all our fellow human beings who were affected by the tragedy. And we wanted to do something about it – to rush to the aid of the victims (as many people did), to find and punish the bomber, and to make sure that this sort of tragedy could never happen again. Our emotions tell us that the world is not as it *should* be and that we should *do* something about it. Imagine another image of children dancing and playing on a beach. We feel their exuberance, their joy, their sense of being alive, their connections with one another. We *know* through our feelings that the world *is* as it should be, that we should appreciate the perfection of that moment, and that we should try to sustain the kind of world that produces such joy and love.

When we sift through the complexities, we find that messages loaded with emotion have two essential meanings: a judgment of good or bad and an imperative to keep things as they are or to change things. This is the core of emotional theory, as described earlier. The two key components of the emotional process are appraising the situation (and the most basic appraisal is good/bad) and a tendency to act or refrain from action (Frijda et al., 1989). Anger stems from the judgment that something is wrong (often unjust) and that action should be taken to fix it. Love stems from the judgment that something is right and that action should be taken to sustain it. In two words: emotion orients us to the *good* and to the *should*: to things that we value and to things that we feel we ought to do.

Morality deals with exactly those same issues. To behave morally is to judge right and wrong, good and bad, and to behave accordingly. Telling the truth is considered morally correct (good and advisable) most of the time because it produces positive effects, and society works better when truth can be assumed. Moral standards get hazier when the truth produces more harm than good ("That dress is hideous!") or when fabrications produce more good than harm ("Santa Claus will come down the chimney tonight!"). Much of moral theory focuses on assessing the degree of good or harm that comes from an action (or inaction in the case of sins of omission), considering who gets to decide (the deceiver, the deceived, disinterested observers), and imagining what the world would be like if everyone behaved accordingly (e.g., Bok, 1978).

None of this is to say, of course, that feeling a particular emotion in a certain situation is inherently right from a moral point of view. An angry person is righteous from her own point of view (at least at the moment she is feeling the anger), but not necessarily from the point of view of anyone else judging her. It is too much to expect emotion to point us in the *right* moral direction or even in a *single* moral direction. It is not uncommon to be torn between anger and shame, between sympathy and disgust, or between the opposing moral outrage of two groups (the abortion debate comes to mind). The important thing to recognize, however, is that emotion and not only reason stands at the foundation of moral assessment and moral action.

Judgments about emotions are open to discussion, even discussion about whether judgments should be made at all. As Clark (1997: 203) states: "Judges do not judge in a vacuum. They know that others are likely to judge their judgments." We curse tennis judges who make bad calls, and we criticize people who judge others' feelings too much, too harshly, or not harshly enough. For example, I might condemn someone for not showing enough sympathy for a disabled person. Then someone else might come along and condemn my condemnation because disabled people don't want sympathy; they want to be treated normally. Because I know this could happen, I am careful to take others' views into account in making my judgments of my own and others' emotions. I need not agree with everyone else, but I am likely to consider them because I might be asked to justify my own judgments, not to mention my own emotions.

Emotions, to be sure, do not solve the problem of what our moral standards should be, but they do draw attention to, assert, and celebrate whatever moral standards we hold. Greenspan (1995: 189) says that emotions provide indirect knowledge about our own ethical standards when we feel inclined to act in certain ways. Disgust, for example, tells us what we find contaminating either physically or morally (Miller, 1997). Guilt and shame call us to task for not behaving in accord with the values that we hold dear. As Parish (1994: 216) says: "surges of painful affect will fill the gap between what you have done and what you should have done" [or at least believe that you should have done].

To appeal again to the weaving metaphor, we might say that when we weave emotional messages; our patterns are often stories about how we *ought to* make judgments and act. They are morality plays that are woven into the very fabric of social existence and made vivid by the colors of emotion. The glories of war are outlined by the colors of the Bayeux tapestry, and the tragedy of ruined lives is made vivid in the colors of the AIDS quilt. The good, bad, and the ugly show up in living color (Tangney, 1991), and they reflect and define the moral stances of the weavers.

Emotion Messages Communicate Standards for Right and Wrong

Many authors have argued that we do not reason our way to conceptions of morality, at least not in everyday life. Instead, we feel moral violations in our guts. And that is good, because if we only thought about them, we might never say or do anything. Feelings, however, include the urge to act. In Solomon's words (1990: 33):

> Justice begins not with Socratic insights but with the promptings of some basic emotions, among them envy, jealousy, and resentment, a sense of being personally cheated or neglected, and the desire to get even – but also, of course, those basic feelings of sharing, compassion, sympathy, and generosity that cynics have forever refused to acknowledge.

Leaders of social movements are not usually philosophers who *think* about morality, but they *are* very often victims who *feel* the effects of immoral systems themselves (Nelson Mandela of apartheid, Saint Patrick of slavery), and sometimes they are both victims *and* philosophers (Mohandas Gandhi). Those who have behaved immorally or have benefited from immoral systems may also feel guilt or shame and be goaded to action. Many a saint has been a former sinner. *Feeling* moral outrage, more than just *thinking* it, leads people to speak out and act. Moral feelings, however, are not always radical; they can also be deeply conservative. Shame can make members of downtrodden groups feel that they deserve their oppression, suppressing their actions and stifling their voices. Pride and hubris reinforces the feeling that one deserves privilege by virtue of superiority. Embarrassment and fear (or the anticipation of them) enforce playing by the rules, and so on (Solomon, 1989).

Communicating Anger and Guilt at Injustice

When we believe we are the victims of injustice, our immediate response is often anger (Mikula, Scherer, & Athenstaedt, 1998). Injustice is not the only thing that makes us angry, to be sure; we also get angry in amoral situations when our goals are simply frustrated (such as missing the bus when trying to get to work). Yet anger is especially powerful and enduring when we believe we are treated unfairly – when others do not play by the rules (Averill, 1982). Anger serves as a wake-up call, a motivator, an energizer, and a source of empowerment (for good or for ill) for the individual who experiences it. An angry person feels self-righteous and strong, which is not a bad way to feel. It makes us want to get even or set things right. Anger can be a passion that engages important moral principles, takes precedence over other goals, and is pursued with great persistence, even in the face of great risk (Frijda et al., 1991: 217–220). Passionate anger (especially in the form of righteous indignation or outrage) can fuel lifelong crusades that make enormous strides against injustice (as in the case of Dr. Martin Luther King) or cycles of murderous vengeance that give people even more grounds for hate and rage (the Serbs and Croatians come to mind).

Expressing Anger at Injustice. When an angry person expresses her anger (whether in word or in deed), the perceived injustice is put on the table to be dealt with by everyone involved – the presumed victim, the presumed perpetrator, and perhaps interested parties or onlookers as well. Expressed anger serves as a warning to potential rule violators to stop in their tracks or to make amends, and it doesn't take sophisticated moral theories to figure this out. Many a toddler has been stopped from playing with fragile valuables by a well-timed and angry "No!" and many a dog has been kept from dragging her master around by the leash with an angry "Bad dog!" When the angry person has as much power as people do over their children and pets, the offender has little choice but to follow their rules. Whimpers protesting the injustice are not likely to be much of a challenge to the status quo. When power is more equally balanced, however, it is a different story. Justice and injustice become more negotiable, and anger does not necessarily produce the desired effect.

When anger does not have the expected result, the angry person is primed for action. He may take further verbal action (such as more persuasion or increasingly demanding threats), but he may also take physical action in order to "teach them a lesson," "get even," or "set things right." Physical action may even precede or supersede verbal or nonverbal warnings, especially if the angry person is highly impulsive or if he believes words are weak, ineffectual, or are not to be trusted. In a working-class Chicago neighborhood code named "Teamsterville," the prevalent view was that "real men don't talk, they act." In one episode, "the question was put to the group worker, who was not a native of Teamsterville [by 13- to 14-year-old Teamsterville boys]: 'What would you do if a guy insulted your wife?' The group worker responded that he did not know, that it would depend on the situation. The answer did not satisfy the boys, who pressed the question by asking, 'But you'd hit him wouldn't you?' " (Philipsen, 1992: 25).

Taking action to correct an injustice, however, is a tricky business because it is difficult to know what is truly just, and it is easy to overcorrect and create even more injustice, at least from someone else's perspective. Baumeister (1997: 40–47) describes a consistent bias in judgment that makes it nearly impossible to strike the perfect balance. Perpetrators of violence or other harmful acts consistently underestimate the harm they cause to victims compared to the victims' perceptions,[1] and/or victims overestimate the harm they suffer com-

---

[1] In one particularly striking case, Baumeister cites Scully, *Understanding sexual violence* (London: HarperCollins, 1990), p. 130. One serial murderer/rapist said that "he had always made sure to be 'kind and gentle' with them [his victims], at least 'until I started to kill them.' "

pared to perpetrators' perceptions. Moreover, perpetrators see the harm as accidental or justified, whereas victims see it as voluntary and unjustified (Averill, 1993). You can see the cycle developing. I insult your wife, which you see as an egregious offense but I see as a momentary, trivial lapse of etiquette. So you ask me to apologize (or you hit me), which I see as unnecessarily demeaning (or overreacting). Then I need to correct that new injustice by some comment that is even more offensive (or I hit you back – harder). You get the idea. If not, read about the many examples of cycles of revenge documented in *Wild Justice* (Jacoby, 1983). The odd thing about revenge is that often it is not really intended to correct injustice (since the harm often cannot be undone, e.g., victims brought back to life), but rather to cause the perpetrator pain in equal measure to the pain he caused the victim (or maybe a little more, to be safe). What is most unjust is that the victim suffered (and perhaps continues to suffer), while the perpetrator goes his merry way. Revenge equalizes the suffering and the power to inflict suffering (Frijda, 1994).

Is the desire for revenge, then, a moral or an immoral emotion? Frijda (1994: 286) argues that "[w]hen the offense is real and unacceptable, desire for revenge is acceptable" because it supports the moral order by which we all strive to live. But if it is based on imagined or exaggerated offenses, if it is out of proportion to the magnitude of the offense, or if the offense is within acceptable bounds (e.g., a slight rebuff or understandable error), the desire for revenge destabilizes the moral order. The hard part is knowing the difference and channeling the desire for revenge into actions that promote justice, not further injustice. In Jacoby's words (1983: 5), "Establishment of a balance between the restraint that enables people to live with one another and the ineradicable impulse to retaliate when harm is inflicted has always been one of the essential tasks of civilization." In addition, punishment (whether through revenge or the law) sends a powerful moral message to the offender and to everyone else: An important moral principle is at issue; we will not tolerate violations, and WE MEAN IT! (Burgh, 1987: 330).

Negotiating Anger Messages. The accused person has two basic choices. He can either argue that the other person's anger is unjustified (perhaps responding in anger to the false accusation) or he can admit the wrong (express guilt and remorse) and do what he can to correct it. Armon-Jones (1986: 67–71) suggests that one can challenge other people's feelings (anger being one example) on three grounds. First, one can argue that the anger was based on misinformation or misinterpretation of the relevant information. For example, I might say, "You are wrong to think that I left you out of the decision; I asked for your input right before the meeting." Second, one can argue that the anger is out of proportion to the offense. I might say, "Okay, I didn't consult you as much as I should have, but it doesn't warrant getting THAT angry." Third, one can argue about the moral standard that was violated. "You have no right to be angry because I have no obligation to consult you; in fact, you should be grateful that I asked for your advice at all." This last argument shows clearly that anger is grounded in implicit norms, values, and rules that function as moral standards but that are themselves debatable.

Implicit standards become explicit when we get into arguments about them. An excellent example is Clarence Thomas's response to accusations that he had sexually harassed Anita Hill (in the 1991 U.S. Senate hearings). Partly (perhaps even largely) through nonverbal expressions of righteous indignation, he made the argument that the true injustice was that he, a respectable African American, should be humiliated by being subjected to such accusations (a "high-tech lynching for uppity blacks"; Mayer & Abramson, 1994: 299). It is a difficult argument to challenge because, from Thomas's perspective, everyone involved in the trial was committing a sure injustice (subjecting him to accusations) in order to investigate a possible injustice (the sexual harassment). In some people's view, the means did not justify the end. In other people's view, they did. They thought that the embarrassment of a public trial was a small price to pay for keeping a man who abused women off the Supreme Court. Responding to anger with counteranger is an enticing choice because anger makes you feel self-righteous and strong. Nevertheless, the situation can easily get out of hand, especially if there is no one who is able to mediate the dispute. Responding with expressions of guilt and remorse, on the other hand, requires swallowing your pride and makes you feel weak and fallible.

Communicating Guilt and Remorse. Just as expressions of anger from victims uphold standards of justice, expressions of guilt from perpetrators ratify those standards. Open expressions of guilt, in essence, communicate this message: "I recognize that I have violated a standard, I take responsibility for it, I feel the pain of guilt and remorse, and I condemn the violation publicly." Communicating guilt specifically to the victim may also help to satisfy his desire for revenge by recognizing that he (the victim) now has the power to make the accused suffer (emotionally, at least) (Baumeister, et al., 1994). Public expressions of collective guilt (discussed earlier as apologies) go a long way toward legitimizing the moral standard that was violated and toward redeeming the self-respect of the victims or the victimized group.

There are also biases in judgment that work against accepting blame (and guilt) for an unjust or immoral act. People in general want to retain their belief in a just world, and so when they see someone victimized, they tend to blame the victim for her own suffering (Lerner, 1980). She must have done something to deserve it. There are innumerable examples – poor people must be lazy, battered wives must have got out of line, he was too stupid to ask for help. Perpetrators of injustice and onlookers alike find this bias very convenient, even when they have no evidence to support it. Victims, on the other hand, tend to want to see themselves as blameless, even though in many cases they actually did contribute to the problem (such as when escalating arguments lead to violence; Gottfredson & Hirschi, 1990, cited in Baumeister, 1997: 53).

Assuming that the perpetrator does take responsibility, we find an interesting counterpart to vengeance in penance, though penance is less common in the West these days and tends to be associated with punitive religion. Self-flagellation is one of the more dramatic examples of religious penance; secular ones include contributing to charity or making public confessions. Like vengeance, penance can seldom right the original wrong, but it can balance the suffering. Penance serves three important functions, especially if it is prescribed by a religious or secular authority. First, it produces tangible, verifiable hardship or pain (not just emotional pain, which can be faked), so the victim knows exactly how the perpetrator is suffering. Thus it deflects revenge, by man in its secular form and by God in its religious form (Mitchell, 1990: 50). Second, penance helps to alleviate authentic feelings of guilt on the part of the perpetrator when the penance is fulfilled. Third, penance gives the perpetrator a way to earn readmission to respectable society and gives society a way to know that readmission is justified. Moral order is restored, and everyone, even the formerly unjust, is part of the moral community again. Forgiveness may be in order, but it is not a naive, spineless forgiveness that takes no stand against injustice (for an insightful discussion of forgiveness and mercy, see Jacoby, 1983: 331–362).

Getting Even with Gratitude. Until now, we have considered only malevolent injustice (when one person causes unfair harm or hardship to
someone else), but there is also a benevolent side to injustice. This
happens when one person gives another pleasures or benefits that are
beyond what is expected and what one is able to give in return. There
is a "get-even" or "set-things-right" emotion to take care of this too;
it is called *gratitude* (Solomon, 1990: 257). Saying "thank you" may not
exactly restore the balance, but at least it recognizes it and celebrates
important moral virtues such as generosity and selflessness. The more
archaic "much obliged," on the other hand, makes explicit the responsibilities that come with an exchange that is out of balance. Even if the
gift isn't particularly valued (the much maligned holiday fruitcake
comes to mind), it is appropriate to express gratitude for the act of
giving, if not for the gift. A truly honest recipient might say, "You are
so thoughtful!" instead of "How tasty!" The gracious response, as
everyone knows, is to minimize the value of the gift ("It was nothing"
or, these days, "No problem" – in Spanish "*de nada*," in French "*de
rien*"), to reframe the gift as a benefit to the giver ("My pleasure"), or
to indicate that it was indeed freely given ("You're welcome").

Real gratitude serves more as an emotional commitment to reciprocate in the future when the appropriate occasion arises. If the river
is flooding and my neighbors come over to help me sandbag my
house, I express my gratitude, but I will never have a chance to repay
them. But if their barn catches fire and I do not respond, or if I respond
only grudgingly, I obviously do not "get it" and deserve moral condemnation (McConnell, 1993: 81). That is when real gratitude counts.
Gifts in return for gifts, like the suffering returned in revenge, should
be appropriate and commensurate (Schwartz, 1967; Solomon, 1989:
368). And like revenge, repaying a gift is a tricky business. Reciprocated gifts should be of equal value, and that is always a matter of
opinion. Reciprocated gifts must be chosen and timed just right. If a
good friend gives you a ride home and you offer to pay her in cash,
she will probably be offended ("I didn't do that for MONEY!"). Or if
you water her plants while she is away and she offers to come over
and mow your lawn immediately, you may be offended ("You don't
have to do that now; I know that you'll water my plants whenever
I'm away") (Clark & Mills, 1979; McConnell, 1993: 51–53). How gratitude and reciprocity are handled not only depends on the kind of
relationship between people, but it also helps to define the relationship. People who have close (or *communal*) relationships give each

other personal, nonmaterial gifts (such as affection and support), expect to have a long-term connection, and base their exchanges on need, not payback (Miller & Berg, 1984). So if you pay me back when I am not in need, if you give me something that is not chosen specifically for me, or if you insist on paying me back right away, you are implying that ours is not a close relationship. Instead, you feel compelled to set things right immediately and with impersonal resources because you don't want a personal entanglement with me. Alternatively, close friends get into a cycle of giving that is so complex and enduring that it is impossible after a while to know what is fair and balanced – but nobody cares. Losing track of who benefits most may truly be the opposite of the vicious cycle of revenge in which both parties are obsessed with balancing the suffering.

Connecting with Others Through Sympathy, Love, and Caring

Justice is not the only important social value to be upheld by emotional forces; so are social connections themselves. Traditional Western ethical theory tends to focus on abstract principles more than on the experiences and interrelationships of people in their particular situations. Recent formulations of *systems* of justice and *rules* of morality (Kohlberg, 1981; Rawls, 1971) have been counterbalanced by moral frameworks oriented to caring and loving relationships (Baier, 1994; Gilligan, 1982). Certainly we need justice to make a society work, but just as certainly we need love and caring. As Baier suggests, if we had only justice without love, we would all die in the cradle for lack of loving caregivers to sustain us. One can argue that when we care for children, we are paying back the system that nurtured us as children. This may be true, but it doesn't *feel* like the right reason to me. Love, sympathy, and caring are just as real, and perhaps more powerful and persistent motivations for moral behavior (and sometimes immoral behavior, to be sure), as are anger and guilt. You could just as well say that anger and guilt are emotions that one must resort to only if love and caring fail.

Loving Connections with Others. Love is the emotion that makes us want to connect with others, in as many different ways as there are varieties of love – physically when cuddling a child or making love with one's partner, experientially or emotionally when having fun with friends or sharing an intimate experience, or spiritually when worshiping God or communing with nature (Sternberg & Barnes, 1988). Love compels us to nurse babies, make friends, find lovers, be together, enjoy each other, stick together in times of distress, and mourn each other's passing. Because loved ones are highly valued, we want to act in their best interests. The phrase *caring for someone*, of course, has the dual meanings of "loving" and "nurturing." Love might even be considered an inherently moral emotion in the sense that it fosters social bonds, makes the world a better place, and generally leads to good consequences all around – that is, except for a few exceptions such as thwarted rivals, unrequited love, self-sacrificing love, obsessive love, excessively dependent love, and love that leads to any number of dire consequences such as pining away, double suicide, or abandoning children (to name only a few).

If love is so natural, so necessary, and usually so nice, why do we have so many moral prescriptions about it? Love your neighbor. Do not love your secretary (at least not in THAT way). Love your mother. Love all your children equally. It's hard to get love exactly right. To adapt what Aristotle said about anger: "We praise a man who feels [love] on the right grounds and for the right persons and also in the right manner at the right moment and for the right length of time":[2] Society gives guidelines that are in some cases very clear and very strict. We may delegitimate feelings that do not fit the cultural ideal for love as "puppy love," "just an infatuation," or "not real love." Because so much hinges on romantic love, we get powerful messages (though varied and sometimes subtle ones) about what is good romantic love and what is bad romantic love. If you don't believe me, just listen to popular music for a few hours. Another reason love needs some moral force behind it is that it is sometimes hard to muster love when you need it (such as toward a screaming baby at 2:00 A.M. or toward a screaming father when you come in after the curfew). You need to be reminded that love is the proper way to feel and loving is the proper way to behave.

Just as expressions of anger and guilt appeal to and validate moral commitments to justice, expressions of love appeal to and validate the need for connection and caring. Messages of love and affection give us a basis for building bonds and confidence that those bonds are steadfast. In tentative relationships, expressions of love are explora-

---

[2] Cited in the *Columbia Dictionary of Quotations* (1993). New York: Columbia University Press.

tions of possibilities. Most of the time, affection is expressed in subtle and sometimes ambiguous nonverbal messages (such as the yawn/ stretch/arm-around-the-shoulder maneuver of young boys or a shy child finally crawling into your lap) (Baxter & Wilmot, 1984). As any skittish suitor knows, the first statement of "I love you" can be a bombshell (Owen, 1987) and a turning point for the relationship (Baxter & Bullis, 1986). In established relationships, verbal statements of love usually provide assurance of continued bonds rather than or in addition to authentic expressions of feelings at that moment. As Kurt Vonnegut quipped: "If somebody says, 'I love you,' to me, I feel as though I had a pistol pointed at my head. What can anybody reply under such conditions but that which the pistol-holder requires? 'I love you, *too*.'[3]

Even if genuinely intended, it is not always easy to communicate love and to provide assurance that the social bond is intact. As with all abstract concepts (and especially with emotions), people do not necessarily agree on what is a sincere expression of love. It's the old refrain: "If you really loved me, you'd . . .": "If you really loved me, you'd take me out to a romantic dinner" – "But I fixed your carbure-tor!" or alternatively, "If you really loved me, you'd have sex with me" – "If you really loved me, you wouldn't ask me to have sex with you," and so on. We may not even agree on whether verbal expres-sions of love and affection are needed at all. As a person from an inexpressive family, I find exchanges of "I love you" – "I love you too" between parents and children somewhat bizarre. I am tempted to judge them as stating the obvious in a way that seems rather ludicrous, but I know that this is probably not the interpretation of those who do it. I also wonder if this practice has become more prevalent as the divorce rate has risen and kids and parents alike really do need the reassurance.

If love is the ultimate enforcer of the moral order (fostering loving families, loving neighbors, even loving the unlovable), it is also the ultimate reason for disrupting the moral order. No one believes that breaking up families is a good thing if it can be avoided, but love (or lack thereof) is commonly considered to be a legitimate excuse. If we take romantic love seriously as a reason to get married, then to be fair we have to take the lack of romantic love (or love of another) seriously

---

[3] Vonnegut (1994) cited in *The Columbia Dictionary of Quotations.* (1993) New York: Columbia University Press

as a reason to get unmarried. "Your mom and I split up because we don't love each other anymore" is a refrain heard regularly. Whether or not it is honest, it serves as a legitimate excuse. It's funny how the same excuse does not work for child or parental abandonment ("I'm leaving you, Mom/Dad/kid, because I just don't love you anymore"), although perhaps if it did, we would have less child and elder abuse. In parental and filial relationships, one has a moral responsibility to conjure up and sustain the appropriate love. Our cultural beliefs do not support the notion of "falling in love" with one's parents or children, and so they do not support the notion of "falling out of love" with them either. Romantic love is seen as less controllable and therefore somewhat less subject to moral censure, at least in some circles.

Sympathy and Empathy with Others' Misfortunes. The feeling that may come closest to inherently moral feeling is sympathy – feeling bad that another person is in pain, has suffered misfortune, or simply is feeling bad. Empathy may go even a step beyond sympathy from feeling *your own* feelings of distress at another's distress (sympathy) to taking the other person's perspective so vividly that you feel *his* distress (true empathy). Clark (1997) argues that "sympathy is a crucial emotion that provides glue for social bonds, the building blocks of society," because it "holds people together in times of trouble" (p. 5), "connects the unfortunate to the fortunate" (p. 16), and "creates ties of obligation and reciprocity" (p. 20).

It is hard to defend the opposites of sympathy and empathy – indifference or even pleasure at another's plight – except as a way of feeling better ourselves. There is little doubt that sympathy and empathy lead to good works most of the time, although not always. Batson and Olesen (1991; also Eisenberg & Miller, 1987) have reviewed evidence for the connection between empathy and altruism and concluded that it cannot be explained away by the alternative explanation that we really help others for our own sake. Nevertheless, "the range of people and problems that evoke empathy and hence altruistic motivation is limited, and altruistic concerns can be and often are overridden by self-concerns" (Batson & Oleson, 1991: 82–83). There are also conditions under which empathy does not lead to helping, such as when overwhelming personal distress prevents you from doing the right thing, such as giving artificial resuscitation or telling people an unpleasant truth (Davis & Kraus, 1991). Nevertheless, if managed well, empathic distress may be no more likely to prevent effective action on behalf of others than our own distress is to prevent action for ourselves.

Empathy and sympathy may lead to good works, but what good does it do to communicate them to others? At the very least, expressions of sympathy celebrate the value of staying in touch with others' distress and "being there" for them in symbolic ways. Even if I do not really feel sad that a relative of a friend has died, sending a sympathy card reminds me (and others) that it is the *right* way to feel. In addition, receiving sympathy from others keeps isolation and loneliness at bay, especially when the suffering is over a loss. "Mere" expressions of sympathy can be substitutes for tangible assistance, to be sure, but they can also lead one to appropriate feelings and helpful action (Clark, 1997).

Messages fostering sympathy and empathy can be radical in the sense that they draw our attention to heartlessness and hypocrisy, or when they elevate the value of caring for others over alternative values such as personal financial comfort (as most appeals for charities do) or other forms of justice such as equity (e.g., wages for work). It seems that the more personal and vivid the message, the more easily empathy comes to us, especially if the needy are also portrayed as blameless. Examples of this abound on the daily news – stories of victims of natural disasters, crime, and poverty, especially during the holidays, when our sympathetic sensibilities are supposed to be heightened. Only a Scrooge would feel nothing for the travails of Tiny Tim. On the other hand, sympathy follows rules (Clark, 1997: 159–181). You cannot make claims to sympathy on false grounds (e.g., hypochondria); you cannot claim too much (incessant complaining); you cannot ignore all offers of sympathy if you expect to get any in the future ("I don't need your sympathy"); and you have to reciprocate the sympathy that has been given to you ("Where were you when I needed you?").

"Sinful" Emotions – Hate, Jealousy, and Envy

You would think that sinful emotions such as hate, jealousy, and envy would be the very antithesis of morality, but Solomon (1989) argues that they have their own places in enforcing and challenging the moral order (see also Armon-Jones, 1986). Hate seems unabashedly immoral because it makes you want to harm others. But what about hating people who want to harm you, your loved ones, or even people you have never met? What is morally correct – hate for a terrorist or sympathy for a terrorist? The answer is not obvious, any more than is the distinction between a terrorist and a freedom fighter. As Sommers posed the question: "Is the hatred of evil a negative emotion?" (Solomon, 1989). Perhaps not, but you have to be very sure about what is evil. Hate reinforces moral values by mobilizing feelings against behaviors, people, and moral systems that work against those values. To war propagandists, mobilizing hate for the enemy is more important than mobilizing love for the motherland. And pure hatred requires pure evil, which often must be manufactured (Baumeister, 1997). In his discussion of the emotions of war, Gray (1959: 146) notes that "increasingly, we cannot fight without an image of the enemy as totally evil, for whom any mercy or sympathy is incongruous, if not traitorous."

How to deal with hate speech is a pressing and controversial issue these days (e.g., see Leets & Giles, 1997). Even among people who defend free speech, hate speech is condemned because it is directed toward groups of people (usually religious, ethnic, or value-based minorities) and may incite violence. In addition, hate speech is demeaning and threatening to the targeted group, even if it never leads to action. Nevertheless, we should take a look at the moral side of hate and ask if we as a society might better manage the values that hatemongers are defending. If the value is racial privilege, then we have a moral right and responsibility to despise hate speech, but if the underlying value is the ability to provide a decent living for one's family, then we may be too quick to dismiss legitimate concerns when their vehicle is hate speech. In general, it may be easier to recognize the immoral side of emotions that we presume are moral than to recognize the moral side of emotions we assume are immoral.

Jealousy is another "sinful" emotion that protects values. It is a complex emotion blended primarily from anger-, sadness-, and fear-like feelings (Sharpsteen, 1991) that mobilizes us to protect our attachments with people whom we value. Is that so wrong? Jealousy sends the message "You are important to me," which is why being the object of jealousy can be very flattering (and, when managed well, has exactly this effect). But jealousy has a bad reputation these days because it can easily go wrong. If one person believes he has an absolute right to the attachment of another (which gives the other no right to break the attachment), jealousy can be abusive (White & Mullen, 1989: Chap. 8). Jealousy can also be unrealistic, such as when your husband's lunch with another woman or your wife's attractive clothes are interpreted as an inherent threat to the relationship (Chap. 7). Of course, we have moral guidelines for jealousy, as we do for most emotions. Nowadays in the United States, it is acceptable and even appropriate for husbands to be jealous of rivals for their wives' affection, but not for children to be jealous of new arrivals' demands on their parents' time, energy, and love (Stearns, 1989).

People tend to downplay the intensity of their jealousy when communicating it to others (either to the target of the jealousy or to someone else), especially compared to other, more acceptable emotions such as sadness (Zammuner & Frijda, 1994). Talking about jealousy and the situations that produce it, however, can be helpful in managing it. Helpful techniques used in therapy include problem solving, role playing, role reversal, and even exaggerating the conflict to the point of absurdity (White & Mullen, 1989: 270–272). In everyday life, communicative responses to jealousy run the whole gamut from integrative communication (e.g., trying to reach an understanding with one's partner) and compensatory restoration (e.g., sending gifts) to signs of possession ("She's taken") and surveillance (spying on the partner) to manipulation (flirting with others) and violence (pushing, slapping, and destroying possessions) (Guerrero & Andersen, 1998: 171–172). Consequences can also range from the "brightest" form – rekindling relational and sexual bonds – to the "darkest" form – murder.

The third sinful emotion is envy – wanting something another person has – which is closely akin to anger at injustice when things are distributed unfairly (Smith, 1991). What first leaps to mind is envy of material goods – the neighbor's house, the boss's golf clubs – but we also envy nonmaterial things such as accomplishments, talents, or even happiness. I read a story today called "Water Babies: Why I Love to Swim" by Oliver Sacks (*The New Yorker*, May 26, 1997) which triggered my envy of people who feel at home in the water and take great pleasure from swimming. That kind of envy is innocuous enough and illustrates the good side of envy (nonmalicious envy); envy may goad us to acquire or accomplish something we value. On the whole, though, we think of envy as an immoral emotion (formerly known as a *deadly sin*) because it is often malicious – wanting to deprive the other person of something you value rather than acquiring it yourself. It can be especially corrosive when we focus on the unfairness of life in general and envy everyone who has something we don't (Parrott, 1991: 11). People with advantages, of course, serve to benefit by demonizing envy, whereas people who want a more level playing field serve to benefit from encouraging it.

Schoek (1966) argues that envy is particularly unmentionable in the United States because Americans do not want to admit that they are not all equals. Even in supposedly open-minded U.S. academic circles, envy is maligned (pp. 125–128). In fact, the term *envy* seems to have fallen out of use almost completely, *jealousy* serving as an inaccurate but perhaps more permissible substitute (Parrott, 1991: 7, 24). Schoek (1966: 31) writes, "There can be no doubt that we have the rarest and also the most unequivocal evidence for the role of envy when the envious man ultimately admits publicly to his own envy and confesses that he has harmed another person from that motive. So far I have read only one such admission. . . ." Schoek goes on to explain that the confessor actually "hides behind the less painful . . . term *jealousy*." The explicit portrayal of Salieri's malicious envy of Mozart's talent in the film *Amadeus* may have been a breakthrough in broaching the subject of envy, but from it we learn that envy destroys genius (see also Pushkin, 1832/1964, cited in Smith, 1991).

The irony is that at the same time that we consider envy unmentionable in polite circles, it is virtually a constant message (perhaps THE constant message) in advertising. You should have what they have; you should look the way she does; you should drink what he drinks. If someone else has it, why shouldn't you? Messages that cultivate envy, of course, implicitly cultivate certain values – in this case, having the best, or looking the best as befits a consumer culture. Occasionally, we hear messages about "being the best" in the sense of acquiring skills (in the army) or in excelling in competition (in sports) but rarely in the moral sense. As Schoek (1966) writes: "No system of ethics, no religion, no popular wisdom recorded in proverbs, no moral fables and no rules of behavior among primitive people have ever made a virtue of envy. . . . Why? Because in any group the envious man is inevitably a disturber of the peace" (p. 33) and "[t]here can be little doubt as to the economically inhibiting effect of the envy-motive" (p. 413). It seems that Schoek was not thinking of the consumer society.

Communicating Shame for Social Failure

Certainly the emotions we have discussed so far – anger, guilt, love, sympathy, hate, jealousy, and envy – have enormous power to enforce and challenge moral standards, especially in their most benevolent or malevolent forms. Even so, shame puts them all to shame. Shame has been called the "*master emotion* in all societies, both traditional and modern," because it can be used to control almost any other emotion (Scheff, 1995: 1055, citing Elias, 1978; see also Lewis, 1971; Tomkins, 1963). It is the ultimate moral weapon before which we all cringe because it is the most strongly evaluative, the most painful, and probably the most powerful emotion of them all.

Shame involves a condemnation of the entire person as *no good* (either being ashamed oneself or shaming someone else) (Lewis, 1992). It is closely related to guilt, but it is more powerful because guilt is limited to condemning an action, whereas shame condemns the person as a whole. Guilt makes you want to correct the transgression; shame makes you want to hide, disappear, or die (Lewis, 1993: 569). Shame is also "one of the most *painful* emotions that it is possible for a human being to suffer" (Turner, 1995: 1060) because it involves a complete negation of self. It is so painful that many people choose excruciating physical pain in order to avoid it. For example, it is still a common practice for Muslim girls to undergo genital mutilation willingly in order to avoid the shame of being different (and of shaming their families). If people are willing to cause themselves great pain to avoid shame, then they are certainly willing to hurt others, even to murder them (Scheff, 1994).

It is easy to illustrate the power that shame has to control other emotions. You can stop someone from being angry, sad, joyous, or even hateful by laughing at her derisively or making fun of her (a common technique of childhood socialization, I might add, because it is so effective; Lewis, 1992). Wurmser (1995: 26) argues that shame serves as a screen against more important anxieties, but marital therapists Johnson and Greenberg disagree. They say "[t]he only emotion people never seem to transform other feelings into is shame. We may experience our loneliness as lust, our sadness as anger, and our anger as fear. But we never seem to choose shame. Shame is always unwelcome" (1994:78).

Shame is a broad-spectrum enforcer of social standards; it wipes out the whole self instead of targeting specific behaviors, as guilt does. In that sense, guilt may be more helpful than shame because guilt makes you want to solve the problem, but shame makes you want to withdraw and hide from it. One experiment illustrates this point well. Toddlers were brought in to play with a toy that was designed to fall apart shortly after it was used. When it broke, some of the toddlers looked away and had tense facial expressions but tried to fix the toy, demonstrating guilt; others looked away "and their bodies appear[ed] to collapse" – a sign of shame even in small children (Alessandri & Lewis, 1993: 339). Compounding the problem is meta-shame (shame about being ashamed), which makes people reluctant to admit their shame even to themselves, much less to do anything about it. One way to confront shame is to ask someone, "What makes it so hard for you to apologize, to say, 'I'm sorry' or 'I'm wrong, I made a mistake'?" Apologizing "helps to develop, in small doses, tolerance for shame" (Balcom, Lee, & Tager, 1995: 62).

The irony is that shame, the ultimate moral enforcer, may also fuel the most morally reprehensible acts of which humanity is capable. Shame is more likely to bring someone in line with moral standards when it is acknowledged (at least privately) and is permitted to dissipate of its own accord. Bypassed or unacknowledged shame is a different matter (Lewis, 1987). Most often the *screen affect* (the one shame hides behind) is anger (or, more accurately, rage), which compels retribution with a fury. Scheff and Retzinger have analyzed the shame–rage cycle in domestic violence (Retzinger, 1991), the role of shame in suicide (Scheff, 1990), national shame as a cause of World War I (Scheff, 1994), and the importance of humiliated fury to Adolf Hitler's appeal and his policies (Scheff & Retzinger, 1991). A parallel analysis of the role of the Vietnam War as a shaming experience for the United States and its subsequent influence on the 1991 Persian Gulf War has been done as well (Kaufman, 1992).

Not only is shame the moral enforcer par excellence, it also intensifies other emotions that enforce moral values. Scheff (1990) argues that shame is an indicator that the social bond is threatened and attains much of its power from the need for love and belonging. Frijda (1994) claims that damage to one's self-esteem or to that of one's group puts greater emotional force behind the desire for vengeance. Because the self-esteem that may be regained through vengeance is "so deep, so vital, . . . it is worth losses in other respects. . . . Loss of life is among these losses." In other words, being dead may be preferable to being no good. Certainly depression coupled with shame can be suicidal. White and Mullen (1989: 180, 265–266) report that shame is commonly experienced as part of pathological and normal jealousy, and envy is often associated with feelings of inferiority (Parrott, 1991: 13). It seems that especially when emotions are intense and prolonged, it is worth looking for an underpinning in shame.

Even though popular opinion might be that shame is to be avoided because it is so painful, no serious theorists would argue that any society can get along without it. "Shame is a powerful human mechanism, a normal and necessary part of a well-functioning society" said Retzinger (1995: 32). It is certainly NOT the case that people everywhere and forever have been ashamed of nakedness, sex, urination, or defecation, as you might think (Elias, 1978; Nathanson, 1992: 431–454), but it probably is the case that all people feel shame when they fail to conform to the important values of their society. In present U.S. society, it might be shameful to be illiterate (perhaps even computer illiterate in some subcultures) because reading and writing are essential competencies, whereas among the Ifaluk it is shameful not to give others food because food sharing is essential to their survival (Lutz, 1988). A shameless society has no means to bring individuals in line with the essential values of the group, and a shameless individual is beyond social and moral control because he is no longer concerned with the social bond. He is a condemned man (in terms of society's regard for him), and he has nothing to lose. He is perhaps the only true outlaw because a normal outlaw at least follows the laws of other outlaws.

Cultivating and Judging Emotional Character

If we *feel* morality, it makes sense that we would try to cultivate character by encouraging the right emotions and discouraging the wrong ones. We also *judge* other people's moral character based on how *they* feel. If you doubt it, think of the question "What kind of person would feel . . . ?" What kind of person would feel happy to see another suffering? Or alternatively, what kind of person would feel *nothing* when murdering someone? It is clear from these questions that moral character is judged on the basis of expressed emotions (to be sure), but with important moral transgression we are trying to see through the expressions to the genuine feelings as well. It may not be enough to fake the appropriate expression (as would be the case with remorse for a murder); you must also feel the remorse.

Why do we bother? Why is it worse to be a shameless hussy than to be just a regular hussy? Why is it worse to be a gleeful torturer than it is to be a reluctant torturer? Why don't we just settle for behaving well and leave feelings well enough alone? Well, sometimes we do. Sometimes sending a thank-you card for a gift is sufficient, and we don't worry much about whether it was sent out of real, heartfelt gratitude. The little secret that everybody knows is that gift exchanges are sometimes pro forma and that the artificial gratitude that accompanies them is too. Similarly, you might say, "I'm sorry I interrupted you," not out of true sorrow (after all, how much sorrow does this really deserve?), but as a social nicety that recognizes a minor gaffe. A small rule was broken and no real harm was done, so words are good enough; we don't require the feelings too. There are many times, however, when actions and words are *not* good enough. It is important to be genuinely sorry or truly grateful when the social value at stake is important and the consequences are grave. Who would accept a pro forma apology from a hit-and-run driver or lip-service gratitude for a donated kidney? If the person does not recognize the value of life and death, we've got a major problem. As Hochschild (1983: 82) puts it: "Guilt upholds feeling rules from the inside: it is an internal acknowledgment of an unpaid psychological debt. Even 'I should feel guilty' is a nod in the direction of guilt, a weaker confirmation of what is owed."

Feelings also serve as commitments to future behavior (Frank, 1998). My fury promises revenge; my love promises caring. They assure us that a person has internalized certain values (Armon-Jones, 1986: 80) and is behaving as expected because she wants to, not because she has to (a distinction that psychologists label as *intrinsic* or *extrinsic* motivation). Kohn has made a strong case for the value of intrinsic over extrinsic motivation in *Punished by Rewards* (1993) (for a classic work, see Deci & Ryan, 1985). As any parent will tell you, getting a child to do homework is much easier and better for everyone involved if she loves it than if she hates it and is forced to do it. The same is true for good works. If a person has moral feelings, she is carrying the motivation to do good around with her all the time. She will do good and avoid wrong when no one is looking, when there is no reward or punishment to be had, and perhaps even when she must put herself at risk. Better yet, she does not have to be taught each acceptable or unacceptable behavior piecemeal, and she can be morally creative because her feelings will tell her the right thing to do when novel situations arise.

She may even rethink her culture's system of morals to capture a more inclusive or more applicable one (as perhaps did the first non-slave to oppose slavery). Doing what others expect is seldom creative, but following your feelings sometimes is. Solomon's (1990) "passion for justice" could be, as would disgust at overconsumption. Ignoring your feelings may be revolutionary too if you refuse to be shamed into hating the enemy or adoring the king. Tina Turner's line "What's love got to do with it?" is in a sense revolutionary because it challenges love as sufficient justification for close connections. Refusal to feel (or at least to act on) fear and hatred is one of the premises of nonviolent protest. Transforming feelings of fear, shame, and depression into feelings conducive to protest and activism is one of the goals of feminist organizations (Taylor, 1995: 229).

Cultivating Moral Character Through Emotions

Aristotle said it well: "we ought to have been brought up in a particular way from our very youth, as Plato says, so as both to delight in and to be pained by the things that we ought; for this is the right education" (McKeon, 1941: 954). Empathy provides an excellent example. As noted earlier, the capacity for empathy is evident in 2-year-olds, and even then, empathy can motivate prosocial behavior (Thompson, 1987: 130–133). Early experiences such as secure and affectionate attachments to adults, empathic models, and intimate childhood friendships encourage empathy. It is interesting to note, however, that calm and well-reasoned messages pointing out how a child has hurt another do not seem to be enough. Instead, the "emotional role model" needs to show intense emotion himself in order to indicate to the child that this is important and the child should feel bad (Barnett, 1987: 149–158). Yet, natural as empathy may seem, it can easily be overridden through socialization. Abused children respond to other children's distress first with comfort, but if that does not work, with verbal and physical abuse (Klimes-Dougan & Kistner, 1990). They have learned from their own role models that a little empathy may be okay at first, but if that doesn't relieve the suffering, it's time to stop empathizing and start punishing.

Nothing teaches empathy like direct experience, and being ⁀ victim of immoral behavior (injustice, harm, or lack of love) can be an important way of sensitizing children and adults to its harmful effects. But victimization can also be caustic if effective avenues of response are blocked. One of the impulses behind vengeance (or so people say) is to give the perpetrator the same direct experience that the victim had to teach him a lesson, but being a victim is more likely to convince someone that they should do *anything* (moral or immoral) to make sure that they are not on the receiving end ever again, which often means identifying with the aggressor and perhaps eventually becoming one (Graham & Rawlings, 1991).

Hearing vivid descriptions of the pain that victims suffer can also instill remorse, assuming there is some grain of caring and connection around which it can crystallize. Mothers Against Drunk Driving (MADD) uses this technique. Drivers who have been arrested for being drunk come to a meeting where they hear wrenching stories of the physical and emotional pain suffered by victims and their families. After such an experience, it is hard to minimize the effects of your actions on possible or actual victims. Programs in Australia and New Zealand take this process one step further to create what Braithwaite calls *reintegration ceremonies* for juvenile offenders (Braithwaite & Mugford, 1994). The offender along with his or her supporters (family, teachers, etc.), is brought together with the victim and his or her supporters under the supervision of a coordinator (police officer, juvenile worker). Both sides describe the offense from their point of view, with the coordinator representing the public interest as well. "In this ceremony, identities are in a social crucible. The vision that an offender holds of himself as a 'tough guy' or that victims have of him as a 'mindless hooligan' are challenged, altered, and recreated (for example, as a 'good lad who has strayed into bad ways') . . . disapproval of a bad act is communicated while sustaining the identity of the actor as good. Shame is transmitted within a continuum of respect for the wrongdoer" (Braithwaite & Mugford, 1994: 141–142). Offenders usually apologize (Samoans often on their knees), and victims finish the ceremony more concerned with getting the offender back on track than with punishment. After the ceremony, victims and offenders commonly shake hands, sometimes hug, and even have dinner together afterward!

Clearly, moral character can be developed through messages from loved ones, teachers, celebrities, and any other role models who encourage feelings that defend and promote the right values. Solomon (1990) wants us to cultivate a "passion for justice," and programs such as reintegration ceremonies promote empathy and compassion (on both sides of crime). Of course, the opposite is true as well. Messages that portray other people as less than human (Bosmajian, 1983) encourage complacency or perhaps even satisfaction with injustice, and they discourage empathy. Messages that minimize guilt in order to build self-esteem (e.g., "My kid can do no wrong") do us a disservice in two ways. Not only do they gloss over the consequences of wrongdoing, but they also may teach children that they are globally good or bad (rather than children who are basically good but occasionally engage in bad acts), making them inclined toward either hubris or shame, neither of which makes good citizens (Lewis, 1992).

Judging Character Via Feelings

If morality and character can be found and cultivated in emotion, then it must be possible to judge people's character based on the emotions they feel. We do this all the time, and we also know that other people are judging our moral character based on our emotions; that's why we follow display rules. Sadness and loss provide many useful examples. Laughing at a funeral is insensitive and shows disrespect for the deceased; crying shows that you really cared and that you are of good moral character. Any mother who loved her child would be distraught at the child's accidental death. The real killer would show some signs of guilt; the falsely accused would be outraged. As I argued earlier in this chapter, emotions *are* good indicators of someone's moral character, and we use expressions to judge them (Oakley, 1992).

Here are some recent or well-known examples. Example A is the Azaria Chamberlain case. It became famous in Australia and was popularized by the film *A Cry in the Dark* and documented in the film *Baby Azaria*. An infant disappeared from the tent on a family camping trip, and police suspected that the mother had killed the infant because she showed so little emotion. Many people who followed the case and the trial agreed; no mother could be so unfeeling about her child's death unless she had done the killing herself. Example B occurred when U.S. President Bill Clinton was criticized for "walking along after [Commerce Secretary Ron] Brown's funeral, laughing at something he was being told – then going all somber when the camera was trained on him. This was offered as proof that the President is a phony" (Grief analysis, 1996). No person who was as close to Ron Brown as Clinton was would laugh at his funeral. Example C is actually two similar cases. Both U.S. Senator Edmund Muskie and Representative Pat Schroeder were criticized for shedding tears at press conferences, Muskie when his wife was maligned and Schroeder when she announced that she would not run for president. Politicians who cry do not have their feelings under control, are obviously weak, and are unfit for office.

These people seem to be flouting social values by not feeling as they should (in Example A), feeling as they should not (Example B), or losing control of their feelings and showing them in public (Example C). We should all be outraged. Or should we? Are there other explanations for the feelings they expressed besides "bad character"? In the first case, clearly there was. Compelling physical evidence indicated that the Australian infant in fact was killed by wild dingos, and Mrs. Chamberlain was acquitted. She showed little emotion because she belonged to a religious group that valued stoicism and acceptance of God's will. The lesson here is that emotional expressions are never completely trustworthy indicators of experienced emotions, as was discussed earlier. When judging others' character based on the emotions they feel, it is important to remember that no one can interpret emotions infallibly, and there is no infallible one-to-one correspondence between feelings and actions (especially murder).

The case of President Clinton is also controversial, but even the *Time* magazine commentator claimed that judging Clinton as "phony" based on laughing at a funeral was harsh because many people laugh at funerals for many good reasons. A humorous story about the deceased, for instance, might be both respectful and funny. In addition, laughter is known to be common in moments of tension and stress (Bales, 1950). Judging emotional character by isolated incidents is much less trustworthy than judging an overall pattern of feelings in a variety of contexts. We should also recognize that people laugh out of sorrow and tension, cry out of sadness or joy, and show no feelings at all either out of apathy or because an emotion is too overwhelming to express. And are Clinton's feelings really any of our business when we have a public record of his policies on which to base our votes?

The cases of Muskie and Schroeder raise yet a different issue because here we enter the realm of gender and emotion politics. Many people came forward to defend both Muskie and Schroeder's tears on the grounds that they were expressing appropriate emotions and showing proper moral character (Sullivan, 1993; Sullivan & Goldzwig, 1994). Any politician who loved his wife would and should be upset when she is maligned. Any politician who became so frustrated with the political system that she could not run for president and retain her values would and should feel great anger and sorrow. People lined up on both sides on the more general question of what emotions (and what moral stances that underlie them) should be expected from people, especially people who serve the public trust. Schroeder herself stated the issue well: "The critics who seemed the most insane to me were those who said they wouldn't want the person who had a 'finger on the button' to be someone who cries. I answered that I wouldn't want that person to be someone who *doesn't* cry" (Schroeder, 1989: 165, cited in Sullivan, 1990: 24). As the Schroeder quotation illustrates, change is made possible by people who are willing to flout others' evaluations and refuse to be shamed into conformity.

The question then remains: What are the morally correct emotions to feel, if any at all? When, how, why, and what *should* we feel (or avoid feeling) in order to behave ethically and have moral character? When, how, why, and by what standards should we judge the feelings of others? And what ethical concerns should we have in mind when using messages to influence others' feelings and, through them, their actions? Of course, there are no firm answers to these questions, only moral and ethical considerations that we can explore in part by turning to philosophers who have reflected on the ethics of emotion.

Challenging and Defending Emotion-Based Morality

In my opinion, it is good that we seldom find indisputable solutions to moral questions because morality (like all the other human capabilities and resources, including emotions) should be flexible enough to respond to changing circumstances. Neither rigid moral strictures nor unrestrained permissiveness serves us well, but an ongoing and reflective conversation about proper emotional experience, expression, and action does. What should we consider when we debate whether an emotional expression defends or undermines the moral order? Here are some guidelines to consider:

Arguing Control

One argument goes like this: A person in an emotional state has no choice but to act based on that state. He was driven by uncontrollable jealousy to murder his wife's lover.[4] She stabbed him because her anger was out of control (Averill, 1993). He was compelled by love to reveal state secrets. She said those cruel things because she was humiliated. Powerful emotional states challenge the moral order because people cannot be held accountable for their emotions or the actions that result from them. No one can control strong feelings, and we do not hold people accountable for things they cannot control. That is why they fall into the special category called *crimes of passion*. A slightly modified version of this argument is based on the *ventilationist* model of emotion – that pent-up emotion must be released, so homicidal rage must inevitably result in, well, homicide.

The counterargument is that, on the contrary, emotions can be controlled and that claiming to be out of control emotionally is only an excuse, much like blaming alcohol or drugs. In fact, the parallel with alcohol and drugs plays out further because people make the choice at some point to come under the influence of a strong emotion, just as they choose to drink or to take drugs. You may be "insanely" jealous of your wife's lover or "deliriously" in love with a spy, but adults in this society can and should be expected to manage their emotions well enough to refrain from harmful acts or even harmful words.

What does the literature on emotion tell us about this argument? It tells us that there is evidence for both sides, but more for the latter than for the former. Emotions are defined by action tendencies but they are only *tendencies*, not certainties, and coping is also an integral part of the emotion process (Frijda, 1986). It is not unreasonable to expect people to cope with their emotions in ways that uphold the moral order, but it is easier to control emotions in some circumstances than others. Among the most promising techniques are getting or staying away from the circumstances that are likely to facilitate strong emotion (as Catholics say, "Avoid the occasions of sin") and practicing emotion control through *deep acting* (rethinking the situation to calm yourself down). The controversy surrounding Muskie and Schroeder had to do with whether the issues that upset them were important enough to warrant strong emotion (as displayed in their

---

[4] Berscheid (1990) uses the scenario of a jealous husband shooting his wife's lover as a way to explore various theorists' perspectives on how to define emotion, but she does not address the issue of whether he is morally responsible, even if it is clear that he is in an emotional state.

messages) and whether they could be trusted to control their feelings when control clearly *was* warranted. Notice, however, that the same question was not raised about Clarence Thomas's display of anger, no doubt because his anger was considered to be more justified than their tears, but perhaps also because it was a display of strength, not of weakness.

There are also some broader ethical questions lurking within the issue of control. Do messages in the public forum (such as televised courtroom trials) support the idea that we can and should hold people morally accountable for their emotions or, alternatively, do they support the idea that strong emotions serve as legitimate excuses for wrongdoing? To a large extent, emotions are as controllable as we believe and train them to be, so we need to reflect on our shared "implicit moral philosophies" and how well they work. Another issue is whether our collective discourse directs the moral force of shame and envy toward things that people can control. For example, Karen (1992: 58) points out the prevalence of "class shame," which shames people for important aspects of their identities that they cannot control. Also, because Americans think of themselves as a classless society, "class shame crosses the line . . . from a shared burden to [a] sense of personal defect." Along those same lines, Smith (1991: 90) and Schoek (1966) grapple with the moral implications of envying other people's natural abilities or characteristics (as Salieri did Mozart's). Such envy is misplaced, they contend, because no one has any control over their beauty or natural talents. Nevertheless, beauty and talent are developed through experiences, training, and artifice that are controllable and hence appropriate objects of envy. In concrete terms, I might not be justified in envying my neighbor's musical talents, but I could envy her lessons and her Steinway grand piano.

Arguing the Facts

At first glance, it seems absurd to talk about evaluating the facts of an emotion. After all, emotion is not rational; facts have nothing to do it. But facts and reason *do* underlie emotion, and this is easy to demonstrate. Anger changes to embarrassment when you find out that your boss did not call you in to give you more work, but to give you a surprise party. It would be wrong (not to mention stupid) to continue to be angry with your boss once you learned the truth. But reason, not emotion, is the real problem, as Hume pointed out when he said that passion "must be accompanied with some false judgment, in order to its being unreasonable; and even then it is not the passion, properly speaking, which is unreasonable, but the judgment" (1738/1995: 401). Delusional jealousy based on imagined events or ridiculous interpretations of real events (White & Mullen, 1989) is based on factual or interpretive error, not irrational emotions. Jealousy would be perfectly appropriate and perhaps judged as moral if the imagined events were really true.

Solomon (1980: 261) argues that "[s]ince normative judgments can be changed through influence, argument, and evidence, and since I can go about on my own seeking influence, provoking argument, and looking for evidence, I am as responsible for my emotions as I am for the judgments I make." We might take this argument a step further to argue that since other people's judgments can be changed through your influence, your arguments, and the evidence you provide, then you are also responsible for the emotions they feel. Consider the morality of using emotional appeals to persuade others to do something when the persuader knows perfectly well that the feelings being induced are inconsistent with any reasonable interpretation of the facts. Is this, in effect, emotional deception on a par with lying about the facts? To use a benign example, is it ethical to strike fear into the hearts of little children who will not go to bed by telling them that the boogie man is going to get them rather than tell them the less persuasive truth, which is that they will be grouchy in the morning? To use a more malignant example, so to speak, recent arguments have claimed that it is immoral to produce advertisements that portray cigarette smoking as fun or cool because smoking is now firmly linked to cancer, and there is nothing fun or cool about cancer (as the Joe Chemo parody ads show vividly).

We can also argue about whether a situation is important enough to warrant strong feelings. Part of the task of raising children is to help them distinguish between important moral transgressions that deserve intense emotions (like feeling REALLY BAD that you shoplifted) and less important things (like feeling just a little guilty that you didn't brush your teeth). Part of the task of resocializing criminals is to make sure that they recognize and feel remorse proportional to the magnitude of their crimes, especially given their tendency to underestimate the damage done. We can also argue about whether our decision makers have the proper emotional sensibilities. Pat Schroeder did not want someone who was unable to feel the full horror of nuclear holocaust to make decisions about using nuclear weapons. Others did not want her to be president if she was inclined to react so strongly to frustration. We all walk something of an emotional/moral tightrope, and we ask people in positions of authority to walk an even narrower one.

Arguing Values

Moral issues often arise at fault lines between values, and advocates line up on each side. Public speeches often celebrate values that are widely shared, but even then it is easy to find protesters who challenge them. On the anniversaries of great battles, we hear speeches inviting us to feel gratitude and respect for those who died serving their country, but in the background we hear war protesters arguing that the value of human life transcends the value of patriotism. On Columbus Day in the United States, we hear speeches celebrating the courage and perseverance of the Europeans who explored the New World, but in the background we might hear voices reminding us that such courage and perseverance resulted in genocide.

Great public moral debates, as well as personal ones, revolve around which of two or more cherished but opposing values should hold sway. Because one position always has a slight edge over the other in terms of public policy, one position challenges the moral order and the other defends it. These are not abstract moral debates; they are gut-wrenching. In the abortion debate, the values upheld by both sides are explicit – the right to life versus the right to choose. In the capital punishment debate, justice competes with compassion. The slavery debate hinged on preserving what at the time seemed to be the natural social and moral order in the face of appeals for equal rights for all men. The debate over the treatment of the native inhabitants of the New World focused on the opposing values of religious conversion and compassion. We can argue whether these high-minded values were what was really at stake, as opposed to economic advantage, but they sound lofty. The irony about value-related terms like *freedom* or *justice* is that they are frustratingly vague and yet command deep emotional allegiance.

Conflicts of values and the powerful emotions that accompany them are not limited to the public sphere. As discussed earlier, the transition from traditional sex roles to parallel division of labor has put many women in the position of having to choose between their sense of justice and their need for connection or, put in emotional terms, between anger and love (Hochschild, 1989a, 1989b). Memmi (1957/1990) has described in vivid detail the emotional struggles inherent in the roles of colonizer and colonized, whether one accepts or challenges the colonial system. The colonizer who *challenges* the colonial order is torn between belonging to a group whose values he does not share (other colonizers) and sharing values with a group to which he will never fully belong (the colonized). The colonizer who *accepts* the system is torn between guilt for benefiting from it and pride based on the belief that he is inherently superior and the colonized people inherently inferior. Colonized people are wracked by shame if they believe themselves to be inferior (as the moral order declares), anger if they do not believe it, hope if they aspire to being part of the system of power, and frustration when their voice is not heard. Memmi concludes his analysis by saying, "What is apparent at the end of this path – if the two portraits are accurate – is that it is impossible for the colonial situation to last because it is impossible to arrange it properly" (p. 212). From an emotional point of view, the tensions are profound and irreconcilable.

Arguing Hypocrisy

If the values are agreed upon and do not themselves need to be argued, what still can be argued is whether they are being followed properly. By celebrating a moral ideal and drawing attention to our failure to live by it, it may also be possible to slide over any controversy surrounding the ideal itself. Dr. Martin Luther King, Jr.'s, 1963 "I Have a Dream" speech is one of the most powerful speeches of all time because of the vivid and emotionally evocative imagery used to inspire us to pursue the ideals of freedom, justice, and equality and to remind us that we have not yet achieved them. Black people have been "battered by the storms of persecution" and "come fresh from narrow jail cells," and yet Dr. King had a dream of an Alabama where "little black boys and little black girls will be able to join hands with little white boys and little white girls as sisters and brothers" and a vision of all people being "Free at last!"

Arguing Awareness and Voice

In the end, if there are no moral grounds that hold stable and no ultimate moral authority, then perhaps the best we can hope for is that all interested voices are heard. This is the *ideal speech situation* advocated by Habermas, in which participants are able to voice opinions and come to agreement based on the strength of the legitimate arguments, and no parties are hindered either internally or externally from expressing their views (Thompson & Held, 1982). Habermas would argue that because important values are at stake, moral debates should include criminals and victims, the enslaved and the free, women and men, the colonizers and the colonized. No debate is fully moral when any party with interests at stake is excluded.

Taking Habermas's view a step further, we might ask how it applies to emotional messages. First, it requires awareness of one's emotions and the ability to articulate them as an integral part of rational arguments. Second, it requires that all parties believe that there is a basis for negotiating and agreeing about emotion. A useful discussion cannot be a matter of "my emotions can beat up your emotions" because they are stronger, but rather, emotions should be used to uncover implicit values and what they mean to the parties involved. In fact, I doubt that a complete picture of what the situation means to all parties can be created unless they speak with passion. Third, it requires that no parties lose their voices because of shame or the feeling that they are not worthy to be part of the discussion. It is not difficult to silence another person by shaming her; her natural reaction is to want to withdraw.

Pathos, Logos, and Ethos Revisited

Effective moral rhetoric requires three basic ingredients: pathos (emotion or passion), logos (logic or reason), and ethos (character) (McKeon, 1941). After analyzing the emotional underpinning of moral discussion, we now have a richer appreciation of how all three work in concert. Morality based on pathos can be misguided without logos (if the anger is based on factual errors) and transitory without ethos (if you feel guilty now but not tomorrow). Morality based on logos can be impotent without pathos (if you try to persuade with bland statistics) and manipulative without ethos (if you rouse the rabble with ill intent). Morality based on ethos can be inflexible and indisputable without pathos and logos (if she is assumed to be ethical, regardless of feelings or facts). Pathos, logos, and ethos together, however, give us a braided thread that is much stronger than any one of its individual strands.

Emotivism versus Moral Emotionality Today

A popular view of emotion today is that emotions are neither moral nor immoral; they are what they are. We must accept any emotions that we or others feel simply because they are authentic. One person's feelings are as good as another's, and emotions are not debatable. There is justification for this position in the sense that it is important to recognize and acknowledge your own and other people's feelings, and sometimes other people's feelings are none of our business. But emotions are neither inherently ethical nor beyond the scope of ethical consideration. As I have argued throughout this chapter, they are ethically significant, as Greenspan (1995: 188) says: "essentially a kind of perception of moral saliences." The argument that emotion is neither ethical nor unethical, but instead ethically meaningless (*emotivism*, as it was called), had its heyday in philosophy at the peak of confidence in rationality and science (the 1940s and 1950s; Ayer, 1946/1995). Today few philosophers believe in emotivism due to the efforts of many of their colleagues who have tackled emotion with a few more decades of knowledge at their disposal and perhaps a little disillusionment with science (e.g., de Sousa, 1987; Greenspan, 1995; Rorty, 1980; Solomon, 1993). It is hard now to be well informed about emotion and believe "My emotions, good or bad."

The closest we come is to believing that intense emotions are bad, crazy, uncool, and perhaps even just plain wrong. This is a change from the Victorian belief that intense emotions could and should be harnessed for the public good (Stearns, 1994). Victorians might have seen intense anger as righteous indignation that reflected well on a man's character when directed toward appropriate goals (e.g., challenging injustice), though the same was probably not true for women. Today we may be more likely to see it as fanatical, going off the deep end, or being out of control (heaven forbid). For Victorian women, passionate mother love was valorized as the peak of moral feeling and the core of a stable society. Today it is more likely to be seen as excessive, controlling, and clingy, and the woman as somebody who obviously needs to "get a life." The norm of channeling justifiable emotions toward moral ends seems to have been overridden by the ideal of moderation of intensity, no matter how important the moral imperative (Stearns, 1994).

Another popular ethical stance toward emotion is that "good" emotions are "feel-good" emotions and that "bad" emotions are "feel-bad" emotions. For example, guilt and sadness are bad because they make you feel bad, so you really should get over them as soon as you can, taking drugs like Prozac or otherwise comforting yourself in whatever ways work. The emotional meaning of life is to strive for the pleasant and avoid the unpleasant. Living *"the* good life" is the same thing as "living *a* good life" (Solomon, 1990). That might be well and good except for the uncomfortable fact that the actions that make you feel good may make others feel bad and may have negative implications for the well-being of society. It is undoubtedly unpleasant for you to feel guilty about cheating on your taxes and pleasant to feel glee that you pulled one over on the government, but your cheating makes me feel bad because I have to pay your share and because it clearly decreases the resource base of society.

Having a world full of happy people is the stuff of utopias but also of dystopias such as *Brave New World*, with its "feelies" instead of movies and happiness found in soma pills (Huxley, 1932/1989). As an alternative, writers like Moore (1992) and Hillman (1960/1997) challenge us to explore the depths of anguish and despair in order to arrive at a deeper and more embracing appreciation and understanding of life in all its complexity. To return to the weaving metaphor, they would say that you cannot weave a tapestry that teaches people how they should live without using drab and gloomy colors.

In the next chapter, we shall see that people from different cultures and historical periods have created a great array of ways of feeling and communicating emotion. Their emotional meanings are not morally neutral, as we shall see; rather, they are tuned to their unique life circumstances. One of the great joys of living in a time and place where there are anthropologists, historians, and books is that we can glimpse strange yet familiar emotional lives.

7. How Is Emotional Communication Grounded in Common Human Experience and Diverse Cultures?

> We cannot feel strongly toward the totally unlike because it is unimaginable, unrealizable; nor yet toward the wholly like because it is stale – identity must always be dull company. The power of other natures over us lies in a stimulating difference that causes excitement and opens communication, in ideas similar to our own but not identical, in states of mind attainable but not actual. . . .
>
> C. H. Cooley (1902/1964: 153)

Are we all humans who can understand each other's hearts in ways that transcend our differences, or are our emotions so strongly shaped by our personal, cultural, and historical circumstances that we can never grasp the feelings of strangers? Stated in everyday terms, can a North American understand the *liget* that the Ilongot (of the Philippines) feel, and can an Ilongot understand North American *anger*? Can we read *The Odyssey* and understand the Homeric "spirit of battle" or look at the sorrow on the faces in a 14th-century Flemish painting and grasp the meaning of those expressions for the painter and for all the people who have looked at it over the centuries? Do people from different cultures have the same repertoire of emotions? These are profound questions because they address our ability to transcend our own limited life experiences and to learn from others who are different from ourselves, as the chapter-opening quotation implies.

Cross-cultural and transhistorical emotional understanding also has significant practical consequences. These days we find ourselves communicating with a much wider range of people than we did before the mass media, the Internet, and the jet plane connected people in a global web of messages. In the past (and still in many places now), you could live your entire life communicating almost exclusively with people like yourself. You had no access to and probably no interest in writings from long ago (except for holy texts that were interpreted for you). Now that situation has changed dramatically for many people. You may find yourself trying to make a joke during a lecture in Spain, only to have it embarrass everyone (Iglesias, 1996). Or you may find yourself trying to negotiate a contract in China, Japan, or Korea, give an honest and clear "no" answer to a proposal, and inadvertently offend people by being so direct and unapologetic (F. Li, personal communication). Or you may find yourself trying to understand why Jesse Jackson's speeches are so emotionally powerful by trying to understand the traditions of African American rhetoric (Kochman, 1981).

After several cycles of debate in the academic community over whether emotion and its expression are universal across cultures or differ from one culture to another, there is now a widespread consensus that neither extreme position is tenable; there is some truth to both sides. For a sampling of scholars who find the debate between extreme positions tiresome and unproductive, we can cite Besnier (1995a: 560), Leavitt (1996: 515), Levy (1984a: 217), Lutz and White (1986: 408), Parish (1994: 295), and Wierzbicka (1995: 40). I think Lofland (1985: 172) states the emerging consensus best: "It is not a question of *whether* all humans are like or unlike all other humans. Rather, it is – and this is far more complex – a question of *how* humans are alike and *how* they differ."

If we focus on communication, the issue shifts slightly to the question "How do people go about the difficult task of understanding the feelings of someone from a different culture, and in what ways are they likely to succeed or fail?" (Ellsworth, 1994: 24). In a certain sense, this question is the same one that has guided the rest of this book: How do we communicate emotion with others, and how are we likely to succeed or fail? Because no two people are alike, communication is always fallible. But when we try to cross cultural and historical gaps, we make a qualitative leap in difficulty because systems of meaning can be quite different as well.

To develop the metaphor of weaving a tapestry, we might recognize that weavers use different patterns that make their fabrics distinct. Anyone can see the differences between a Navajo rug, a French medieval tapestry, and an Iranian gabbeh, even if they cannot tell you from what culture they came. The patterns and skills needed to create these weavings have been passed down through generations of masters and apprentices, all using the standard patterns and yet adapting them to their unique visions. The patterns used by each culture communicate information about its relationship with the earth and raw materials, about momentous historical events, about cultural myths, and much more. To some extent, one must know the code to understand the meaning, although some weavings are more representational and others more symbolic. Nevertheless, each pattern speaks to important elements of the human experience. The variations rely on different arrays of colors (emotions) and a range of types of thread (cues), but they all use the same basic resources to create the unique patterns that constitute an important aspect of their way of life (emotional philosophies or ideologies).

In thinking about communicating emotion across cultural and historical gaps, I feel obliged to issue three warnings. First, it is easy to assume that easy communication is good communication, but it isn't; it is just easier. Certainly, if you need to communicate fear to a child who is about to run into the street, easy is good because your goal is a quick, appropriate change in behavior. But if your communicative goal is more ambitious – such as to develop a rich and subtle sense of another person's feelings and way of life – communication is more difficult. If, in addition, that other person has lived a life very different from yours, participates in a radically different society or social role, and has feelings that are not the same as yours, communication is much more challenging. International negotiators in government and business confront this practical problem every day. The reward for grappling with it is to live vicariously beyond your own time and place. That is the gift we have been given by the many anthropologists who have shared with us what they learned about the emotional lives of people in other cultures and the historians who have tried to decipher emotional life in other times. The people they describe seem quite alien to us in some ways (as we no doubt would to them), but in other ways they are quite familiar. Historians have an even more difficult task than anthropologists do because they cannot communicate directly with people who are long dead, but instead must rely on written records and other artifacts. We cannot pretend to understand deeply the culture of honor in Icelandic sagas or even the feelings of Hamlet or Lear as Shakespeare intended them, but to the extent that we can, our own lives are expanded and enriched.

Second, we must avoid thinking of differences among cultures and among historical periods as distinct and fixed. Individuals differ. The Utku Eskimos (Canada) tend to be emotionally controlled, but one man, Inuttiaq was unusually intense and assertive by Utku standards (Briggs, 1970: 41–74). All members of a culture are not equally guided by it. When Oriya Hindus in Orissa, India, were asked to describe an image of the Great Mother Goddess Kali, many respondents agreed about its emotional meaning, but others gave unusual accounts, and still others were "cultural duds" who seemed to have no clue (Menon & Schweder, 1994). Cultures change. In the past, the Ilongot celebrated and managed *liget* through head-hunting, but due to pressure from the Philippine government, they no longer hunt heads but express great nostalgia for head-hunting and the feelings that gave it meaning. Emotional messages can even be a force in producing cultural changes, such as when an Egyptian Bedouin recorded poems on a cassette about his lost love, and thus elicited sympathy for his plight and challenged the authority of traditional elders to arrange marriages (Abu-Lughod, 1990).

Third, this chapter and much of the research that serves as its foundation are based on a model of translation, which may be very different from the process of learning a language but is a useful first step. Translating a word or phrase involves providing another word or phrase from a familiar language that comes close to its meaning. Translation is never exact and always distorts the term being translated by forcing it into a framework that never fits exactly. This is abundantly clear with emotion terms. *Song* or *liget* can be translated into *anger*, but only with enormous distortion. Nevertheless, as Leavitt (1996: 530) writes, "[w]hile one cannot directly experience what other people experience, it should be possible to construct intelligible and potentially sense-able models of their experience by using one's own as material on which to work."

The point I want to make, however, is a larger one. Most emotion scholars, including myself, adopt a modern Western view of emotion, and we translate foreign views of emotion into our own (e.g., Hawaiian *aloha* is like love). That makes sense as a way of understanding emotional diversity *from our point of view* (or, to extend the metaphor, to force it into our language), but we cannot forget that our view of emotion is no more objective than American English is objective. For example, I began this book by outlining a process model of emotion that frames emotion as primarily an individual phenomenon, but other cultures define emotion as primarily social or interactive, so they might begin a book with situations in which emotion is produced (we would probably say that emotion "happens"). In this book there is an entire chapter on the control of negative emotions because that is a pressing concern for contemporary Americans, but there is very little on how emotion is generated and shared in groups and communities, which is a much more important concern in many other cultures.

That is not to say, however, that there are no shared emotional processes that transcend cultures (a sort of emotional Esperanto, sign language, or directly understandable code). It is also not to say that there is no way of analyzing emotional phenomena from an objective (or intersubjective) point of view. Ultimately, scholars aspire to and work toward a general theory of human emotion (no doubt with its culture-specific conditions) rather than a separate theory for every culture that exists or has ever existed. It can be exhilarating to recognize what we share, blended with what we do not share, as physical, emotional, cultural, and linguistic human beings.

Anyone who has lived in another culture long enough experiences emotional "bilingualism," but any single book, much less a single chapter, is much too short to accomplish that. The content of this chapter parallels the main issues of the previous six chapters, and obviously contains only the highlights of cultural and historical research that qualify or elaborate those issues. If you want to learn a bit more of another emotional "language" rather than learning some simple translations, I urge you to immerse yourself in at least one extended anthropological account of the emotional life in another culture. I have been most influenced by Briggs (1970), who has written about the Utku Eskimos of Canada; Lutz (1988b) who has focused on the Ifaluk islands of Micronesia; Rosaldo (1980) whose concern is the Ilongot of the Philippines; and Wikan (1990), who has described the Balinese (Indonesia). To save you the trouble of reading these authors' names repeatedly, assume that when I refer to each group, I am referring to the sources just named. You will read about many other people, places, and times as well.

How Important Is Emotion in Everyday Interaction?

In what ways is emotion the same or different across cultures and historical periods, and what does our answer imply for the importance of emotion in face-to-face interaction? Fortunately, the process model of emotion works well as a framework to analyze emotional diversity because each component can be analyzed separately; then we can consider how the pieces fit together as a set. Mesquita and Frijda

(1992) have done a thorough and detailed review of cross-cultural similarities and differences in the emotion process, from which I draw heavily in the following section.

Cause/Object/Antecedents

Do people everywhere and always have emotions about or in response to the same kinds of events? The answer is, as you would expect, yes and no. Because humans share the same biological and social processes, some events are good candidates for universal antecedents to emotion because they have important consequences for survival (confronting fear, acquiring resources) or because they are grounded in universal problems of social life (negotiating conflicting goals, living up to social standards, losing significant relationships, and acquiring intangible resources such as prestige or affection) (Lutz, 1988a: 400). But events that are biologically or socially important do not necessarily have the same emotional meaning everywhere and always; meaning is shaped by specific circumstances and by the person's culture. If we can approach one generalization about emotion and culture, it would be that the more general the emotion antecedent is, the more likely it is to be common across cultures, but the specific types of events that produce emotions vary widely across culture and time, as do their emotional meanings (Shaver, Wu, & Schwartz, 1992). Let's begin with death.

"Death itself is certainly one universal of the human condition. But the *experience* of death is a variable" (Shaver et al., 1992: 177–181). Lofland (1985) develops this point by describing how and why the experience of grief varies across cultures. People who experience the death of others as a regular part of their lives (in places and times with high mortality rates), who have strong attachments to many other people (such as same-sex friendship groups, extended families, and whole communities), and who do not have time or privacy to grieve (crops to tend and small houses) will experience the death of a family member differently than people who rarely confront death, who almost never have death in their homes, who have only a few very intense attachments to others (relatively speaking), and who have the time and privacy to go through an extended grieving process, especially when it is expected by others. For example, Mexican culture lives with death – in its literature, on its murals, in its food (eating *pan de los muertos* – bread of the dead – after offering some to the spirits of the dead), and on the streets during the "Day of the Dead" festivals (Younoszai, 1993).

Social interaction among the living is almost certainly a universal source of emotion, perhaps more in non-Western cultures than in Western ones. Among Europeans, Japanese, and Americans, social relationships were reported to be the most common sources of sadness, anger, and joy and one of the most common sources of fear. White (1994: 229–230) says that for A'ara speakers, nearly all examples of emotion involved other people (all for shame and somewhat fewer for fear). Communicative events such as getting letters from relatives living abroad (for the Nukulaelae, Besnier, 1995b) or giving a speech (for Tahitians, Levy, 1973) may be especially likely to arouse emotion.

The meanings of specific interactional events, such as insults, however, vary substantially across cultures. On the small Pacific island of Ifaluk, failing to share food is supremely insulting, but if you offered to share your fries in an American fast-food joint, you would receive some very odd looks. To avoid insulting others, you have to know their social norms. Even then, what is accepted and even enjoyed by them may not be okay for you. Women who call themselves and each other "girl," African Americans who call each other "nigger," or gays who call each other "queer" use those terms with affection, but they take them as insults from out-group members.

Well, then, if it is so easy to give offense, perhaps a smile coupled with a friendly and enthusiastic attitude can provide the transcultural social lubricant that you need to get through difficult encounters. That may be true for Americans, but we know that the Japanese, for example, do not view smiles as positively as Americans do (Matsumoto & Kudoh, 1993). Foreigners in the United States are often insulted by the shallowness of Americans' friendliness, finding their enthusiasm exaggerated (Wierzbicka, 1994: 185–189). Well, if smiles may not work, perhaps you could ask them questions about themselves – surely interest in the other person shows good intentions across the globe. If you did so with Hawaiians, they would consider you intrusive and rude, violating their personal boundaries with what to them is a nosy question or personal probe (Ito, 1985: 304).

Appraisals

What about the basic ways of appraising events that result in emotional reactions? Do they differ among cultures? Some of the basic responses seem to be universal, although, again, the specifics vary (Ellsworth, 1994; Mesquita & Frijda, 1992). People everywhere tend to orient to novelty as a stimulus for emotion, but what is novel varies tremendously from culture to culture. The film *The Gods Must Be Crazy* shows us how truly bizarre the !Kung (Bushmen) of the Kalahari find the completely ordinary (and, to Westerners, transparent) practice of changing activities based on changes in the clock. Another universal dimension may be the very rapid appraisal of something as positive or negative (in the sense of "good for me"/"bad for me"), but again, such a response is based strongly on familiarity, which, of course, varies a great deal (Zajonc, 1980). I, for one, would not be too keen on the frozen fish eyes that are a familiar treat for Eskimo children, and they surely would not trade them for gummy bears. Many cultures also make distinctions among emotions in terms of fairness, morality, goal consistency, implications for self-esteem, who or what is responsible, and coping possibilities (Mesquita & Frijda, 1992: 185).

Different cultures also have tendencies toward different appraisals (Mesquita & Frijda, 1992: 186). We might think of them as appraisal biases, except that there is no standard that we can hold up as unbiased. Members of relatively individualistic cultures, for example, tend to make appraisals based on individual achievements and characteristics, whereas members of more collectivist cultures tend to make appraisals based on relationships and others' expectations (Markus & Kitayama, 1994: 89–90). Here is a recent example. Masako Owada, a "bright, highly educated, fast-track member of the Foreign Ministry," gave up her career and autonomy to marry, out of duty, Crown Prince Naruhito of Japan. "From many European-American perspectives, the Princess' decision was 'obviously' self-sacrificing and 'naturally' accompanied by the emotion of unhappiness," but from many Japanese perspectives, "she may indeed have felt content or 'good' as a result of her decision to respond to the desires and expectations of others and marry into the royal family."

If appraisal tendencies are general and far-reaching enough, we may call them *emotional ideologies* (Myers, 1979, cited in Heelas, 1996: 187). To borrow some examples from Mesquita and Frijda (1992): "The Utku Eskimos, much more than any of us, are used to extreme hardship and discomfort. Their philosophy, therefore, is that such things must be tolerated, not flailed against," so anger and aggression are extremely rare (quoting Solomon, 1978: 193–194). Anger is also rare for the Tahitians, who put "an emphasis on the substitutability of goals and desired objects, which are assumed to be in adequate supply. If you lose one woman, you will get another" (quoting Levy, 1973: 288). On the other hand, the Ilongot emotion that we would call anger (*liget*) is both celebrated and suspect; "*liget* can generate both chaos and concentration, distress and industry, a loss of sense and reason, and an experience of clarification and release" (Rosaldo, 1980: 47). Before the 19th century in Western Europe and colonial North America "undue grief could denote undue attachment to worldly ties" and so was considered downright heretical, whereas a mere century later, grief was indulged and admired (Stearns & Knapp, 1996: 133).

Physiological Changes

We know very little about how people's physiological reactions vary across cultures (Mesquita & Frijda, 1992), but we do know that some people emphasize physiology more than others and describe their internal states differently. Many cultures locate emotion in organs of the body, but the specific organ of emotion varies. The Austronesian language Mangap-Mbula of New Guinea uses terms such as *kete-(i)malmal* (translated as "liver fight" or anger in English) and *kete-kutkut* (translated as "liver beats" or anxious in English) (Wierzbicka, 1994: 148). Other emotional centers are the heart and lungs (for Homeric Greeks), the stomach (for the Gahuku-Gama), the intestines (Tahitians, Maori), and the heart (Ilongot, Yoruba, Americans) (Heelas, 1996: 180–181). One can imagine some interesting Valentine's Day cards, such as those with anatomically correct pictures of the heart.

Kövecses (1995) notes that the metaphor of the body as container, emotions as fluids in the container, and even anger as a hot fluid in the container is found in English, Hungarian, Chinese, Tahitian, and Wolof, with variations primarily in how emotion is controlled (add Venezuelan Spanish from Shaver et al., 1992). Kövecses argues that this is too much of a coincidence, so the commonalities are probably based on common physiological reactions (body heat, internal pressure, and redness). Evidence has also been found for cross-cultural similarity in physiological responses such as heart rate acceleration with fear and anger and deceleration with sadness (Ekman, Levenson, & Friesen, 1983).

When people from 27 different countries were asked to report physiological indicators of various emotions, Wallbott and Scherer (1988:

44–48; Scherer & Wallbott, 1994: 326) found more differences between emotions than between cultures, especially in terms of arousal and temperature. What we do not know, however, is whether people are reporting real physiological indicators of emotion or their own stereotypes of what bodily feelings go along with what emotions (Rimé, Philippot, & Cisamolo, 1990). In some cultures, people report no physiological changes at all when they describe their emotions spontaneously (Mesquita & Frijda, 1992: 189) and in others, physiological changes are recognized but take their meanings from the cultural context (Brenneis, 1995).

Action Tendencies, Action, and Expression

Little is known about variations in how people are inclined to act or not to act when they are feeling different emotions (Mesquita & Frijda, 1992). Some national differences are striking: "It appears that, when jealous, the French get mad, the Dutch get sad, the Germans would rather not fight about it, the Italians don't want to talk about it, and the Americans are concerned about what their friends think!" (Bryson, 1991: 191). The sexes, however, react to jealousy in very similar ways, except in the United States, where "men are more likely to respond with violence and then to experience remorse at their actions" (p. 189). Comparisons between Ugandans' (who spoke either Luganda or English) and Americans' feelings of anger showed that Ugandans felt impulses toward either moving away from others (including crying) or extreme aggression (killing and severe mutilation), whereas Americans reported impulses toward moderate aggression (striking out, hurting, etc.) (Davitz, 1969: 183).

Emotional Experience

One of the most important conditions for experiencing emotion in many cultures is the presence of other people. Levenson, Ekman, Heider, and Friesen (1992) report a dramatic example. When Americans posed positive and negative facial expressions, they showed corresponding physiological reactions and reported feeling positive or negative emotions. Yet when the Minangkabau of western Sumatra posed the same expressions, they showed the same corresponding physiological patterns, but they did not report any change in feeling.

The authors speculate that the Minangkabau do not think of emotional states as occurring when they are alone, so facial expressions and physiological changes were not indicators of emotions for them.

Emotion Talk

The vocabularies of emotion terms found in different cultures can tell us a great deal about how they conceptualize emotion, what emotions are described in words, how emotions are categorized, and so on, although it is important not to jump to conclusions about emotional experience based on vocabulary alone. For example, we would not want to claim that if a language has no word for "joy," its speakers never feel what English speakers would call joy. Nor would we want to say that people with more words for emotion have more emotionally varied lives than people with fewer words. Such a claim was made by the anthropologists Sapir (1921) and Whorf (1956) early in this century, but its strong form (as stated here) has not held up well under research scrutiny, although language may have some power to shape perceptions of emotion. For example, Miller (1993: 101) argues that convenient, simple emotion terms tend to act as "evaluative magnets" that encourage us to lump together closely related feelings.

In trying to understand emotion terminology from other cultures, we immediately run into translation problems. Start with the term *emotion*. To study the emotion words in a culture, you have to have a working definition of what emotion is so that you know what counts and what doesn't. Unfortunately, there is often no clear distinction between emotions and nonemotions. Some words clearly refer to emotions (e.g., love), some clearly do not (e.g., intelligence), and some are not clearly one or the other (e.g., indecision) (Shaver et al., 1987). To compound the problem, not all languages even have a term like *emotion* that can be used to include or exclude other terms, and if they do, it may not mean the same as the English word. German has the term *fühlen*, meaning "to feel," but it does not distinguish between mental and physical feelings, and French has the terms *sentir* ("to feel") and *émotion*, but the latter refers to overwhelming feelings and would not include ordinary feelings like *tristesse* (sadness) (Wierzbicka, 1994: 150–152).

In any case, there are extremes. The Ommura of Papua New Guinea simply do not refer to emotion in communication; they think of internal states as "vague and incommunicable" (Hallpike, 1979: 397). A small indigenous group in Malaysia, the Chewong, have eight emotion terms, whereas the neighboring Malays have 230. American English has about 400, and Taiwanese has about 750 (Heelas, 1996: 174). Emotion words also change over time, leading to some words being added or emphasized more (*limerence, stress, depression*) and others falling into disuse or even becoming extinct (*accidie, melancholy*) (Harré & Finlay-Jones, 1986).

Assuming that if we can decide on a working definition of emotion, we can compare emotion words across languages and cultures in order (1) to find the common categories or "families" of emotion within each culture, (2) to understand the basis for grouping some emotions together but not others, and (3) to compare categories across cultures. American English speakers, for example, group emotion words into the basic categories of love, joy, anger, sadness, and fear, based primarily on the appraisals of good/bad and intense/weak. Ifaluk speakers group their emotions based on the situation: situations of good fortune (such as having a boyfriend/girlfriend), situations of danger (e.g., walking on the chief's property), situations of connection and loss (e.g., going off to a distant island to high school), situations of human error (e.g., going fishing and catching very little), and situations of inability (having to eat a food you don't like) (Lutz, 1986). Emotion categorizations have also been done for three cultures in Indonesia (Heider, 1991), for Samoa (Gerber, 1985), and for China (Shaver et al., 1992).

Single emotion words and even clusters of emotions never translate exactly between cultures (Romney, Moore, & Rusch, 1997; Russell & Sato, 1995), but whether there are basic emotion categories that bear rough correspondences is a matter of debate. Shaver and colleagues (1992) argue that our joy and love look much like emotions of good fortune to the Ifaluk, our fear looks like their emotions of danger, our sadness looks like their connection and loss, and our anger corresponds roughly to their emotions of human error. The only unusual one is emotions of inability, but the authors argue on technical grounds that it should not really count as a category (p. 203). The analogy that is often used in this debate involves color terms. Some cultures may have words like *puce, chartreuse*, and *taupe*, but basic colors are still the foundation for all the nuances. On the other side are scholars arguing that there are no natural divisions between emotions and that it is a serious distortion of the actual meaning of words to force even rough correspondence (Wierzbicka, 1994). Heider (1991:

88) offers an intermediate position based on his analysis of Indonesian emotion words, arguing that some emotion words and even clusters of emotion words do correspond across cultures and others do not. Practically speaking, you can find yourself in big trouble on Ifaluk if you think that their term *song* is equivalent to our *anger* because you might be deluded into thinking that *anger/song* functions the same in both cultures, but knowing that there is a rough correspondence might be a good start.

Emotion in Everyday Interaction

How important is emotion in everyday interaction in other cultures? If by important we mean common, we get mixed reports. Heelas, (1996: 193) says that the Chewong (Malaysia) report little emotion in interaction, and Heider (1991: 4) says that in Indonesia "[a]ctual emotion scenes or outburst are relatively rare in daily life, and they are usually kept relatively private." Wierzbicka (1994: 151) notes that in American conversations displays of emotion are unusual, whereas in Russian conversations emotions are normal and their absence reveals a "deadening of a person's duša (heart or soul)." Similarly, in French and German cultures, "the idea that *les sentiments* or *Gefühle* should be viewed as a departure from the normal state of composure would strike most people as bizarre" (Wierzbicka, 1994: 150–152). In some cultures, social interaction is *the* place to find emotion because, if it is not shared, it is not emotional (Brenneis, 1990).

If we interpret important to mean that emotions are valued, they vary from adored to ignored. In rural China, displays of emotion are "by Western standards, most vividly expressive," but they are considered neither dangerous nor useful for achieving any goal; they are simply ignored (Potter, 1988: 188). Differences can be found in the United States between European Americans, who tend to value emotional self-restraint, and African Americans, who tend to value emotional expressiveness as powerful, exciting, and energizing. In Maori (New Zealand) meetings, "speech is meant to be from the heart rather than in a more prepared way from the head" (Strongman & Strongman, 1996: 201). Several cultures do not value the heart over the head or vice versa; rather, they strive to make them work together. Some make no distinction at all between emotion and reason. In the Ifaluk (Micronesia) language, *nunuwan* covers both, and the Balinese (Indonesia) "do not recognize feeling (*perasaan*) to be distinct from thought (*pikiran*), but regard both as aspects of one integral process – *keneh* – which is best translated as feeling/thought" (Wikan, 1980: 35). They feel sorry for Westerners who think/feel separately (pp. 267–283).

How and Why is Emotion Communicated?

How well are we able to communicate across experiential gulfs? Anthropologists who have joined other cultures and tried to understand them in depth give us mixed reports from their own experience. On the one hand, Middleton (1989: 194) argues that Briggs was frustrated in her ability to decipher the facial expressions of the Utku Eskimos with confidence. On the other hand, Levy (1984b: 410) says that "aside from one or two temporarily confusing gestures, expressive behavior in both places [Tahiti and Nepal] was not hard for me to understand." Setting aside the possibility that the Utku were simply more inscrutable than the Tahitians or Nepalese (which certainly is possible) or that Briggs was more obtuse than Levy, let's assume for the moment that they are both right. The expressions of people in exotic cultures must provide some foothold for studying their emotions; otherwise, there would be no place to start to understand them. But if emotions were very easy to understand, anthropologists would not need to spend years studying Utku or Tahitian feelings. That is the conclusion supported by much of the research; communicating emotion between cultures seems to be easy at a relatively superficial level and quite difficult at a deeper and more subtle level, just as it is within cultures.

Accounts of the first contacts between the Maori of New Zealand and the first European visitors provide several interesting examples. One member of Captain Cook's expedition reports a Maori war dance in which "each man jump'd with a swinging motion at the same instant of time to the right and left" Warriors "distended their Mouths, Lolling out their tongues and Turned up the White of their Eyes, the whole Accompanied with a strong Hoarse Song, calculated in my Opinion to Chear Each Other and Intimidate their Enemies" (Gore, 1769, quoted in Salmond, 1991: 126). Just so. This is easily recognized today as the *haka*. During another incident one frustrated Maori " 'turned up his breach and made the usual sign of contempt amongst the Billingsgate ladies' – the first recorded instance of the ritual insult known as *whakapohane*, or exposure of the anus" (Monkhouse, 1769, cited in Salmond, 1991:145).

But it did not always go so well. A French expedition that reached New Zealand during the same year as Cook mistakenly interpreted the *whakapohane* not as insult but as lasciviousness (Salmond, 1991: 345). Worse yet, when the captain of the ship, Surville, went to get water, he was harangued in a loud voice and stared at by an old Maori man. Because Surville was annoyed, he tied a piece of red ribbon to the old man's spear, and "from then on he ceased his harangues and seemed happy" (Monkhouse, 1769, cited in Salmond, 1991: 330). In fact, the old man was probably a *tohunga* (priest) trying to *maaktu* (stare fixedly, bewitch) Surville. When Surville tied a red ribbon to the old man's spear, he was, in essence, confronting the gods head on. As Salmond notes (Salmond, 1991: 330), "to claim that the old man was 'happy' about this was undoubtedly an error of cosmological proportions."

How Is Emotion Communicated?

What is striking in anthropologists' accounts is that people everywhere seem to use a wide variety of cues to communicate emotion. For example, the Ifaluk show *song* (justifiable anger) by

> one or several of the following maneuvers, including a refusal to speak or, more dramatically, eat with the offending party; dropping the markers of polite and "calm" speech; running away from the household or refusing to eat at all; facial expressions associated with disapproval, including pouting or a "locked" mouth, "lit-up" or "lantern" eyes, gestures, particularly brusque movements; declarations of *song* and the reasons for it to one's kin and neighbors; throwing or hitting material objects; and in some cases, a fast or the threat of suicide or other personal harm. (Lutz, 1988b: 174)

Ilongot *liget* (anger/energy/passion) is "manifested in hard work, fine ornaments, or forceful speeches; it is to recognize a passionate vibrato in a fellow's singing, a show of muscular grace and tension in a dance" (Rosaldo, 1980: 46). The Utku Eskimos are renowned for their emotion control, but small children "are snuffed, cuddled, cooed at, talked to, and played with endlessly, the men as demonstrative as the women" (Briggs, 1970: 70). It is not hard to find examples of people around the globe and across history communicating emotion through their faces, their voices, their bodies, and their words. Precisely how they do that, however, can vary considerably.

The Balinese distinguish among emotions based primarily on the *face.* They expect a clear and bright face (*mue cedang* or *cerah muka*), about which, they say, "we can see from the eyes, the eyes cannot lie." But the face can also be *layu* (withered, faded, languished), *muram* (cloudy, gloomy, sorrowful), *seram* (hideous, horrible, frightening), or *nyebend* (grave, stern) (Wikan, 1990: 52). When the Maori (New Zealand) do the *haka* (war chant), they stick out their tongues. To express surprise/embarrassment/fear, Oriya women of Bhubaneswar (India) show this face: "the tongue extends out and downward and is bitten between the teeth, the eyebrows rise, and the eyes widen, bulge, and cross" (Schweder, 1991: 246, cited in Mesquita & Frijda, 1992: 194).

Vocal cues include Irvine's (1990: 137) observation that among the Wolof of Senegal, the expressive speech of the griots (bardic or poet-singer class) can be six times faster than the inexpressive speech of nobles. Brenneis (1995: 248) says that "In Bhatgaon (Fiji), villagers comment that they frequently pick up on the emotional flavor of an event through observing and participating in styles of interaction and talk. Rapid, strongly interlocked talk with frequently exaggerated intonational contours marks *tamashabhaw* [a situation of playfulness or fun] as surely as does its label." The ancient Greek and Latin epic poets Homer, Vergil, and Ovid often wrote about stupefaction in their characters through "the sudden silence, an unexpected rupture of conversational pattern, an abrupt change of pace in statement and response" (Lateiner, 1992: 265).

There is evidence of *physiological* cues to emotion in the ancient Icelandic sagas (legendary family narratives). "[E]ven though it would not have been the saga way for people to talk about emotions, their bodies were not always so obliging" (Miller, 1993: 101). Reddening (in anger to us) was mentioned frequently, and tears and swelling were not uncommon. Nowadays Bali is the only culture known in the world (of 73 studied) in which the natural response to hearing of the death of a loved one is to laugh (but they cry as well) (Wikan, 1990: 123). The Ifaluk (South Pacific), on the other hand, "cry big" at funerals (Lutz, 1988b: 100). Darwin (1872/1965) cites many accounts of people all over the world blushing.

Gestures and body movements also express emotion in many cultures. Brenneis (1990: 118) says that "the word in local Hindi for emotion (*bhaw*) is the same as that for gesture or display" and that the Hindi word for anger (*qussa*) also means 'fist' (p. 119). People around the globe also communicate emotion through their *actions*. The Utku Eskimos refuse to speak to and interact with people who provoke their anger. An Ilongot (of the Philippines) might hunt heads as an expression of *liget*. At the extreme of inaction, "the Balinese often react to unfamiliar or frightening events by falling asleep" (Bateson & Mead, 1942, cited in Mesquita & Frijda, 1992: 196). The Utku described the emotion term *niviuq* to Briggs (1970: 316) as "to want to kiss," to touch, or to be physically near someone. On the other hand, Briggs states that before living with the Utku, "I had never imagined that sulking could be such an aggressive act" (p. 138).

Verbal cues to emotion can be microscopic or macroscopic. Irvine (1990: 128) notes that the differences in emotional expressiveness between Wolof (Senegal) griots and nobles show up in grammatical, phonological, and phonetic differences. At a more macroscopic level, we hear Egyptian Bedouin love and British Victorian grief expressed intensely, and often through story and song (Abu-Lughod, 1990; Stearns & Knapp, 1996: 134). Recurrent themes of the Norse sagas testify to ancient Icelanders' overriding concern with honor and humiliation (Miller, 1993). People on Nukulaelae (Polynesia) verbally express their concerns about emotions (especially anger) by gossiping about angry people and episodes of anger, but also by acting out others' emotions both verbally and vocally (Besnier, 1995c).

Expressiveness

Enormous differences in expressiveness exist across cultures, just as they do within cultures. The Balinese, for example, are at the highly inexpressive end of the continuum when it comes to negative feelings. They are expected to express positive feelings and keep negative feelings hidden, but they are sensitively attuned to subtle nuances that might hint at negative feelings. They "rely on a host of indications (*ciri-ciri/tampe-tampe*) to ferret out another's heart" (Wikan, 1990: 97). We can see the extremely expressive end of the continuum at Gusii funerals, where "widows of the deceased were expected to tear off their clothes, cover themselves with ashes, and put on articles of the dead husband's clothing as they lamented his death and danced on his grave ... continuously on this and the next day, becoming completely exhausted" (LeVine, 1992: 87).

All other differences in expressiveness pale by comparison to those found between the griot caste and the noble castes of the Wolof of Senegal (Irvine; 1990). "One of the main roles of griots is to serve as expressive vehicles for the ideas and feelings of noble patrons – to communicate for them energetically and persuasively, especially in the public arena" (p. 256). To wit:

> Political meetings, villagewide celebrations, and the feasts given by prominent families are good examples. The griot stands and shouts as loudly as possible to the assembled crowd; he sways and jabs at the air with dramatic and forceful gestures, pointing at his addressees and holding up the money he has received in largesse. The veins in his forehead and neck stand out from the effort of the performance. His voice rises into falsetto pitch, and the rate of his utterance increases to more than 300 syllables a minute. Meanwhile, the higher-rank persons present, especially the highest nobles, remain seated, silent, and motionless, until moved to some action such as handing the griot a gift or (at a political meeting) making a terse comment. (p. 137)

Moreover, Irvine observes that the griot-noble model permeates interaction even between relative social equals, so that one participant takes on the griotlike expressive role (even if he or she is not a griot by social class) and the other person takes on the noblelike inexpressive role (even if not really of the nobility), relatively speaking.

The Wolof example also raises an issue that has not come up earlier in this book: *Whose* emotions are being communicated? In Western culture it is assumed that you express emotions for yourself. Among the Wolof, however, "emotional displays may be, and even must be, performed on someone else's behalf . . . there can be a disjunction between the 'owner' and the displayer of feeling." (Irvine, 1995: 257). Irvine explains that "If griots are expressive vehicles, 'transmitting' and magnifying the messages of others (like expressive microphones, to which villagers sometimes compared them), then much of what they express is not ultimately their own" (pp. 256–257). She reports a case in which one Wolof chief invited another to his house: "each had his griot mediator, and after the initial greetings the conversation was entirely taken over by the griots, who conversed with each other on their nobles' behalf. The chiefs themselves simply sat in silence" (1990: 145).

In Western cultures, it is rare for people to communicate feelings for others. Some exceptions are quoting characters in stories (such as when a parent reading a story to a child says, " 'I must stop this Christmas from coming . . . but HOW?' said the Grinch"), spokespersons who express feeling on behalf of public officials (such as vice-presidents expressing presidents' grief at funerals of foreign dignitaries), or one teenager telling another, "Jason really likes you" (a fine way to avoid the potential embarrassment of direct confrontation). I suppose that on the whole, though, Westerners assume that each person feels his own emotions, so he is in the best position to communicate them to others, whereas the Wolof assume that people can know each other's emotions and that certain types of people are better suited by temperament to do the expressing.

Emotional Accuracy

One of the earliest questions that Western researchers asked about emotional communication was how accurately facial expressions of emotions could be identified across cultures (Ekman, Sorenson, & Friesen, 1969). That question has guided (or plagued, depending on your point of view) the research ever since and is still a source of controversy today. Here is the basic research paradigm (which includes some variations): You photograph some good examples of prototypic facial expressions for basic emotions – anger, sadness, fear, joy, disgust, surprise; then you show the pictures to people far removed from Western influence and measure how accurately they can identify those faces as sad, happy, afraid, and so on. Ekman's paradigm has produced decades of research showing that people from widely disparate cultures can identify facial expressions at better than chance levels, thus supporting the universalist position. For decades, these findings have been accepted as orthodoxy, but there are also objections on several grounds, some methodological and some cultural (Ekman, 1994; Russell, 1994).

It is easy to see the accuracy cup as half full or half empty, depending on your point of view. One objection is that researchers are loading the dice by picking ideal examples of the most typical emotions, and accuracy is much lower when the full range of emotions and expressions is used. Levy (1984b: 409) believes that people can pick up general tendencies, but the boundaries get fuzzy. A second and related question is, what level of accuracy is good enough? Generally, we expect accuracy to be better than chance, but better than chance still is not necessarily very good. It depends on your goals. Personally, I would not want to go on an expedition into the jungle (rain forest or urban) knowing only that I could identify my guide's emotions at a level better than chance. I might be able to distinguish good from bad feelings (Russell, 1994), which might be good enough for deciding whether to walk past the snake but not for deciding whether to intimidate, pacify, or negotiate with that *other* group. Van Brakel (1993, cited in Wierzbicka, 1995: 35) says that "what the data gathered . . . may show is that people often make appropriate guesses at other people's emotions, even cross-culturally, just as they often make appropriate guesses about people's beliefs, intentions, and so on; but this is a far cry from stating [that] there's universal agreement on what, say, a prototypical sad expression is, let alone agreement on what, in general, is a sad expression."

Van Brakel hints at another objection to this research, which is ethnocentrism in the sense that Western (specifically American) facial expressions and emotion terms are typically used as *the* basic expressions and the criteria for accuracy (Wierzbicka, 1995). To be fair, we should ask the Ifaluk to pose expressions of "emotions of good fortune" or "emotions of loss and connection" and check to see if Americans could recognize them as equivalent to "joy," "sadness," or "seeing a venomous snake." Still, even if culturally unbiased, such a procedure oversimplifies meaning. In Heelas's words (1996: 175): "Although such terms [basic emotion words] involve distinctions which allow translation in terms of our emotion concepts, they also derive their meaning by including states of affairs which do not suit our concepts; which do not suit our understanding of what counts as being afraid, being angry and the like." Moreover, many people in other cultures would not even ask about accuracy because it assumes an individual, internal state model of emotion that is hidden and is expressed rather than a model in which participants enact an emotional event or situation together in public.

Emotional Understanding

From a purely practical point of view, it makes more sense to be concerned about emotional understanding than about accuracy. It is probably more important to know *why* someone is responding negatively to your actions (i.e., what the eliciting event was) than whether they are feeling angry, sad, or afraid. A great deal can hinge on whether they think your actions are your fault, their fault, or due to circumstances (appraisal). No doubt it matters whether they are inclined to attack, give up, or run (action tendencies). In other words, emotional understanding can be very helpful in deciding *your* course of action based on *their* emotional states.

Is emotional understanding itself an ethnocentric idea? The answer is, again, yes and no. Yes, many members of non-Western cultures do not consider emotions to be legitimate if they occur only *within individuals*, so it makes no sense to try to understand other people's subjective emotions. As mentioned earlier, the Ommura of Papua New Guinea know that people have subjective mental and emotional states, but they consider them to be vague and incommunicable (Hallpike, 1979: 397). It is what people do openly that counts. Yet, as White (1994: 235–236) says: "Research in a wide range of languages and cultures indicates that when people talk about emotion, they are not talking primarily about states inside the individual, nor are they talking about responses or events outside their person. Rather, they are talking about processes that *mediate or link* persons, actions, and events" (emphasis mine). Just as Westerners recognize that the Ommura deemphasize the private, subjective experience of emotion, the Ommura could accuse Westerners of neglecting the public, social, and moral aspects.

I will speculate that even when Westerners try to understand each other's emotions, they *do* consider the social and moral ways in which an individual relates to a social situation, even though they may think they are understanding private feelings. Consider this example. Your roommate is afraid of giving a speech tomorrow, and you are trying to understand his feelings. Despite the apparently individualistic nature of his feelings, what he really cares about is how others in the class are going to judge his speech. You reassure him that even if the speech doesn't go well, others in the class will still like and respect him. He may be inclined to postpone the speech to another day, but you convince him to give it because postponing would be a hardship on other people. You are discussing, as White would say, the emotional processes that link the person (especially his competence), his actions (his speech), and the social setting in which they occur (the class), with emphasis on the social and moral implications (what they will think, what he should do). It is a description of emotional understanding that might satisfy some of the Oceanic peoples that White is trying to represent, perhaps even the Ommura.

Emotional Coincidence

To many non-Western people, the fact that people often have similar reactions to the same event is not just coincidence; it is how emotion works. Brenneis says that in Bhatgaon (Fiji), moods are located primarily in events themselves; they are not thought of as internal states that coincide with shared events. For example, *prembhaw* (amity) occurs in weekly meetings of religious groups and does not just happen but is "made" or "built" (*karna* or *banana*) (Brenneis, 1995: 245). Pintupi Australian aborigines see emotions as bound to social activities, saying, "Yayayi was 'not a happy place' (*pukulpa wiya ngarrin*) and . . . several men suggested that a 'sing' should be organized to stop the fighting and make people 'happy' " (Myers, 1979: 353). Westerners also talk of emotions as located in events ("fun" parties, "sad" occasions, "inspiring" speeches), although a more individualistic perspective emphasizes the fun, sadness, or inspiration felt by individuals on those occasions, whereas a more collectivist perspective emphasizes the jointly created and shared feelings.

Emotional Contagion and Empathy

The Balinese are exquisitely and explicitly aware of the power of emotional contagion. One Balinese man said, "You must manage your heart so that you can forget your sadness. Otherwise, if you are sad, it may spread onto another" (Wikan, 1990: 144). Expressing your own feelings openly is "considered shameful (*ngidalem*) or selfish. It is to impose one's own concerns on people who have enough with their own" (p. 49). In fact, "feelings are treated *as if* they were social belongings," and "one owes it [appropriate feeling] to the social collective, one owes it to one's family, and one owes it to oneself. And the reason one owes it is that feelings are dangerous, they are contagious, they are the source of health and welfare, and they may predispose one to death" (p. 100). As Wikan's informant, Suriati, recognized when she moved away from Bali, "It is so much easier to be happy in Bali, there are so many smiles" (p. 111).

In collectivist cultures, empathy is not really an issue, but rather seems to be a normal and unproblematic part of everyday life. In individualized cultures, you may have to go out of your way to take another person's point of view and feel his feelings, but in collectivist cultures, emotions are not as strictly divided between yours and mine. Collective identity also makes for shared emotions even in cultures that are not particularly collectivist in orientation. In Spanish, there is a term, *vergüenza ajena*, which means "embarrassment or shame that is felt by observing another person's action whether the actor feels it or not . . . for instance, it is pretty common to listen to people complain about politicians' performances and scandals and also about the *vergüenza ajena'* these cause them" (Iglesias, 1996: 125). Observers may or may not be empathizing with a politician's shame or embarrassment (because he may not be ashamed or embarrassed), but they experience *vergüenza ajena* because the politician's behavior reflects on all Spaniards.

The fine distinctions that Western academics make among varieties of emotional connections also make little or no sense from many non-Western points of view. Chances are that these cultures do not distinguish among the feelings that you "catch" from another person (contagion), the feelings that you adopt from imagining another's situation (empathy), the feelings that you have about another's situation (sympathy), or the thoughts that you have about another's feelings (understanding). Their distinctions may instead be between socially appropriate feelings or socially inappropriate feelings, or between social feelings that count as emotions and individualized feelings that count as only something comparable to what we would call "sensations" (Brenneis, 1990).

Evoking Shared Feelings

In many cultures, an important function of messages is to produce shared feelings in the audience, and the message sender's own subjective feelings are largely irrelevant. For example, "Professional *qawwali* [Sufi Muslim devotional music of Pakistan and India] musicians use a range of performance devices not to express their own sense of religious ecstasy but to draw it forth from members of the congregation (Brenneis, 1990: 115). Appadurai (1990: 109) explains how evoking shared feelings works in Hindu India:

> In the creation of 'communities of sentiment,' standardized verbal and gestural forms are used, and there is no assumption of any correspondence between the words and gestures and the internal emotional world of the 'actor.' What matters are the emotional *effects* of praise, which, when it is properly 'performed,' creates a generalized mood of adoration or admiration or wonder that unites the one who praises, the object of this praise, and the audience, if there is one.

In many cases, the audience is not standing by passively waiting to have their emotions manipulated but instead is an active, integral part of the process of creating shared feelings.

The Issue of Confidence

We might also ask how much confidence people have in their ability to understand other people's feelings. Frijda and Mesquita (1994) conducted a study of Turkish, Surinamese, and Dutch people living in the Netherlands and found some interesting differences among these cultures in their confidence. "Not only did the Turkish respondents, on the average, expect other people to think, feel, and react as they had under similar circumstances, they assumed that other people would also behave as they had." Compared to the Turkish, the Dutch expressed more reservations about other people's interpretations and reactions, and the Surinamese thought others would interpret the situation more or less as they did but might react differently (pp. 69–71). In Samoa, Gerber (1985) found people to be so reserved about their ability to understand the inner states even of other people they knew well (as did Margaret Mead) that they would not answer her "why" questions about other people. "Samoans frequently say, with the full force of self-evident conventional wisdom, 'we cannot know what is in another person's depths,' or 'we cannot tell what another person is thinking' " (p. 133). Only when Gerber responded, "Yes, I know – but why do you think, in your *own* mind, that he did this?" would they say 'well, . . . in my *own* mind. . . . ' "

In a sense, the Turks have adopted a universalist position on emotion and its expression, and in doing so place themselves at risk not only of misinterpreting the feelings of others, but also of not even realizing what mistakes they are making. If we take the Samoans' public reaction seriously, we would have to put them at the other extreme as not even cultural relativists but complete relativists. Their caution may lead them to miss opportunities to understand others and recognize human commonalities.

Are Emotional Messages Spontaneous or Strategic?

All cultures deal with the tension between spontaneously expressing and strategically communicating emotion, but they resolve it in different ways. We see this clearly in the variations among philosophies and techniques of emotion management across time and place. One important philosophical distinction is between valuing emotional excess or emotional restraint. Dionysian cultures (so named after the Greek god of wine) "regard the majority of emotions as vital to both themselves and the social order," whereas Apollonian cultures (named after the god of the law) "regard the majority of emotions as dangerous threats to themselves and to their institutions" (Heelas, 1996: 178–179, borrowed from Benedict, 1935, who borrowed from Nietzsche, who borrowed from the Greeks).

Characterizing whole cultures as either Apollonian or Dionysian is no doubt an oversimplification, but it reflects an important tension. We can see that tension in the ambivalence toward love in 20th century U.S. culture. Love is celebrated as a peak experience in life ("Your love has lifted me higher"), the wellspring of many forms of art ("How do I love thee? Let me count the ways"), and a prime mover in life ("All you need is love"). Yet at the same time, we know that love can lead to disaster (think of many country Western songs) and needs to be managed ("You can't hurry love"). The Ilongots (of the Philippines) resolve the tension between emotional extremes and emotional constraint by balancing knowledge and passion. They are strongly ambivalent about the emotion that is focal in their culture, *liget*, which translates roughly as anger, passion, and energy rolled into one. " 'Without *liget* to move our hearts," Ilongots have told Rosaldo, "there would be no human life." Yet at the same time "[t]he energy that is *liget* can generate both chaos and concentration, distress and industry, a loss of sense and reason, and an experience of clarification and release" (Rosaldo, 1980: 47). *Liget* is more than a necessary evil; it is a vital life force that must be handled for the good of all.

History also reveals an ongoing tension between emotional spontaneity and control. Elias (1978, 1994) analyzed texts about manners (primarily table manners) back to the 13th century in Europe and concluded that the "civilizing process" is grounded in the control of emotion, especially shame, embarrassment, and disgust. Although Elias's thesis is controversial in its strong forms (civilization = emotion control or emotion control has increased linearly over time), he and other historians have documented interesting historical changes both toward and away from emotion control. Stearns and Knapp (1996), for instance, describe evidence for an intensification of grief by the early 19th century in Western Europe and colonial North American, culminating in a "Victorian grief culture" that included "poetic lessons" about death in *McGuffy's Reader*, popular parlor songs about death, and even "death kits" for children's dolls that included mourning apparel and caskets. (Can you imagine a mourning Barbie doll?) But public opinion swung back in the opposite direction beginning early in the 20th century, resulting in the less indulgent and more restrained "therapeutic" approach to grief that is with us today.

Philosophies and Strategies

Mesquita and Frijda (1992: 198) say that "regulation processes [both restrictive and prescriptive] probably are the most widely recognized source of historical as well as cultural variation in emotional phenomena." We might even call them different philosophies of emotion control. For example, Confucians, the Pintupi (Australia), and in some regard the Ilongots use "learning models" (emotion controlled by knowledge), whereas Buddhists in Thailand and northern Nepal favor cognitive strategies (managing feelings through thoughts) (Heelas, 1996: 189). The Ifaluk (South Pacific) use a sociotherapeutic approach to manage *song* (justifiable anger) when they call in an advisor to mediate, as do the A'ara (South Pacific) when they engage in community-based "disentangling" (White, 1990). Still other techniques include making sacrifices to the gods (Chewong of Malaysia) or removing fear by rituals such as crawling between the legs of a high-born woman or chief (Maori of New Zealand) (Heelas, 1996: 189). The Ilongots formerly managed *liget* not only through *beya* (knowledge), but also by hunting heads or, more precisely, by throwing the victim's head to the ground (Rosaldo, 1980: 137–176). The African Dinka make sacrifices, not only to placate the gods but also to manage distressful emotions (Lienhardt, 1961, cited in Heelas, 1996: 189).

Many ways of managing emotion look exotic to outsiders, but others look more familiar. The Ilongots negotiate *liget* and other feelings through public oratorical debate (*purung*). The Utkus (Canada) may use their ultimate weapon, social ostracism, to bring into line children or anthropologists who cannot manage their anger. The Balinese may laugh at and make fun of people who cannot manage their grief. The Ifaluk (South Pacific) advise others to "separate the good from the bad, or divide the head, and then to throw away disruptive thoughts/emotions" (Lutz, 1988b: 97). Ancient Icelanders managed shame and anger by taking revenge (Miller, 1993).

Emotion control can be used not only to restrain the spontaneous emotions of individuals but also to generate emotions, often in a group. The Balinese do not just try to repress their grief; they also try to generate laughter, good feeling, and light-heartedness in its place. Wierzbicka (1994: 175) reports that the Polish language is rich in verbs that imply "[a] kind of voluntary (unchecked) wallowing in a feeling" that "suggest that the experiencer is acting out an involuntary impulse, amplifying it, and giving it full vent." For the Bhatgaon villagers of Fiji, "true *bhaw* (feelings) are 'built' or 'made' " (*banana, karna*) ... for example, speakers frequently use the phrase *prembhaw banana cahiye* ('we must build amity') ... [s]imilarly, an oral invitation to drop by a friend's house is often defined as a chance to 'make' *tamash-abhaw* ('fun')" (Brenneis, 1990: 119).

What Is Real?

What then, is "real" or "genuine" emotion? Wierzbicka (1994: 173) gives an example of the problem, taken from Hoffman, whose emotional philosophy came into contrast with that of her Polish immigrant mother.

> Once, when my mother was very miserable, I told her, full of my newly acquired American wisdom, that she should try to control her feelings. "What do you mean?" she asked, as if this was an idea offered by a member of a computer species. "How can I do that? They are my feelings." My mother cannot imagine tampering with her feelings, which are the most authentic part of her, which are her. (1989: 269)

To people such as those in Bhatgaon (Fiji), however, real emotion is felt and generated in joint performance, whereas individual feelings are fleeting, trivial, and not to be taken as seriously as collective sentiment. It is hard to imagine Hoffman's mother discussing emotion management with someone from Bhatgaon. "Building amity" would probably be seen by her as manipulative and artificial (if it was conceivable at all); you can almost hear her saying, "How can I do that? They are not my feelings." But people from Bhatgaon would probably see Hoffman's mother as self-centered and at the mercy of fleeting moods; you can almost hear them ask, "How can you trust emotions that only 'happen' to you and are not 'built' intentionally?"

How Is Emotional Meaning Constructed Through Communication?

Several cultures hold what we call the *ventilationist* view of emotional suppression; that is, if emotion is not "released" in some way, bad things will happen, often physical illness. We know that the ancient

Greeks debated the value of drama for providing emotional release, with Aristotle arguing the merits of catharsis (whether as medical purgation or as insight has been an issue ever since) (Scheff, 1979: 20–21). According to Heelas, the Utku Eskimos talk about repression and catharsis (1996: 185; see Heelas, 1983: 394), but at the same time, they recognize the inevitability of certain hardships and sorrows and try to bear them with equanimity (Briggs, 1970: 365). The Ifaluk of Micronesia believe that mature persons rid themselves of unwanted thoughts and feelings through verbal expression, and "the lack of expression is seen as a possible precursor to illness or as a sign of mental incapacity," except for the absolute sanction against expression through violence (or even loud or impolite words) (Lutz, 1988b: 96–97). For Nukulaelae Islanders of the Central Pacific, letters are a means of emotional catharsis, "to an extent and of a kind that is rarely found in oral communication" (Besnier, 1995b: 114).

By contrast, on Bali (Indonesia), it is not considered therapeutic but rather dangerous to disclose negative feelings because they weaken the *bayu* (life force) and erode strength. " 'You shall conquer sadness and anger, or you will be sick and our life be in danger' is a cultural proposition of self-evident insight and wisdom" (Wikan, 1990: 270). And "like the Balinese, the Chinese believe that the excessive expression of feelings will disturb the harmony of the body and lead to illness" (Kleinman, cited in Georges, 1995: 20). According to Sun (1991: 32) "when a person is troubled or emotionally distraught – i.e., harbouring 'selfish' feelings – he or she is usually advised to 'think it through' (*xiangtong*) or to 'view things clearly' (*kankai*), 'meaning to put things in a wider and broader context, to see oneself in relation to the total scheme of things, and to exert more self-control." This is quite different from the ventilationist perspective, but it is still consistent with the ancient Greek notion of *katharsis* as clarification. It emphasizes "placid flexibility" in light of a resignation to "bad things and good things" (Sun, 1991: 32).

Dilemmas of Disclosure

The Balinese seldom confess or ventilate strong feelings because they believe that it weakens their bodies, but that is not the only reason. Wikan's informant, Suriati, feared that others would mock her for showing sadness at the death of her fiancé. "They will say, 'Oh, you're a widow!' and they will laugh" (1990: 11). This sounds cruel, but according to Balinese emotional logic, mocking laughter is intended to be therapeutic: "not left at peace to be sad, she becomes an object of a kind of shock treatment whereby the humiliation felt at being the object of laughter shakes her out of self-pitying ways and impresses upon her the supreme value of self-protection and care for others" (p. 171). The Balinese also recognize that if they express negative feelings, others may take advantage of their weakened state to use black magic against them. Close relations are no more trustworthy than strangers, perhaps less so, because "hurt and offense can easily be caused, even inadvertently and unwillingly. And the other person is ideally positioned in terms of sorcery revenge" (p. 83). Writing poetry to express sadness is a common Balinese practice, but the poems are not shared with others.

Fortunately for the Balinese, and for many others as well, there is a safe haven in a professional counselor or healer; on Bali it is the traditional healer, the *balian*. In Wikan's words (1990: 233), "[t]he balian provides an island of hope and encouragement in a sea of fear and distrust." The balian listens to patients and tells them what is wrong. The patient must also believe in the balian and be *cocok* (in harmony) with him or the cure will not work (p. 232). "With them [balians] feelings may be given free vent, fears voiced, and interpersonal problems exposed" (p. 263). In a similar vein, members of a community in Puebla, Mexico, who hold indigenous conceptions of emotional trauma (*susto*) think of it as "soul-loss," in which "a fright causes the loss of the spirit (*tonalli*), and this in turn induces malaise" (Signorini, 1982: 315). The soul is restored by an elaborate ritual in which a healer seeks the cause of the *susto* in a dream, asks approval for the healing ritual of God and his saints, then calls the lost *tonalli* and invites it back into the body (p. 316).

In the South Pacific there is a type of emotional healing ritual called *disentangling*, which is grounded in the belief that hidden negative emotions may cause illness and misfortune, but which does not distinguish clearly among the roles of patient, counselor, and observer/ audience. Members of a family or community meet to talk about interpersonal conflicts and "bad feelings" in order to defuse their destructive potential (White, 1990: 53). But the primary purpose of disentangling is not individual catharsis. "In most cases there is no overt concern for the emotional needs of persons as individuals (i.e., as defined separately from relations with others) and little nonverbal evidence that cathartic release is accomplished in some unrecognized way. The events that are most therapeutic in orientation are primarily concerned with reestablishing social and emotional ties among related persons" (Watson-Gegeo & White, 1990: 12). Similarly, the *pancayat* (public event for the mediation of disputes in Bhatgaon, Fiji) "is said to lead not to the stimulation and release of individual feelings but to a shared experience of some sort" (Brenneis, 1990: 217).

The Canadian Ojibwa also used confession to heal serious illness because they believed that illness was caused by social transgression. Unlike the private confessions made in therapists' offices, however, Ojibwa confessions were public statements made to the group, which also "provided a public forum for stating and restating the core values of Ojibwan culture to members of the group as well as a venue for the socialization of children" (Georges, 1995: 16). The African Ndembu go one step further. The "Ndembu healer orchestrates the confessions of not only the patient, but also those of relatives, neighbors, and other members of the community who must all confess in order that the sick person get well" (Georges, 1995: 17). We might call this *sociotherapy* because the primary goal is to resolve the problem socially, although individual catharsis may also play a part.

How Is Emotional Meaning Both Personal and Social?

Markus and Kitayama (1991) argue that there are two predominant forms of the self that guide emotional experience and expression. One is a more personal self that is *independent* of others, autonomous, made up of unique features, and serves as an internal guide to behavior. This view is most common in the United States and northern Europe (individualistic or low-context cultures). The other view is a more social self that is *interdependent* with others, founded in connection and belonging, and responding flexibly to exigencies in the social situation. This is the view that is most common in Asia, Africa, Latin America, and many parts of southern Europe (collectivist or high-context cultures: Hall, 1977; Hofstede, 1980). Parish (1994: 129) says that in American culture "you can 'lose your identity' in relationships; you 'find yourself' by separating and distancing." Newars (from Nepal) " 'find themselves' in relationships and 'lose themselves' by separating."

According to Markus and Kitayama (1991: 236), people with independent selves become experts at the expression and experience of self-focused emotions such as anger or pride, whereas people with interdependent selves become expert at other-focused emotions such as sympathy or shame. "For those with independent selves, emotional expressions may literally 'express' or reveal the inner feelings such as anger, sadness, and fear. For those with interdependent selves, however, an emotional expression may be more often regarded as a public instrumental action that may or may not be related directly to the inner feelings." Each type of emotion and its expression comes from the self and so is felt as real and genuine, but what is meant by the *self* differs.

The extent to which emotional expressions are more personal or social may also depend on how much people think and talk about them. Heelas (1996: 192) says that "[e]motion talk functions as a kind of spotlight. . . . Emotional elements which have no light thrown on them remain in the dark. And emotions which are focused on become enriched and highlighted in experience." Anthropologists make the useful distinction between hypercognized emotions (those that are thought and talked about a lot) and hypocognized emotions (those that receive little attention and elaboration). Levy (1984a: 227) says that hypercognition "involves a kind of shaping, simplifying, selecting, and standardizing" of emotions through talk, whereas hypocognition leaves emotion in the private realm of "tacit knowledge and preconscious processes." In the United States today, I would point to love as a hypercognized emotion that is talked about, sung about, written about, watched on TV and in movies, and virtually inescapable in the mass media. Shame, on the other hand, is hypocognized in the United States; it is rarely talked about and is perhaps even too shameful to mention in public. In China, however, shame is hypercognized (Shaver et al., 1992).

Emotion Socialization

Differences between hypercognized and hypocognized emotions show up early in small children's emotion knowledge. Shaver et al. (1992: 199) report that "Only 10% of American mothers thought their 30-to 35-month-old children understood ashamed. . . . In contrast, 95% of Chinese mothers of children in the same age group said that these children could understand shame/shyness." How do these differences come about? Lutz and White (1986: 424) say that several studies in other cultures "show emotion to be a frequent topic in child/caregiver conversations and a frequent strategy in their interactions."

No one doubts that messages about emotion help to socialize children in all cultures, but scholars take different positions on how emotion socialization actually works.

> For the universalist, socialization processes work on a set of universal, distinct, internal feelings as well as on a more general emotionality; the child learns to mute or heighten the expression (and perhaps also the subjective experience) of each, much as one adjusts the volume on a radio. Socialization processes also structure the child's environment in ways that make the experience of some emotions more likely. For the constructionist, emotional socialization is the process by which the child is introduced into an emotional life constituted by the discourse of adults with each other and with the young. (Lutz & White, 1986: 424–425)[1]

It is easy to find evidence for both universal and constructionist positions in stories of childhood socialization. For example, Utku Eskimos learn to be nearly anger-free, but they are not born that way. Briggs (1970: 10) reported that Saarak, a 3-year-old, screamed in anger and frustration "when others were a little slow in bending to her will." The Utku expect children to be easily angered because they have no *ihuma* (mind, thought, reason, or understanding), but they don't take anger seriously and may even laugh if the child is not hungry, cold, or ill (p. 111). But if a child loses his temper after age 5 or 6, when he should have developed sufficient *ihuma*, "one of his elders may inquire with scathing quietness: 'Does one think, mistakenly, that he is using his *ihuma*?'" (p. 112). Older children, such as Saarak's sister Raigili, are expected to control their own anger even when assailed by a demanding little sister. In Briggs's words: "It is not easy to learn to relinquish one's toys or one's chewing gum to an insistent little hand, or laughingly to permit the baby to destroy one's proud handiwork" (p. 137). Raigili had her indirect and surreptitious ways of getting back at Saarak and her parents. She might pinch Saarak under the quilt or snatch her toy when adults' backs were turned, but Raigili responded primarily with sullenness: "a passive, but total, resistance to social overtures" (p. 137). She had already learned the Utku way of managing others' emotions – by threatening to disrupt social bonds. After hearing these stories, it is hard to argue that Utku children are born into a world without anger and therefore never experience anger. On the other hand, it is not just that their anger is muted; children old enough to have *ihuma* are gradually brought into the shared emotional

---

[1] Reprinted with permission from the *Annual Review of Anthropology*, Vol. 15, 1986.

life of the group through talk about emotions and clearly communicated expectations about how to control anger. This example offers a reconciliation of the universalist and constructionist views articulated by Lutz and White.

Emotional Communication and Social Roles

All adult Utku are expected to control their anger, but expectations for emotion control often depend at least in part on the person's role in the social order. All of the Ifaluk (South Pacific) are supposed to feel *fago* (compassion/caring), but the higher one's position is in the social hierarchy on Ifaluk, the more frequent and compelling are the contexts in which one is called on to *fago* (compassion/love/sadness) and to take care of (*gamwelar*) others. The Ilongots (Philippines) value *liget* (anger/energy/passion), but it is assumed that young unmarried men have an abundance of *liget* that is reduced by age and "sending forth shoots" (fatherhood). The Balinese all value a "clear and bright face," but not all to the same degree. "[A] young man whose girlfriend dies may act quiet and grave (*nyebeng*), but a marriageable girl stricken with a similar fate should exhibit unmistakable laughter and cheerfulness. . . . Older people may even show deep sorrow . . . and [h]ighly positioned, powerful men will even say, 'Oh no, people will not laugh if they see you sad!' And they are right. No one would – at them" (Wikan, 1990: 24).

As discussed earlier, the Wolof (Senegal) have a caste system based on what they believe are the inherent emotional temperaments of nobles and griots. "Stolidity and sangfroid are normative characteristics of the nobility, who are supposed to be more solid and 'heavy' than the typical lower-caste person who is considered to be relatively 'light-weight,' motile, even volatile. . . ." Nobles take responsible action and do great deeds, but only when roused and enlivened by griots, so that each caste complements the other, not only in terms of duties but also emotionally. And both are appreciated. In the words of one Wolof villager: "What would you rather have – a car that does not move, or a car that can only go a thousand kilometers an hour? . . . Neither one. . . . What you need is both a strong engine and a good set of brakes" (Irvine, 1990: 153).

Communicating emotion is an important way to negotiate roles. One of the most dramatic examples is the well-known phenomenon in Malaysia of "running *amok*," which resulted in apparently random homicidal attacks. A Malay native describes *amok* like this: 'Anger and shame affects overwhelm the spirit, primitive instincts are unleashed, the savage beast that lies sleeping in every human being bursts out of its cage and rages in a wild and reckless fury of destruction' (van Wulfften Palthe, 1936, cited in Winzeler, 1990: 117). Wild and reckless though it may be, the beast seemed to know where it was welcome. *Amok* thrived in traditional Malay culture and not outside of it. Chinese and Arabs living in Malaysia would occasionally go *amok*, but Malays living in Europe never did. *Amok* was common in a traditional Batavian hospital, but stopped when the patients were transferred to a European-style hospital (Winzeler, 1990: 111). And *amok* was not without purpose. "In its original conscious form, amok was an approved form of social control which restricted the abuses of the power of the Malayan ruling sector" (p. 117). One would think twice about harshly punishing a peasant who might run amok.

Other, more benign Malaysian emotions provide justifications or appeals for help during role transitions. When Malaysian men and women approach the age of 25 and remain unmarried, they are especially susceptible to "*gila kahwin*, a desperate need to get married to set up home, and to have children. Observable symptoms of *gila kahwin* may be seen in a person's behaviour towards the opposite sex; in a woman, public flirtation, expressed envy of a friend's married state, children, willingness to accept just any proposal, and the like. The symptoms are less obvious in a man but may be demonstrated in the vacant singing of popular love songs or, in desperate situations, a request to his parents to get him a bride of their choice" (Karim, 1990: 34). Widowed and otherwise socially marginalized Malaysian Indonesians (most often women) are especially susceptible to episodes of *latah*, during which their speech becomes disorganized, they utter obscenities, and they have a compulsion to mimic the speech or actions of onlookers – all involuntary, or so they say after the episode is over (Kenny, 1990: 125). *Latah* victims are "persons in search of a place which they may not be able to find and . . . may broadcast their plight to others" through *latah* (p. 138).

In Malaysia, *amok*, *gila kahwin*, and *latah* are involuntary but nevertheless culturally sanctioned ways of negotiating changing social roles through emotional expression, but emotional expression can also be used intentionally to change the way things are done. Abu-Lughod (1990) describes how an Egyptian Bedouin taped and played love songs on cassettes as a way of protesting arranged marriages. One lyric goes like this: "My warnings are to the old man who imprisons the freedom of youths, who's forgotten a thing called love, affection, desire and burning flames, who's forgotten how strong is the fire of lovers" (p. 40).

Solidified Social Routines and Rituals

Middleton (1989: 193) says that ceremonies are "public events that communicate emotions and guide their expression along the desired channels." In more communal societies, interpersonal problem-solving may blend seamlessly into social ritual. When one Ifaluk confronts another in *song* (justifiable anger), they tend to follow a socially prescribed routine or *script* for managing potential social disruptions. It is not quite a ritual, but is not done ad lib either. The offended party expresses her *song* in a variety of ways, both to the offending party and to others. The offending party, then, is expected to feel the complementary emotion *metagu* (fear/anxiety) and sometimes to make a payback (*paluwen*) – an apology, payment of a fine, or gift of a valued object. Often an "emotional advisor" is called onto the scene, primarily to calm down the offended party by speaking gently to her or him. An emotional advisor might say something like this: "Sweetheart you shouldn't fight because you are a man. If you fight, people will laugh at you. Throw out your 'thoughts/feelings' about that person because she is crazy and confused. . . . If you fight your sister's children will be 'panicked/frightened (*rus*)' " (Lutz, 1988b: 174–176).

It is interesting to note how many rituals surrounding role transitions such as marriage serve the function of managing emotion. Young men and women in colonial America, for example, often tried to conjure up images of lovers, a practice that appears magical to our eyes but that nonetheless served as a face-saving device. As Gillis (1988: 94) says: "Knowing that he or she had been conjured, the dream lover could choose to accept or reject without loss of face or hurt feelings to either party, a device which, in a village community where the roles of lover, friend, and coworker overlapped, was essential to preserving communal solidarity." Rings were exchanged at betrothal because "The ring finger was thought to give direct access to the heart, and precious metals, especially gold, were guaranteed to stir the passions" (p. 99). After betrothal came the "posting of banns," which was "a time of teasing, ritual joking, which tested the couple's willingness to go through with the wedding but also worked to counteract tensions that were invariably present when any single persons were removed from the pool of eligible mates" (p. 100). A sibling who had been passed over in marriage might be forced to "dance shoeless or in green stockings, acting out his or her envy, and thereby reconciling the person to the new situation" (p. 103).

Not only is ritual used to manage emotion, but emotion is also used to reinforce the meaning of rituals. Whitehouse (1996: 710) argued that the absolute and lasting terror produced during Melanesian initiation rituals results in "flashbulb memories" that imprint "a stock of very vivid, disturbing and perhaps enlightening memories which are consciously turned over in the minds of initiates for years to come, and indeed may accompany them to the grave." The shared terror also produces strong bonds among the initiates. "The bonds of solidarity once forged cannot easily be revoked or extended. They encompass those people who actually endured the terrifying experience together, and separate them forever from the rest of humanity" (p. 712).

Funeral rituals have also changed in response to changing views of death. Stearns and Knapp (1996: 137) note that in the 19th century, embalming and the use of cosmetics on corpses became more common "to direct emotions away from decaying flesh to the bittersweet grief at a loved one's loss." Especially for children's deaths, "gravestone euphemisms about death as sleep, or as going home, expressed the grief-induced need to see death as something less than final." Cultural variations occur too, ranging from the exhausting wailing of Gusii (African) funerals to the merriment (relatively speaking) of the Irish wake. For the Hmong, reed pipes are vital to funeral rituals because they guide the souls of the deceased through the journey from the world of the living to the world of the spirits (Bliatout, 1993: 86). The American Lakota Sioux sometimes perform the ritual of *wanagi yuha* (retaining the person's spirit) by taking a piece of the dead person's hair and keeping in it one's home for a year, "often speaking to the dead person, who is understood to be present in the hair" (Brokenleg & Middleton, 1993: 110). The Judaic tradition may include a "meal of consolation" prepared by friends and relatives that often includes symbolic foods such as eggs, which are a sign of life and rebirth (Cytron, 1993: 119). This is just a sampling.

Across cultures and historical periods, where does responsibility for emotion lie – with the individual or with society? The answer is both. Canadian Utku Eskimo children are socialized by adults to feel and express emotion as Utkus do (suggesting social responsibility), and yet, if they do not conform to expectations, they may be criticized or even ostracized until they do (indicating personal responsibility). The Egyptian Bedouin youth studied by Abu-Lughod (1990) knew that expressing passionate love was both a personal challenge to a widely accepted social practice of arranging marriages and, at the same time, a way to get others to support him in defying his own father and uncles, thus mustering social support for his individual situation. The lesson is that emotional communication is both a personal and a social responsibility, but in addition, it is a way of negotiating between social norms and personal concerns that can be seen in a variety of cultures.

How Do Emotion Messages Communicate Moral Meaning?

Cultures tend to target certain emotional states as ideals that members should strive to attain and to warn people against other emotions that are especially dangerous. Emotional saints and sinners are good barometers of the moral values that are sacred to a culture, although almost nobody fulfills those ideals always and in all situations. St. Catherine of Siena, for example, strove to enact the religious ideal of humility by overcoming disgust by washing sores and drinking pus (Miller, 1997: 157–161), but this is not an ideal that many of us could attain even if we wanted to. Cultural ideals also vary from one situation to another; for example, the Balinese aspire to emotional control (except at cockfights). Festivals and celebrations are also common occasions when the ordinary rules of emotional control are suspended temporarily. Emotional ideals are also dynamic. In early America, for example, jealousy was viewed as righteous in the defense of power, whereas now it is usually seen as petty and immature (at least relatively speaking) (Stearns, 1989).

Emotional Ideals

For the Canadian Utku Eskimos, gentleness is the most highly valued emotion. At the other extreme, "bad temper (*huaq, urulu, ningaq*), stinginess, and unhelpfulness, [are] three of the most damning traits that one Eskimo can ascribe to another" (Briggs, 1970: 195). The Utku also strongly value emotional control over emotional spontaneity; "indeed, the maintenance of equanimity under trying circumstances is *the* essential sign of maturity, of adulthood" (p. 4). And above all, one should control anger. Direct expression of *anger at injustice* is not socially acceptable among the Utku Eskimos even if the expression is subtle and the anger is completely justified, as Briggs learned the hard way (1970: 274–291). She tells the story of an incident in which White Canadian fishermen (*kaplunas*) borrowed for several weeks canoes that belonged to the Utkus, which they needed desperately in order to move camp, set fishing nets, gather food, and ferry people across the river. When the *kaplunas* damaged one canoe and then asked to borrow the only remaining good Utku canoe (which Briggs knew they did not want to lend), she explained the hardship that the Utku would suffer to the *kapluna* guide in a cold voice and without smiling (showing admirable emotional constraint when another *kapluna* like myself might have gone ballistic). Later she suspected that she had violated the Utku emotional/moral code when she noticed that no one was coming to visit her. Her suspicions was verified when she read what someone wrote about her in a letter sent outside the camp. "She is very annoying (*urulu*), because she scolds (*huaq*) and one is tempted to scold her. She gets angry easily. Because she is so annoying, we wish more and more that she would leave" (1970: 286). What to Briggs was more than justified anger and even admirable restraint was to the Utku "getting angry easily."

At the core of morality for the Ifaluk islanders of the South Pacific is the emotion *fago*, which combines *compassion, love, and sadness*. Although it may seem strange to foreigners to combine love and sadness, for the Ifaluk *fago* "refers to one's relationship with a more unfortunate other, rather than to a more atomistic internal feeling such as 'sadness' " (Lutz, 1986: 273). The Ifaluk feel *fago* for disabled people, relatives away from the island, and people singing love songs (Lutz, 1988b: 120). Like the American English word *caring*, *fago* encompasses personal feelings, interpersonal connections, and action (as in 'caring for'). In Lutz's words, the assumption underlying *fago* – "that a durable and automatic link exists between the suffering of one person and the nurturing of others – lies at the heart of Ifaluk emotional and moral life" (p. 121). It is "perhaps the ultimate quality of good people and competent adults . . . individuals will be praised by saying of them 'She [or he] is good. She [has] fago for people' " (p. 140). The value of *fago* for the Ifaluk is not mysterious. They live on a crowded half-square-mile coral atoll that is at most 15 feet above sea level and is regularly hit by typhoons with winds of up to 140 miles per hour. They need each other.

The morally ideal person on Bali (Indonesia) subjugates personal feelings to those of the group. She seldom or never communicates negative emotions that intrude on others' positive feelings and consistently displays a clear and bright face. Wikan (1990: 9) says that *polos* (always calm [*tenang*], never hot-tempered or rash, never asking for much) ranks at the apex of the scale of values by which Balinese are judged. At the nadir of those values are expressions of anger, fear, and especially sadness that "undermines the strength and steadfastness of one's life force" (p. 8) and is also seen as selfish. Venting a feeling of desperation in places outside of the house can be the "clearest and most undeniable sign of madness" (p. 24). Wikan reports the story of Wayan, who fell into despair after being fired from his job and rebelled by writing emphatic letters of protest, scolding and upbraiding his wife, and behaving strangely in public. One of Wayan's former colleagues wrote of his situation: "No, Wayan is not mad, only extreme and deviant, but society does not have concepts to characterize deviance. They call everything mad – *gila*. . . . Society punishes such deviance. It is as if they say 'Who do you think you are to think you will change us, set yourself above everyone else?' " (p. 220). The common good, as defined by conventional moral and emotional standards, is the moral underpinning of emotional expectations on Bali.

In all cultures, however, emotion ideals orient individuals to the moral standards most valued by a society, whether they be compassion, courage, or cheerfulness. Gerber (1985: 153) explains how this works, using Samoa as an example:

> By defining "right" feelings in a consonant manner, adherence to the values of mutual aid and hierarchy is not only made surer; it is rendered less painful. A Samoan gives, therefore, not only because he or she has been trained to view giving as morally correct but also because his or her training has created a disposition to feel such an act as "natural," seeming to arise out of the very depths of his or her being.

Judgments of Character

What is "right" and "natural" emotionally seems absolutely certain from within a culture; conversely, different emotional standards seem absolutely "wrong" and "unnatural" from the outside. Examples abound of character judgments of people from other cultures or subcultures that are based on emotional expressions and are unflattering at best. Kochman (1981) described Black Americans' interpretations of the emotional styles of Whites, and vice versa. "Blacks regard more subdued or restrained expressive outputs [of Whites] as 'cold,' 'dead,' or not 'for real'.... Whites, for their part, favor more modest and subdued outputs, degrading more forceful expressive behavior as 'irresponsible' or in 'bad taste.' " Blacks see Whites as phony and uptight, whereas Whites see Blacks as wild (1981: 107).

A century earlier, Darwin cited Humboldt, who, in Darwin's words, "quotes without a protest the sneer of the Spaniard [toward the Indians], "How can those be trusted, who know not how to blush?" (1872/1965: 318, noted in Harré & Parrott, 1996: 306). Darwin himself argued against the idea that non-Europeans were incapable of blushing (and therefore were shameless) by citing evidence from Hindoos, the Semitic races, Chinese, Malays, Polynesians, and North American Indians and negroes [*sic*] who were observed to blush (1872/1965: 315–318). We may suppose, however, that he made the argument precisely because this was a fairly commonly held belief among his contemporaries.

Levy (1973) notes that the first European visitors to Tahiti (starting in 1766) thought the Tahitians were "expressive, open, easy to read" and had a "lively, clear, engaging expressiveness" . . . or "so they seemed at first" (p. 97). Later the Europeans came to wonder how genuine those expressions were because they could be produced or changed at will. What the Europeans did not understand is that Tahitians do not distinguish between group-generated and individually felt emotions, so that they genuinely felt emotions that could be produced or changed at will (Middleton, 1989: 194). Captain Cook came close, however, in writing that "The chief, his wife and daughter but especially the two latter, hardly every ceased weeping [on Cook's departure]. I will not pretend to say whether it was real or feigned grief they showed on this occasion. Perhaps it was a mixture of both" (cited in Levy, 1973: 97). Unfortunately, we will probably never know what the 18th-century Tahitians thought of the emotional character of the Europeans.

Briggs gives us both sides of the emotional (mis)understanding as a *kapluna* [White woman] living with the Utku Eskimos. She says that European Canadian hunters saw the Utku Eskimos as "obligingly acquiescent" (to use her term, 1970: 276), or perhaps even docile pushovers (to use mine), but the judgments that the Utku made of European North Americans were harsher. "The Utku . . . define unkindness and bad temper more broadly than we do, and condemn it far more stringently, with the result that bad temper and aggressive-ness are two of the first qualities that they notice about us, as indi-cated, for example, by the stories that children bring back from board-ing school. In the Utku view, *kaplunas* are about as bad-tempered as the dogs from which they consider we are descended" (Briggs, 1970: 329).

To What Extent Can We Share Emotional Meanings Across Culture and History?

Is the intercultural emotional communication glass half empty or half full? In teaching this material to undergraduates, I find myself using exotic examples of cultural differences to shatter the myth that on an emotional level we are all alike. Sometimes the students respond by saying, "How can that be?" "How can they have NO words for inner states?" "How can they think of emotion as occurring between, not within, people?" But they also respond at times by saying, "Well, that's a lot like us." "We know that feeling; we just don't think of it as an important emotion." Or "We might respond in a similar way in those circumstances." There is much truth to both sides. The danger is that when we emphasize differences, the contrast makes others seem nonhuman and threatening, but when we emphasize similarities, we may assimilate them into our own narrow view of what is human and fail to understand or appreciate the variations in human emo-tional experience and expression.

Miller (1993: 112) offers what might be the seeds of a partial reso-lution. He writes that "[p]art of the reason that Lear and Hamlet travel so well is that we tell ourselves repeatedly that they do; they are part of a consciously maintained tradition that makes them part of us and not exemplars of the Other." Perhaps the Other can be part of Us if we make it so. Karim (1990: 12) says that "emotion and action consti-tute the workshop of experience on which culture is built." Perhaps it is possible to recognize that the human workshops of experience on the little island that is susceptible to typhoons where the Ifaluk live or the frozen tundra that is the homeland of the Utku will produce different emotional handiwork than the teeming, affluent cities of the West. In a world where people are becoming more deeply interrelated and where technologies prod an incredible rate of change, we need to appreciate many different ways of living, including different ways that humans live their emotional lives.

Epilogue

What Is the Future of Emotional Meaning?

Few people want to take the audacious step of speculating on what our emotional lives will be like in the future, and justifiably so. For one thing, you have to admit your social constructionist tendencies to believe that our emotional futures will vary one whit from the past. If emotion is predetermined in our genes, our emotional tomorrows will be very much like our emotional yesterdays, with change measured not over centuries or millennia but over centuries *of* millennia. Research on the history of emotion has convinced me, however, that this just isn't so. Earlier time periods, even measured in decades, show emotional profiles different from the ones we have now, and we have no reason to believe ours will hold still for the next generation.

Nevertheless, believing *that* emotional meaning will change tells us nothing about *how* it will change. The truth of the matter is – nobody knows. Historians, I believe, give us better-informed speculations than others, but they are inclined to limit their speculations to changes that can be glimpsed now. They are also *very clear* that the one thing we know with certainty from the history of emotion is that we cannot predict anything with certainty. All manner of unforeseen events, technological and cultural developments, changes in demographic patterns, and sheer human serendipity influence the course of history in unpredictable ways. The history of emotion is no exception (Stearns, 1994).

I still believe that knowing that we are probably wrong in our speculation is no reason to refrain from speculating, if for no other reason than that it makes us examine the here-and-now more closely and more critically. Perhaps the trends we see now will be magnified in the future or perhaps they will disappear; we cannot know. We do know, however, that now is the only time we can do anything about

235

them, and if we have learned anything from this book (both you and I), it is that we *can* do something about them both individually and collectively. We can be emotionally creative by paying attention to our feelings, by cultivating certain habits of thought, and by encouraging desired emotional stances in others as well as ourselves.

Perhaps the seeds of emotional change also lurk in dreams, myths, and inchoate urges that are as yet unacknowledged (*hypocognized* in Levy's terms; Levy, 1984b) but that are ready to blossom as the environment becomes more favorable for their growth. Perhaps we will verbalize the inchoate urge to escape the human-dominated world as feeling *wilding*. Perhaps we will create a new word for feelings aroused by aesthetic experience (Lazarus & Lazarus, 1994: 134–135) as *feeling artilated*. Perhaps we will bring the extinct emotion of *accidie* back to life. (It meant "boredom, dejection or even disgust with fulfilling one's religious duty"; Harré & Finlay-Jones, 1986). Perhaps we will invent as many different words for hate as we have for love (*fleeting defatuation, immature puppy hate*, or *mild fondlessness*). Perhaps we will learn to wave all of our fingers from our cars to apologize rather than one finger to accuse. Perhaps we will borrow emotional practices from other cultures – learning not to litigate or fight over disagreements, but to disentangle them (Watson-Gegeo & White, 1990).

We may try to hold on to the emotional status quo, but it will probably be in vain. Whether we want them to or not, our emotional lives are likely to change, if for no other reason than that the rest of our lives are changing and emotions adapt. As Averill and Nunley (1992: 320) write about emotional creativity and change:

> Increasingly, however, the choice is not ours alone to make. Creativity in other spheres – scientific and technological innovations, for example – is changing the way we work, the way we relate to one another, the way we live and die. And the pace is quickening. As individuals and as a society, we are doomed if we are not equally creative in the domain of emotion, if the only ways we know how to respond are the ways fitted to past circumstances.

Work on cultural differences also demonstrates that emotions are attuned and adapted to the circumstances in which people live. In Markus and Kitayama's (1949: 399–340) words, "emotions . . . develop as individuals actively (personally and collectively) adapt and adjust to their immediate sociocultural, semiotic environment. Emotions allow and foster this adaptation and they result from it."

What changes are coming our way, and how do they seem to be

affecting us emotionally? The historian Peter Stearns (1994) has argued that one trend that has gained momentum throughout the 20th century for Americans is to value emotional moderation. In the earlier Victorian era, certain passions, like righteous indignation for men and intense mother love for women, were considered valuable to society, but nowadays even these are considered dangerous. Now Americans are "cool" (that is, emotionally controlled), and strong, intense emotions are seen as threats to personal and social well-being (e.g., "You are losing it – get a grip!"). There are some exceptions, but they are made for intense feelings in domains that are removed from everyday life, like therapy and leisure (e.g., football fan(atic)s and bungy jumping). Rarely is passion that is strongly expressed admired in domains where it counts – on the job, in parenting, or in response to moral transgressions. Using a much more critical tone, Meštrović (1997: 44) describes the current emotional atmosphere as a "bland, mechanical, mass-produced yet oppressive ethic of niceness."

Stearns (1994) does not see any big changes on the horizon, but he does see evidence of a few modifications. Grief may be modified by critics who say that contemporary Americans fight death or hide from death more than is natural or healthy. They offer in its place the hospice movement and a more embracing approach to grieving (pp. 286–287). We can only speculate on what will happen to ways of dying and grieving when death comes for the hugely influential baby boom generation. Stearns also notes that many commentators are also concerned about Americans becoming too free and too violent in their expressions of anger, although this may be yet another example of cracking down on emotions that are out of control (pp. 287–288).

In the last few years, emotion control has been debated on the best-seller lists. Goleman's widely read book *Emotional Intelligence* (1995, drawing on the work of Saarni, Salovey, and others) advanced the thesis that people, especially children, who know how to control their feelings will get along better in the world. On the other side of the debate (and also on the best-seller list) was Moore's *The Care of the Soul* (1992, drawing on work by Hillman), which defended the wisdom of emotions on the grounds that profound truth is to be found by exploring rather than controlling feelings. My own view is that control still reigns (consistent with Stearns), but it is interesting to see that at least the American literati are engaging the issue.

Another notable trend is defining good emotions as "feel-good" emotions and bad emotions as "feel-bad" emotions (Sommers, 1984a,

1984b). According to this view, guilt and sorrow should be avoided, and joy and enthusiasm should know no bounds. Stearns and Knapp argue that "consumerism helped create a new division between pleasant and unpleasant emotions, the former associated with 'happiness' and often with the savoring of material objects or sexual release" (1996: 146; Stearns, 1994: 210–211). The negative emotions, presumably, are associated with unnecessary hardship and deprivation. On a similar note, Miller (1993: 138) observes that "the trivial world of appearance motivates us more, is inescapably present, and hence takes more commitments of time and energy than the serious world of essences. We will elect people to office who steal, lie, commit adultery, betray friends and values they have professed allegiance to, but not people who stumble out of airplanes." What is good is what feels good and what looks good (in other words, what is attractive in the dual sense of having a beautiful appearance and pulling you toward it). What is bad is what feels bad and is repulsive (in the sense of ugly and pushing you away). Viewing emotions solely in terms of personal gratification or attraction rather than in terms of their value for the greater social and moral good is, in the larger historical and cultural scheme of things, unusual indeed.

A related and intriguing trend is for emotions to become more strongly linked to objects and less to other people, perhaps because objects appear to give more unqualified pleasure and are certainly more controllable than other people. Stearns (1994: 212–214) cites the changes in the use of dolls and toys from vehicles for imparting important moral, spiritual, and practical lessons and skills (think of Hopi kachina dolls or toy bows and arrows, for instance) to a source of love, attachment, and emotional comfort (think of Linus's blanket). There are also emotional comforts to be found for adults in goods that are "alluring," "bewitching," and "enticing" (i.e., pleasurable) rather than simply "healthy," "sanitary," or "warm" (functional), or so advertisers would have people believe (Stearns, 1994: 210). Meštrović claims that the marketing of feelings has now gone so far that "advertisements these days sell feelings that have no relationship to the product at all" (1997: 12; Rago, 1989).

Commentators seem to have somewhat opposing views about changes in how people are linked to one another emotionally. On the one hand, it seems that we have turned inward, thinking of our emotions as more personal, subjective, and private (especially the intense or unacceptable ones that we should be able to control). Solomon (1990: 37), for example, notes the rise of "affective individualism" in the sense that "we seem to have more inner feelings and pay more attention to them, but we seem to have fewer feelings about others and the state of the world and pay less attention to them." This is consistent with the view that emotions have come to serve personal gratification rather than social and moral functions.

On the other hand, Meštrović (1997, drawing on Riesman, 1950) argues that our emotions are becoming more strongly shaped by the opinions of others and by the media. "[P]rivate, idiosyncratic and perhaps dissenting emotions must succumb to the emotions of the group, and these group emotions are predetermined and pre-packaged" (p. 55). The media show us how to feel about O. J. Simpson (that he was as much victim as victimizer) and the war in Bosnia (genocide that was not really Americans' concern), to use Meštrović's examples, or, to use mine, that Saddam Hussein is a modern-day Hitler whose expansionism *is* our concern. Meštrović's implicit argument that emotions have been transformed from personal, moral passions into "synthetic, quasi-emotions" manipulated by the culture industry (p. xi) is, in my view, largely overstated given the evidence that emotions have always been shaped in significant ways by the expectations and reactions of others, often through whatever media were available, be they face-to-face interaction, public meetings, or newspapers and books. Nevertheless, he does draw attention to the vast power of the global electronic media to shape the emotions of billions of people because of the sheer scope of their influence.

What I believe may produce the greatest historical change in emotion, however, is not the hegemonic content of the global electronic media, but the ways in which they shape human consciousness. As McLuhan (1964) suggested, the medium itself may be the (emotional) message. Here is the argument, which is pieced together and extrapolated from ideas by Ong (1982), Abram (1996), and Meštrović (1997) but is at root speculative.

In oral cultures (that is, cultures whose primary medium of communication is face-to-face interaction), emotion is immediate, sensual, and interactive. "Communicative meaning is always, in its depths, affective; it remains rooted in the sensual dimensions of experience, born of the body's native capacity to resonate with other bodies and with the landscape as a whole" (Abram, 1996: 74). As Merleau-Ponty (1962, cited in Abram, 1996: 74) describes it, "I do not see anger or a threatening attitude as a psychic fact hidden behind the gesture, I read anger in it. The gesture *does not make me think of anger*, it is anger itself." Heelas (1996: 181) notes that Homeric Greeks identified 'joy' with going to battle "to the extent that the same word (χαρμη) is used for both the emotion and the activity. Joy is 'the spirit of battle.' " Emotion and interaction were inextricable, with each completely penetrating the other.

Things changed, however, with the invention of writing. Writing cultivated the capacity to disengage oneself from involving, sensory, emotional interaction in order to pause and reflect about it. That is, of course, the advantage of writing when it comes to dealing with trauma, as discussed in Chapter 4. You get a different perspective on experience. It seem less vivid, less overwhelming, something you can turn over in your mind (and on paper). But the price you pay is to "deny or deaden that life, promoting a massive distrust of sensorial experience while valorizing an abstract realm of ideas hidden behind or beyond the sensory appearances" (Abram, 1996: 72).[1] Deadening immediate sensory reactions also permits a greater degree of control because you can pause and imagine different ways of construing the situation and different scenarios that might be played out. More important, as literacy becomes widespread, emotional control becomes not only possible but even expected by the culture. It may not be a coincidence that the rise of literacy and the widespread distribution of print correspond to what Elias (1994) called the *civilizing process*, or the rise of social control of emotions that he analyzed from the 13th through the 18th centuries in Western Europe.

Now we are in the throes of the electronic revolution, with its capacity for *virtual* experience, currently in the form of TV, movies, and interactive games (with many new forms to come, no doubt) overlaid on oral and written cultures. No one really knows what effects electronic communication have on our emotions, but we can speculate. First, virtual experience has the immediate and sensory qualities of direct experience, but without the interactive part. A powerful movie, for example, engages our emotions almost as much as a fight with the neighbor, but the difference is that with the neighbor

---

[1] If this strikes you as Platonic, I urge you to read Abram's discussion of how Plato stood "on the threshhold between the oral and written cultures of Greece" (p. 108) and how the two patterns of perception are described and analyzed in the *Phaedrus* (Abram, 1996: Chap. 4).

you can (and probably should) do something other than indulge the feelings. You should talk to him, try to understand his feelings, and perhaps take some action. You don't need to do that at the movies, and you would probably be thrown out if you did (the rare cases in which people talk to the computer or TV notwithstanding). The media permit you to feel a much wider range of compelling human emotions than ordinary life would normally foster *with no consequences whatsoever*. You can experience the terror of being chased by a homicidal maniac, the love of the man or woman of your dreams, or the disgust of being slimed by a space alien, all the while sitting in a comfortable chair eating popcorn. It is the ideal solution for members of a "cool" society who may hunger for intense emotions but are expected to control them in everyday life. That is the good news.

The bad news is that virtual experience may detach emotion from action, with two types of detrimental consequences. One is that the emotional habits of virtual experience may make us disinclined to act on any feelings, whether based on virtual reality or not. The war in the former Yugoslavia is the most meaningful example to Meštrović (as the grandson of a Croatian immigrant). He argues that the world sat by and watched the genocide (aka *ethnic cleansing*) on TV, was horrified, and yet did nothing because "everyone knows that emotions carry no burden, no responsibility to act" (1997: 56). Inaction in the face of genocide is not new to the electronic age, of course, but dramatic and vivid awareness of the actual atrocities coupled with inaction may very well be. In addition, when people witness atrocities, disasters, and other forms of human suffering day after day, year after year, there is the very real risk of emotional overload. The purpose of emotion is, after all, to alert people to situations that deserve priority, but how do you prioritize when one high-priority situation comes after another? Perhaps you give up and become desensitized or you wait to respond only to those situations that touch you personally.

A second consequence of detaching emotional experience from action may be that when people are faced with the opportunity or even the necessity for action prompted by emotion, they do not handle it well. They may not be used to having emotional experiences with real-life consequences, so perhaps they have not developed skills for responding interactively to consequences as they develop (as oral cultures would promote) or responding reflectively by anticipating consequences (as written cultures would promote). Perhaps they are inclined to respond with no concern for consequences at all, as apparently do many of the children whom Goleman (1995) identifies as needing to cultivate their emotional intelligence.

Another possible negative effect of virtual emotional experience is that it makes us suspicious of all of our emotional reactions, period. After all, how is our compassion supposed to know the difference between the victims of a simulated earthquake and those of a real earthquake? It is hard to talk ourselves *out of* being upset when a woman we have been watching for two hours is crushed by a falling building just because it is "only a movie," but it is equally hard to talk ourselves *into* being even more upset about a woman halfway around the world whom we don't even know being crushed by a building because it is "for real." Our emotions may not know the difference between fact and fiction. Meštrović (1997: xv) believes the result is that "ambivalence and ambiguity make emotional stances unlikely." People do not know what to believe or they hear so many equally compelling sides of a story that they cannot figure out what is real, and they have no passionate commitment to anything. And besides, it is more convenient to be able to flip the channel to feel whatever suits us at the moment.

Baudrillard said that in our electronic world "we are becoming like cats, slyly parasitic, enjoying an indifferent domesticity. Nice and snug in 'the social,' our historic passions have withdrawn into the glow of an artificial cosiness, and our half-closed eyes now seek little other than the peaceful parade of television pictures."[2] But I, for one, don't really believe that. Our historic passions were always as much social as physical, and we thrive on thrills as much as on peace. People will strive for rich emotional experiences, even though when, where, and how they experience them will undoubtedly change. Even more than the unexamined life, the unemotional life may not be worth living.

[2] *The Columbia Dictionary of Quotations* (1993). New York: Columbia University Press.

References

Abram, D. (1996). *The spell of the sensuous: Perception and language in a more-than-human world*. New York: Pantheon Books.

Abu-Lughod, L. (1990). Shifting politics in Bedouin love poetry. In C. A. Lutz & L. Abu-Lughod (Eds.), *Language and the politics of emotion* (pp. 24–45). Cambridge: Cambridge University Press.

Adams, P., with Mylander, M. (1993). *Gesundheit!* Rochester, VT: Healing Arts Press.

Albas, C., & Albas, D. (1988). Emotion work and emotion rules: The case of exams. *Qualitative Sociology, 11*, 259–274.

Albrecht, T. L., Burleson, B. R., & Goldsmith, D. (1994). Supportive communication. In M. L. Knapp & G. R. Miller (Eds.), *Handbook of interpersonal communication* (2nd ed.) (pp. 419–449). Thousand Oaks, CA: Sage.

Alessandri, S. M., & Lewis, M. (1993). Parental evaluation and its relation to shame and pride in young children. *Sex Roles, 29*, 335–343.

Andersen, P. A. (1985). Nonverbal immediacy in interpersonal communication. In A. W. Siegman & S. Feldstein (Eds.), *Multichannel integrations of nonverbal behavior* (pp. 1–36). Hillsdale, NJ: Erlbaum.

Andersen, P. A., & Guerrero, L. K. (1998a). The bright side of relational communication: Interpersonal warmth as a social emotion. In P. A. Andersen & L. K. Guerrero (Eds.), *The handbook of communication and emotion* (pp. 303–329). San Diego, CA: Academic Press.

Andersen, P. A., & Guerrero, L. K. (Eds.). (1998b). *The handbook of communication and emotion*. San Diego, CA: Academic Press.

Andersen, P. A., & Guerrero, L. K. (1998c). Principles of communication and emotion in social interaction. In P. A. Andersen & L. K. Guerrero (Eds.), *The handbook of communication and emotion* (pp. 49–96). San Diego, CA: Academic Press.

Andersen, P. A., Guerrero, L. K. Buller, D. B., & Jorgensen, P. F. (1998). An empirical comparison of three theories of nonverbal immediacy exchange. *Human Communication Research, 24*, 501–535.

Appadurai, A. (1990). Topographies of the self: Praise and emotion in Hindu India. In C. A. Lutz & L. Abu-Lughod (Eds.), *Language and the politics of emotion* (pp. 92–112). Cambridge: Cambridge University Press.

243

Argyle, M. (1987). *The psychology of happiness*. London: Methuen.

Argyle, M., & Dean, J. (1965). Eye contact, distance and affiliation. *Sociometry*, *28*, 289–304.

Armon-Jones, C. (1986). The social functions of emotions. In R. Harré (Ed.), *The social construction of emotion* (pp. 57–82). Oxford: Basil Blackwell.

Arnston, P., & Droge, D. (1987). Addressing the value dimension of health communication: A social science perspective. *Journal of Applied Communication Research, 16*, 1–15.

Atkins, C. J., Kaplan, R. M., & Toshima, M. T. (1991). Close relationships in the epidemiology of cardiovascular disease. In W. H. Jones & D. Perlman (Eds.), *Advances in personal relationships* (Vol. 3, pp. 207–231). London: Jessica Kingsley Publishers.

Aune, K. S., Buller, D. B., & Aune, R. K. (1996). Display rule development in romantic relationships: Emotion management and perceived appropriateness of emotions across relationship stages. *Human Communication Research, 23*, 115–145.

Averill, J. R. (1982). *Anger and aggression: An essay on emotion*. New York: Springer-Verlag.

Averill, J. R. (1986). The acquisition of emotions during adulthood. In R. Harré (Ed.), *The social construction of emotion* (pp. 98–115). Oxford: Basil Blackwell.

Averill, J. R. (1993). Illusions of anger. In R. B. Felson & J. T. Tedeschi (Eds.), *Aggression and violence* (pp. 171–192). Washington, DC: American Psychological Association.

Averill, J. R., & Nunley, E. P. (1992). *Voyages of the heart: Living an emotionally creative life*. New York: Macmillan.

Ayer, A. J. (1946/1995). Emotivism. Reprinted in L. P. Pojman (Ed.), *Ethical theory: Classical and contemporary readings* (2nd ed., pp. 412–417). Belmont, CA: Wadsworth.

Backman, C., & Secord, P. (1959). The effect of perceived liking on interpersonal attraction. *Human Relations, 12*, 379–384.

Baier, A. C. (1994). *Moral prejudices: Essays on ethics*. Cambridge, MA: Harvard University Press.

Bailey, F. G. (1983). *The tactical uses of passion*. Ithaca, NY: Cornell University Press.

Balcom, D., Lee, R. G., & Tager, J. (1995). The systemic treatment of shame in couples. *Journal of Marital and Family Therapy, 21*, 55–65.

Bales, R. F. (1950). *Interaction process analysis*. Cambridge, MA: Addison-Wesley.

Banse, R., & Scherer, K. R. (1996). Acoustic profiles in vocal emotion expression. *Journal of Personality and Social Psychology, 70*, 614–636.

Barbee, A. P., Rowatt, T. L., & Cunningham, M. R. (1998). When a friend is in need: Feelings about seeking, giving, and receiving social support. In P. A. Andersen & L. K. Guerrero (Eds.), *Communication and emotion: Theory, research, and applications* (pp. 281–301). San Diego, CA: Academic Press.

Barnett, M. A. (1987). Empathy and related responses in children. In N. Eisenberg & J. Strayer (Eds.), *Empathy and its development* (pp. 146–162). Cambridge: Cambridge University Press.

Barr, C. L., & Kleck, R. E. (1995). Self–other perception of the intensity of facial expressions of emotion: Do we know what we show? *Journal of Personality and Social Psychology, 68,* 608–618.

Batson, C. D., & Oleson, D. C. (1991). Current status of the empathy-altruism hypothesis. In M. S. Clark (Ed.), *Prosocial behavior* (pp. 62–85). Newbury Park, CA: Sage.

Batson, C. D., Turk, C. L., Shaw, L. L., & Klein, T. R. (1995). Information function of empathic emotion: Learning that we value the other's welfare. *Journal of Personality and Social Psychology, 68,* 300–313.

Baumeister, R. F. (1997). *Evil: Inside human violence and cruelty.* New York: W. H. Freeman.

Baumeister, R. F., & Leary, M. (1995). The need to belong: Desire for interpersonal attachments as a fundamental human motivation. *Psychological Bulletin, 117,* 497–529.

Baumeister, R. F., Stillwell, A. M., & Heatherton, T. F. (1994). Guilt: An interpersonal approach. *Psychological Bulletin, 115,* 243–267.

Baumeister, R. F., Stillwell, A., & Wotman, S. R. (1990). Victim and perpetrator accounts of interpersonal conflict: Autobiographical narratives about anger. *Journal of Personality and Social Psychology, 59,* 994–1005.

Baumeister, R. F., & Wotman, S. R. (1992). *Breaking hearts: The two sides of unrequited love.* New York: Guilford Press.

Bavelas, J. B., Black, A., Chovil, N., & Mullet, J. (1990). *Equivocal communication.* Newbury Park, CA: Sage.

Bavelas, J. B., Black, A., Lemery, C. R., & Mullett, J. (1986). "I *show* how you feel": Motor mimicry as a communicative act. *Journal of Personality and Social Psychology, 50,* 322–329.

Baxter, L. A. (1988). A dialectical perspective on communication strategies in relationship development. In S. W. Duck (Ed.), *Handbook of personal relationships* (pp. 257–273). New York: Wiley.

Baxter, L. A., & Bullis, C. (1986). Turning points in developing romantic relationships. *Human Communication Research, 12,* 469–493.

Baxter, L. A., & Wilmot, W. W. (1984). Secret tests: Social strategies for acquiring information about the state of the relationship. *Human Communication Research, 11,* 171–201.

Bellelli, G. (1995). Knowing and labeling emotions: The role of social sharing. In J. A. Russell, J. Fernandez-Dols, A. Manstead, & J. Wellenkamp (Eds.), *Everyday conceptions of emotion* (pp. 491–504). Dordrecht, the Netherlands: Kluwer.

Berscheid, E. (1983). Emotion. In H. H. Kelley, E. Berscheid, A. Christensen, J. H. Harvey, T. L. Huston, G. Levinger, E. McClintock, L. A. Peplua, & D. R. Petersen (Eds.), *Close relationships* (pp. 110–168). New York: W. H. Freeman.

Berscheid, E. (1990). Contemporary vocabularies of emotion. In B. S. Moore & A. M. Isen (Eds.), *Affect and social behavior* (pp. 22–38). Cambridge: Cambridge University Press.

Besnier, N. (1995a). The appeal and pitfalls of cross-disciplinary dialogues. In J. A. Russell, J.-M. Fernandez-Dols, A. S. R. Manstead, & J. C. Wellenkamp (Eds.), *Everyday conceptions of emotion* (pp. 559–570). Dordrecht, the Netherlands: Kluwer.

Besnier, N. (1995b). *Literacy, emotion, and authority.* Cambridge: Cambridge University Press.

Besnier, N. (1995c). The politics of emotion in Nukulaelae gossip. In J. A. Russell, J.-M. Fernandez-Dols, A. S. R. Manstead, & J. C. Wellenkamp (Eds.), *Everyday conceptions of emotion* (pp. 221–240). Dordrecht, the Netherlands: Kluwer.

Blechman, E. A. (1990). *Emotions and the family.* Hillsdale, N. J.: Erlbaum.

Bliatout, B. T. (1993). Hmong death customs: Traditional and acculturated. In D. P. Irish, K. F. Lundquist, & V. J. Nelsen (Eds.), *Ethnic variations in dying, death, and grief* (pp. 79–100). Washington, DC: Taylor & Francis.

Bochner, A. P. (1982). On the efficacy of openness in close relationships. In M. Burgoon (Ed.), *Communication yearbook 5* (pp. 109–124). New Brunswick, NJ: Transaction-ICA.

Bok, S. (1978). *Lying.* New York: Random House.

Bond, M. H. (1993). Emotions and their expression in Chinese culture. *Journal of Nonverbal Behavior, 17,* 245–262.

Booth-Butterfield, M., & Booth-Butterfield, S. (1990). Conceptualizing affect as information in communication production. *Human Communication Research, 16,* 451–476.

Booth-Butterfield, M., & Booth-Butterfield, S. (1994). The affective orientation to communication: Conceptual and empirical distinctions. *Communication Quarterly, 42,* 331–344.

Booth-Butterfield, M., & Booth-Butterfield, S. (1996). Using your emotions: Improving the measurement of affective orientation. *Communication Research Reports, 13,* 157–163.

Borkovec, T. D., Roemer, L., & Kinyon, J. (1995). Disclosure and worry: Opposite sides of the emotional processing coin. In J. W. Pennerbaker (Ed.), *Emotion, disclosure, and health* (pp. 47–70). Washington, DC: American Psychological Association.

Bosmajian, H. (1983). *The language of oppression.* Lanham, MD: University Press of America.

Bowers, J. W., Metts, S. M., & Duncanson, W. T. (1985). Emotion and interpersonal communication. In M. L. Knapp & G. R. Miller (Eds.), *Handbook of interpersonal communication* (pp. 502–559). Beverly Hills, CA: Sage.

Bowlby, J. (1969a). *Attachment and loss:* Vol. 1. *Attachment.* New York: Basic Books.

Bowlby, J. (1969b). *Attachment and loss:* Vol. 2. *Separation.* New York: Basic Books.

Bradford, L., & Petronio, S. (1998). Strategic embarrassment: The culprit of emotion. In P. A. Andersen & L. K. Guerrero (Eds.), *The handbook of communication and emotion* (pp. 99–121). San Diego, CA: Academic Press.

Braithwaite, J., & Mugford, S. (1994). Conditions of successful reintegration ceremonies: Dealing with juvenile offenders. *British Journal of Criminology, 34,* 139–171.

Brenneis, D. (1990). Shared and solitary sentiments: The discourse of friendship, play, and anger in Bhatgaon. In C. A. Lutz & L. Abu-Lughod (Eds.), *Language and the politics of emotion* (pp. 113–125). Cambridge: Cambridge University Press.

Brenneis, D. (1995). Caught in a web of words: Performing theory in a Fiji Indian community. In J. A. Russell, J. Fernandez-Dols, A. Manstead, & J. Wellenkamp (Eds.), *Everyday conceptions of emotion* (pp. 241–250). Dordrecht, the Netherlands: Kluwer.

Briggs, J. L. (1970). *Never in anger*. Cambridge, MA: Harvard University Press.

Brokenleg, M., & Middleton, D. (1993). Native Americans: Adapting, yet retaining. In D. P. Irish, K. F. Lundquist, & V. J. Nelsen (Eds.), *Ethnic variations in dying, death, and grief* (pp. 101–112). Washington, DC: Taylor & Francis.

Brownlow, S., Dixon, A. R., Egbert, C. A., & Radcliffe, R. D. (1997). Perception of movement and dancer characteristics from point-light displays of dance. *The Psychological Record, 47*, 411–422.

Bruder, K. (1992, November). *Emotional experience and expression in a monastic community*. Paper presented to the Speech Communication Association Convention, Chicago.

Bryson, J. B. (1991). Modes of response to jealousy-evoking situations. In P. Salovey (Ed.), *The psychology of jealousy and envy* (pp. 178–207). New York: Guilford Press.

Bucci, W. (1995). The power of the narrative: A multiple code account. In J. W. Pennebaker (Ed.), *Emotion, disclosure and health* (pp. 93–122). Washington, DC: American Psychological Association.

Buck, R. (1984). *The communication of emotion*. New York: Guilford Press.

Buck, R. (1991). Social factors in facial display and communication: A reply to Chovil and others. *Journal of Nonverbal Behavior, 15*, 155–161.

Buck, R., Baron, R., & Barrette, D. (1982). Temporal organization of spontaneous emotional expression: A segmentation analysis. *Journal of Personality and Social Psychology, 42*, 506–517.

Buck, R., Losow, J. I., Murphy, M. M., & Costanzo, P. (1992). Social facilitation and inhibition of emotional expression and communication. *Journal of Personality and Social Psychology, 63*, 962–968.

Burgh, R. (1987). Guilt, punishment, and desert. In F. Schoeman (Ed.), *Responsibility, character, and the emotions* (pp. 316–337). New York: Cambridge University Press.

Burgoon, J. K. (1993). Interpersonal expectations, expectancy violations, and emotional communication. *Journal of Language and Social Psychology, 12*, 30–48.

Burgoon, J. K., & Hale, J. L. (1988). Nonverbal expectancy violations theory: Model elaboration and application to immediacy behaviors. *Communication Monographs, 55*, 58–79.

Burleson, B. R. (1990). Comforting as social support: Relational consequences of supportive behaviors. In S. Duck (Ed.), *Personal relationships and social support* (pp. 66–82). London: Sage.

Burleson, B. R., & Goldsmith, D. J. (1998). How the comforting process works: Alleviating emotional distress through conversationally induced appraisals. In P. A. Andersen & L. K. Guerrero (Eds.), *Communication and emotion* (pp. 245–280). Orlando, FL: Academic Press.

Buttny, R. (1993). *Social accountability in communication*. London: Sage.

Calhoun, C. (1992). Emotional work. In E. B. Cole & S. Coultrap-McQuin (Eds.), *Explorations in feminist ethics* (pp. 117–122). Bloomington, IN: University of Indiana Press.

Camras, L. A., Holland, E. A., & Patterson, M. J. (1993). Facial expression. In M. Lewis & J. M. Haviland (Eds.), *Handbook of emotions* (pp. 199–208). New York: Guilford Press.

Cancian, F. M. (1987). *Love in America: Gender and self-development.* New York: Cambridge University Press.

Candland, D. K. (1977). The persistent problems of emotion. In D. K. Candland, J. P. Fell, E. Keen, A. I. Leshner, R. M. Tarpy, & R. Plutchik (Eds.), *Emotion* (pp. 1–84). Monterey, CA: Brooks/Cole.

Cannon, W. B. (1929/1984). A critical examination of the James–Lange theory of emotions. Reprinted in C. Calhoun & R. C. Solomon (Eds.), *What is an emotion?* (pp. 142–151). New York: Oxford University Press.

Cappella, J. N. (1981). Mutual influence in expressive behavior: Adult–adult and infant–adult interaction. *Psychological Bulletin, 89,* 101–132.

Cappella, J. N. (1993). The facial feedback hypothesis in human interaction: Review and speculation. *Journal of Language and Social Psychology, 12,* 13–29.

Cappella, J. N. (1995). Inoculating against emotional contagion. *Contemporary Psychology, 40,* 636–637.

Cappella, J. N., & Greene, J. O. (1982). A discrepancy-arousal explanation of mutual influence in expressive behavior in adult– and infant–adult interaction. *Communication Monographs, 49,* 89–114.

Carmichael, K. (1991). *Ceremony of innocence: Tears, power and protest.* New York: St. Martin's Press.

Carrera-Levillain, P., & Fernandez-Dols, J. M. (1994). Neutral faces in context: Their emotional meaning and their function. *Journal of Nonverbal Behavior, 18,* 281–299.

Carroll, J. M., & Russell, J. A. (1996). Do facial expressions signal specific emotions? Judging emotion from the face in context. *Journal of Personality and Social Psychology, 70,* 205–218.

Carroll, J. M., & Russell, J. A. (1997). Facial expressions in Hollywood's portrayal of emotion. *Journal of Personality and Social Psychology, 72,* 164–176.

Chelune, G. J., & Associates. (1979). Self disclosure. San Francisco: Jossey-Bass.

Chovil, N. (1991). Social determinants of facial displays. *Journal of Nonverbal Behavior, 15,* 141–153.

Christophe, V., & Rimé, B. (1997). Exposure to the social sharing of emotion: Emotional impact, listener responses and secondary social sharing. *European Journal of Social Psychology, 27,* 37–54.

Clark, C. (1990). Emotions and micropolitics in everyday life: Some patterns and paradoxes of "place." In T. D. Kemper (Ed.), *Research agendas in the sociology of emotions* (pp. 305–353). Albany, NY: SUNY Press.

Clark, C. (1997). *Misery and company.* Chicago: University of Chicago Press.

Clark, H. H. (1985). Language use and language users. In G. Lindzey & E. Aronson (Eds.), *The handbook of social psychology* (Vol. 2, pp. 179–231). New York: Random House.

Clark, H. H. (1992). *Arenas of language use.* Chicago: University of Chicago Press.

Clark, L. F. (1993). Stress and the cognitive-conversational benefits of social interaction. *Journal of Social and Clinical Psychology, 12,* 25–55.

Clark, M. S., & Mills, J. (1979). Interpersonal attraction in exchange and communal relationships. *Journal of Personality and Social Psychology, 37,* 12–24.

Clark, M. S., Pataki, S. P., & Carver, V. H. (1996). Some thoughts and findings on self-presentation of emotions in relationships. In G. J. O. Fletcher & J. Fitness (Eds.), *Knowledge structures in close relationships* (pp. 247–274). Mahwah, NJ: Erlbaum.

Coates, D., Wortman, C. B., & Abbey, A. (1979). Reactions to victims. In I. H. Frieze, D. Bar-Tal, & J. S. Carroll (Eds.), *New approaches to social problems* (pp. 21–52). San Francisco: Jossey-Bass.

Cochran, L., & Claspell, E. (1987). *The meaning of grief.* New York: Greenwood Press.

Cohn, C. (1987). Sex and death in the rational world of defense intellectuals. *Signs: Journal of Women in Culture and Society, 12,* 687–718.

Collins, R. (1990). Stratification, emotional energy, and the transient emotions. In T. D. Kemper (Ed.). *Research agendas in the sociology of emotion* (pp. 27–57). Albany, NY: SUNY Press.

Columbia Dictionary of Quotations. (1993). New York: Columbia University Press.

Conrad, C., & Witte, K. (1994). Is emotional expression repression oppression? Myths of organizational effective regulation. In S. A. Deetz (Ed.), *Communication yearbook 17* (pp. 417–428). Thousand Oaks, CA: Sage.

Cooley, C. H. (1964). *Human nature and the social order.* New York: Schocken Books.

Copp, M. (1998). When emotion work is doomed to fail: Ideological and structural constraints on emotion management. *Symbolic Interaction, 21,* 299–328.

Cosnier, J., Dols, J. M. F., & Fernandez, A. J. (1986). The verbalisation of emotional experience. In K. R. Scherer, H. G. Wallbott, & A. B. Summerfield (Eds.), *Experiencing emotion: A cross-cultural study* (pp. 117–128). Cambridge: Cambridge University Press.

Coupland, N., Giles, H., & Wiemann, J. M. (Eds.) (1991). *"Miscommunication" and problematic talk.* Newbury Park, CA: Sage.

Coyne, J. C. (1976). Depression and the response of others. *Journal of Abnormal Psychology, 85,* 186–193.

Coyne, J. C., Ellard, J. H., & Smith, D. A. (1990). Social support, interdependence, and the dilemmas of helping. In B. R. Sarason, I. G. Sarason, & G. R. Pierce (Eds.), *Social support: An interactional view* (pp. 129–149). New York: Wiley.

Coyne, J. C., & Smith, D. A. F. (1991). Couples coping with a myocardial infarction: A contextual perspective on wives' distress. *Journal of Personality and Social Psychology, 61,* 404–412.

Coyne, J. C., Wortman, C. B., & Lehman, D. R. (1988). The other side of support: Emotional overinvolvement and miscarried helping. In B. H. Gottlieb (Ed.), *Marshalling social support: Formats, processes, and effects* (pp. 305–330). Newbury Park, CA: Sage.

Crozier, W. R. (1990). *Shyness and embarrassment*. Cambridge: Cambridge University Press.

Csikszentmihalyi, M. (1990). *Flow: The psychology of optimal experience*. New York: Harper & Row.

Cupach, W. R., & Metts, S. (1990). Remedial processes in embarrassing predicaments. In J. Anderson (Ed.), *Communication yearbook* (Vol. 13, pp. 323–352). Newbury Park, CA: Sage.

Cutrona, C. E., Suhr, J. A., & MacFarlane, R. (1990). Interpersonal transactions and the psychological sense of support. In S. Duck (Ed.), *Personal relationships and social support* (pp. 30–45). London: Sage.

Cytron, B. D. (1993). To honor the dead and comfort the mourners: Traditions of Judaism. In D. P. Irish, K. F. Lundquist, & V. J. Nelsen (Eds.), *Ethnic variations in dying, death, and grief* (pp. 113–124). Washington, DC: Taylor & Francis.

Dakof, G. A., & Taylor, S. E. (1990). Victims' perceptions of social support: What is helpful from whom? *Journal of Personality and Social Psychology, 58,* 80–89.

Damasio, A. R. (1994). *Descartes' error*. New York: G. P. Putnam's Sons.

Darwin, C. (1872/1965). *The expression of the emotions in man and animals*. Chicago IL: University of Chicago Press.

Davis, D. (1982). Determinants of responsiveness in dyadic interaction. In W. Ickes & E. S. Knowles (Eds.), *Personality, roles, and social behavior* (pp. 85–140). New York: Springer-Verlag.

Davis, M. H., & Kraus, L. A. (1991). Dispositional empathy and social relationships. In W. H. Jones & D. Perlman (Eds.), *Advances in personal relationships* (Vol. 3, pp. 75–115). London: Jessica Kingsley Publishers.

Davitz, J. R. (1969). *The language of emotion*. New York: Academic Press.

Deci, E. L., & Ryan, R. M. (1985). *Intrinsic motivation and self-determination in human behavior*. New York: Plenum Press.

Derlega, V. J., & Berg, J. H. (1987). *Self-disclosure: Theory, research, and therapy*. New York: Plenum Press.

Derlega, V. J., Metts, S., Petronio, S., & Margulis, S. T. (1993). *Self-disclosure*. Newbury Park, CA: Sage.

De Sousa, R. (1980). Self-deceptive emotions. In A. O. Rorty (Ed.), *Explaining emotions* (pp. 283–297). Berkeley CA: University of California Press.

De Sousa, R. (1987). *The rationality of emotion*. Cambridge, MA: MIT Press.

Dillard, J. P. (1991). Rethinking the study of fear appeals: An emotional perspective. *Communication Theory, 4,* 295–323.

Dillard, J. P. (1998). The role of affect in communication, biology, and social relationships. In P. A. Andersen & L. K. Guerrero (Eds.), *The handbook of communication and emotion* (pp. xvii–xxxii). San Diego, CA: Academic Press.

Dindia, K. (1994). The intrapersonal-interpersonal dialectical process of self-disclosure. In S. Duck (Ed.), *Dynamics of relationships* (pp. 27–57). Thousand Oaks, CA: Sage.

Dion, K. K., & Dion K. L. (1996). Cultural perspectives on romantic love. *Personal Relationships, 3,* 5–17.

Downey, G., & Coyne, J. C. (1990). Children of depressed parents: An integrative review. *Psychological Bulletin, 108,* 50–76.

Dunn, J., & Brown, J. (1991). Relationships, talk about feelings, and the development of affect regulation in early childhood. In J. Garber & K. A. Dodge (Eds.), *The development of emotion regulation and dysregulation* (pp. 89–108). Cambridge: Cambridge University Press.

Dunn, J., Brown, J., & Beardsall, L. (1991). Family talk about feeling states and children's later understanding of others' emotions. *Developmental Psychology, 27,* 448–455.

Durkheim, E. (1912/1975). The elementary forms of religious life: The totemic system in Australia. In W. S. F. Pickering (Ed.), *Durkheim on religion* (pp. 102–166). London: Routledge & Kegan Paul.

Edelmann, R. J. (1987). *The psychology of embarrassment.* New York: Wiley.

Edwards, K. (1998). The face of time: Temporal cues in facial expressions of emotion. *Psychological Science, 9,* 270–276.

Egerton, M. (1988). Passionate women and passionate men: Sex differences in accounting for angry and weeping episodes. *British Journal of Social Psychology, 27,* 51–66.

Eidelson, R. J., & Epstein, N. (1982). Cognition and relationship maladjustment: Development of a measure of dysfunctional relationship beliefs. *Journal of Consulting and Clinical Psychology, 50,* 715–720.

Eisenberg, N., & Miller, P. (1987). Empathy, sympathy, and altruism: Empirical and conceptual links. In N. Eisenberg & J. Strayer (Eds.), *Empathy and its development* (pp. 292–316). New York: Cambridge University Press.

Eiser, J. R. (1990). *Social judgment.* Pacific Grove, CA: Brooks/Cole.

Ekman, P. (Ed.). (1982). *Emotion in the human face.* Cambridge: Cambridge University Press.

Ekman, P. (1993). Facial expression and emotion. *American Psychologist, 48,* 384–392.

Ekman, P. (1994). Strong evidence for universals in facial expressions: A reply to Russell's mistaken critique. *Psychological Bulletin, 115,* 268–287.

Ekman, P., & Davidson, R. J. (1994a). Afterword: Can we control our emotions? In P. Ekman & R. J. Davidson (Eds.), *The nature of emotion: Fundamental questions* (pp. 280–281). Oxford: Oxford University Press.

Ekman, P., & Davidson, R. J. (1994b). *The nature of emotion: Fundamental questions.* Oxford: Oxford University Press.

Ekman, P., Davidson, R. J., & Friesen, W. V. (1990). The Duchenne smile: Emotional expression and brain physiology II. *Journal of Personality and Social Psychology, 58,* 342–353.

Ekman, P., & Friesen, W. V. (1975). *Unmasking the face: A guide to recognizing emotions from facial cues.* Englewood Cliffs, NJ: Prentice-Hall.

Ekman, P., Friesen, W. V., O'Sullivan, M., & Scherer, K. (1980). Relative importance of face, body, and speech in judgments of personality and affect. *Journal of Personality and Social Psychology, 38,* 270–277.

Ekman, P., Levenson, R. W., & Friesen, W. V. (1983). Autonomic nervous system activity distinguishes among emotions. *Science, 221,* 1208–1210.

Ekman, P., & Oster, H. (1982). Review of research, 1970–1980. In P. Ekman

(Ed.), *Emotion in the human face* (2nd ed., pp. 147–173). Cambridge: Cambridge University Press.

Ekman, P., Sorenson, E. R., & Friesen, W. V. (1969). Pan-cultural elements in the facial displays of emotion. *Science, 164*, 86–88.

Elias, N. (1978). *The history of manners.* New York: Pantheon.

Elias, N. (1994). *The civilizing process.* (Trans. E. Jephcott). New York: Urizen Books.

Ellsworth, P. C. (1994). Sense, culture and sensibility. In S. Kitayama & H. R. Markus (Eds.), *Emotion and culture* (pp. 23–50). Washington, DC: American Psychological Association.

Emmons, R. A., & Colby, P. M. (1995). Emotional conflict and well-being: Relation to perceived availability, daily utilization, and observer reports of social support. *Journal of Personality and Social Psychology, 68*, 947–959.

Epstein, S. (1984). Controversial issues in emotion theory. In P. Shaver (Ed.), *Review of personality and social psychology* (Vol. 5, pp. 64–88). Beverly Hills, CA: Sage.

Erber, R., Wegner, D M., & Therriault, N. (1996). On being cool and collected: Mood regulation in anticipation of social interaction. *Journal of Personality and Social Psychology, 70*, 757–766.

Ereira, A. (1992). *The heart of the world.* New York: Knopf.

Feeney, J. A., Noller, P., & Roberts, N. (1998). Emotion, attachment, and satisfaction in close relationships. In P. A. Andersen & L. K. Guerrero (Eds.), *The handbook of communication and emotion* (pp. 473–505). San Diego, CA: Academic Press.

Fernandez-Dols, J. M. & Ruiz-Belda, M.-A. (1995a). Are smiles a sign of happiness? Gold medal winner at the Olympic games. *Journal of Personality and Social Psychology, 69*, 1113–1119.

Fernandez-Dols, J. M., & Ruiz-Belda, M.-A. (1995b). Expression of emotion versus expressions of emotions. In J. A. Russell, J. M. Fernandez-Dols, A. S. R. Manstead, & J. C. Wellenkamp (Eds.), *Everyday conceptions of emotion* (pp. 505–522). Dordrecht, the Netherlands: Kluwer.

Fernandez-Dols, J. M., & Ruiz-Belda, M.-A. (1997). Spontaneous facial behavior during intense emotional episodes: Artistic truth and optical truth. In J. A. Russell & J. M. Fernandez-Dols (Eds.) *The psychology of facial expression* (pp. 255–274). Paris: Cambridge University Press.

Fineman, S. (1993). *Emotion in organizations.* Newbury Park, CA: Sage.

Fisher, J. D., Goff, B. A., Nadler, A., & Chinsky, J. M. (1988). Social psychological influences on help seeking and support from peers. In B. H. Gottlieb (Ed.), *Marshalling social support: Formats, processes, and effects* (pp. 305–330). Newbury Park, CA: Sage.

Fitness, J. (1996). Emotion knowledge structures in close relationships. In G. J. O. Fletcher & J. Fitness (Eds.), *Knowledge structures in close relationships* (pp. 195–217). Mahwah, NJ: Erlbaum.

Flam, H. (1993). Fear, loyalty, and greedy organizations. In S. Fineman (Eds.), *Emotion in organizations* (pp. 58–75). London: Sage.

Folger, R., & Baron, R. A. (1996). Violence and hostility at work: A model of reactions to perceived injustice. In G. R. VandenBos & E. Q. Bulatao (Eds.), *Violence on the job* (pp. 51–85). Washington, DC: American Psychological Association.

Folkman, S., & Lazarus, R. S. (1985). If it changes it must be a process: Study of emotion and coping during three stages of a college examination. *Journal of Personality and Social Psychology, 48,* 150–170.

Francis, L. E. (1997). Ideology and interpersonal emotion management: Redefining identity in two support groups. *Social Psychology Quarterly, 60,* 153–171.

Frank, R. H. (1988). *Passions within reason: The strategic role of the emotions.* New York: W. W. Norton.

Frankl, V. E. (1946/1984). *Man's search for meaning* (3rd ed.). New York: Simon & Schuster.

Frick, R. W. (1985). Communicating emotion: The role of prosodic features. *Psychological Bulletin, 97,* 412–429.

Fridlund, A. J. (1991). Sociality of solitary smiling: Potentiation by an implicit audience. *Journal of Personality and Social Psychology, 60,* 229–240.

Fridlund, A. J. (1994). *Human facial expression.* San Diego, CA: Academic Press.

Frijda, N. H. (1986). *The emotions.* Cambridge: Cambridge University Press.

Frijda, N. H. (1993). The place of appraisal in emotion. *Cognition and Emotion, 7,* 357–387.

Frijda, N. H. (1994a). Emotion politics: Manipulation of emotion in social interaction. In N. H. Frijda (Ed.), *ISRE'94: Proceedings of the 8th Conference of the International Society for Research on Emotions* (pp. 39–42). Storrs, CT: ISRE Publications.

Frijda, N. H. (1994b). The lex talionis: On vengeance. In S. H. M. van Goozen, N. E. van de Poll, & J. A. Sergeant (Eds.), *Emotions: Essays on emotion theory* (pp. 263–289). Hillsdale, NJ: Erlbaum.

Frijda, N. H. (1997). Commemorating. In J. W. Pennebaker, D. Paez, & B. Rimé (Eds.), *Collective memory of political events: Social psychological perspectives* (pp. 103–130). Mahwah, NJ: Erlbaum.

Frijda, N. H., Kuipers, P., & ter Schure, E. (1989). Relations among emotion, appraisal, and emotional action readiness. *Journal of Personality and Social Psychology, 57,* 212–228.

Frijda, N. H., & Mesquita, B. (1991). *The various effects of emotion communication.* Paper presented at the sixth meeting of the International Society for Research on Emotion, Saarbrücken, Germany.

Frijda, N. H., & Mesquita, B. (1994). The social roles and functions of emotions. In S. Kitayama & H. R. Markus (Eds.), *Emotion and culture* (pp. 51–87). Washington, DC: American Psychological Association.

Frijda, N. H., Mesquita, B., Sonnemans, J., & van Goozen, S. (1991). The duration of affective phenomena. In K. Strongman (Ed.), *International review of studies on emotion* (Vol. 1, pp. 187–225). New York: Wiley.

Frijda, N. H., & Tcherkasoff, A. (1997). Facial expression as action readiness. In J. A. Russell & J. M. Fernández-Dols (Eds.), *The psychology of facial expression* (pp. 78–102). Paris: Cambridge University Press.

Gaines, J., & Jermier, J. M. (1983). Emotional exhaustion in a high stress organization. *Academy of Management Journal, 26,* 567–586.

Gaines, S. O., Jr. (1998). Communication of emotions in friendships. In P. A. Andersen & L. K. Guerrero (Eds.), *The handbook of communication and emotion* (pp. 507–531). San Diego, CA: Academic Press.

Gallois, C. (1993). The language and communication of emotion: Universal, interpersonal, or intergroup? *American Behavioral Scientist, 36,* 309–338.

Gallois, C., & Callan, V. J. (1986). Decoding emotional messages: Influence of ethnicity, sex, message type, and channel. *Journal of Personality and Social Psychology, 51,* 755–762.

Garfinkel, H. (1956). Conditions of successful degradation ceremonies. *American Journal of Sociology, 61,* 420–424.

Gelles, R. J., & Straus, M. A. (1988). *Intimate violence.* New York: Simon & Schuster.

Georges, E. (1995). A cultural and historical perspective on confession. In J. W. Pennebaker (Ed.), *Emotion, disclosure and health* (pp. 11–22). Washington, DC: American Psychological Association.

Gerber, E. R. (1985). Rage and obligation: Samoan emotion in conflict. In G. M. White & J. Kirkpatrick (Eds.), *Person, self, and experience* (pp. 121–167). Berkeley: University of California Press.

Gilligan, C. (1982). *In a different voice: Psychological theory and women's development.* Cambridge, MA: Harvard University Press.

Gillis, J. R. (1988). From ritual to romance: Toward an alternative history of love. In C. Z. Stearns & P. N. Stearns (Eds.), *Emotion and social change* (pp. 88–121). New York: Holmes & Meier.

Gitter, A. G., Black, H., & Mostofsky, D. (1972). Race and sex in the perception of emotion. *Journal of Social Issues, 28,* 63–78.

Glaser, H. (1993, November). *An alternative use of emotion in organizations: Emotion as a valued resource in egalitarian groups.* Paper presented to the annual convention of the Speech Communication Association, Miami, FL.

Goffman, E. (1959). *The presentation of self in everyday life.* Garden City, NY: Doubleday.

Goldsmith, D. J. (1994). The role of facework in supportive communication. In B. Burleson, T. L. Albrecht, & I. G. Sarason (Eds.), *Communication of social support: Messages, interactions, relationships, and community* (pp. 29–49). Thousand Oaks, CA: Sage.

Goldsmith, D. J., & Dun, S. A. (1997). Sex differences and similarities in the communication of social support. *Journal of Social and Personal Relationships, 14,* 317–337.

Goldsmith, D. J., & Fitch, K. (1997). The normative context of advice as social support. *Human Communication Research, 23,* 454–476.

Goleman, D. (1995). *Emotional intelligence: Why it can matter more than IQ.* New York: Bantam Books.

Gordon, S. L. (1990). Social structural effects on emotions. In T. D. Kemper (Ed.), *Research agendas in the sociology of emotions* (pp. 145–179). Albany, NY: SUNY Press.

Gosselin, P., Kirouac, G., & Doré, F. Y. (1995). Components and recognition of facial expression in the communication of emotion by actors. *Journal of Personality and Social Psychology, 68*, 83–96.

Gotlib, I. H., & Whiffen, V. E. (1991). The interpersonal context of depression: Implications for theory and research. In W. H. Jones & D. Perlman (Eds.), *Advances in personal relationships.* (Vol. 3, pp. 177–206). London: Jessica Kingsley Publishers.

Gottman, J. M. (1979). *Marital interaction: Experimental investigations.* New York: Academic Press.

Gottman, J. M. (1993). Studying emotion in social interaction. In M. Lewis & J. M. Haviland (Eds.), *Handbook of emotions* (pp. 475–487). New York: Guilford Press.

Gottman, J. M. (1994). *What predicts divorce? The relationship between marital processes and marital outcomes.* Hillsdale, NJ: Erlbaum.

Gottman, J. M., Katz, L. F., & Hooven, C. (1997). *Meta-emotion: How families communicate emotionally.* Mahwah, NJ: Erlbaum.

Graham, D. L. R., & Rawlings, E. I. (1991). Bonding with abusive dating partners: Dynamics of Stockholm syndrome. In B. Levy (Ed.), *Dating violence: Young women in danger* (pp. 119–135). Seattle, WA: Seal Press.

Graham, J. W., Gentry, K. W., & Green, J. (1981). The self-presentational nature of emotional expression: Some evidence. *Personality and Social Psychology Bulletin, 7,* 467–474.

Gray, J. G. (1959). *The warriors: Reflections on men in battle.* New York: Harper & Row.

Greenberg, L. S., & Safran, J. D. (1987). *Emotion in psychotherapy: Affect, cognition, and the process of change.* New York: Guilford Press.

Greenspan, P. S. (1995). *Practical guilt: Moral dilemmas, emotions, and social norms.* New York: Oxford University Press.

Grice, H. P. (1975). Logic and conversation. In P. Cole & J. L. Morgan (Eds.), *Syntax and semantics, Vol. 9: Pragmatics* (pp. 113–128). New York: Academic Press.

Grief analysis. (1996, April 22). *Time, 147, 24.*

Gross, J. J., & John, O. P. (1997). Revealing feelings: Facets of emotional expressivity in self-reports, peer ratings, and behavior. *Journal of Personality and Social Psychology, 72,* 435–448.

Guerrero, L. K., & Andersen, P. A. (1998). Jealousy experience and expression in romantic relationships. In P. A. Andersen & L. K. Guerrero (Eds.), *The handbook of communication and emotion* (pp. 156–188). San Diego, CA: Academic Press.

Haas, J. (1978). Learning real feelings: A study of high steel ironworkers' reactions to fear and danger. In J. Haas & W. Shaffir (Eds.), *Shaping identity in Canadian society* (pp. 227–245). Scarborough, Ontario: Prentice-Hall.

Hafen, B. Q., Frandsen, K. J., Karren, K. J., & Hooker, K. R. (1992). *The health effects of attitudes, emotions, relationships.* Provo, UT: EMS Associates.

Hafferty, F. W. (1988). Cadaver stories and the emotional socialization of medical students. *Journal of Health and Social Behavior, 29,* 344–356.

Halberstadt, A. G. (1986). Family socialization of emotional expression and nonverbal communication styles and skills. *Journal of Personality and Social Psychology, 51,* 827–836.

Halberstadt, A. G. (1991). Toward an ecology of expressiveness: Family socialization in particular and a model in general. In R. S. Feldman & B. Rimé (Eds.), *Fundamentals of nonverbal behavior* (pp. 106–160). Cambridge: Cambridge University Press.

Hall, E. T. (1977). *Beyond culture.* New York: Anchor Books.

Hallpike, C. (1979). *The foundations of primitive thought.* New York: Oxford University Press.

Harber, K. D., & Pennebaker, J. W. (1992). Overcoming traumatic memories. In S-A. Christianson (Ed.), *The handbook of emotion and memory: Research and theory* (pp. 359–387). Hillsdale, NJ: Erlbaum.

Harré, R., & Finlay-Jones, R. (1986). Emotion talk across times. In R. Harré (Ed.) *The social construction of emotion* (pp. 220–233). Oxford: Basil Blackwell.

Harré, R., & Parrott, W. G. (1996). *The emotions: Social, cultural, and biological dimensions.* London: Sage.

Harris, P. L. (1989). *Children and emotion.* Oxford: Basil Blackwell.

Hartse, C. M. (1994). The emotional acculturation of Hutterite defectors. *Journal of Anthropological Research, 50,* 69–85.

Hatfield, E. (1984). The dangers of intimacy. In V. J. Derlega (Ed.), *Communication, intimacy, and close relationships* (pp. 207–220). New York: Academic Press.

Hatfield, E., Cacioppo, J. T., & Rapson, R. L. (1994). *Emotional contagion.* Cambridge: Cambridge University Press.

Haviland, J. M., & Goldston, R. B. (1992). Emotion and narrative: The agony and the ecstasy. In K. T. Strongman (Ed.), *International review of studies on emotion* (Vol. 2, pp. 219–247). Chichester: Wiley.

Heelas, P. (1983). Anthropological perspectives on violence: Universals and particulars. *Zygon, 18,* 375–404.

Heelas, P. (1996). Emotion talk across cultures. In R. Harré & W. G. Parrott (Eds.), *The emotions* (pp. 171–199). London: Sage.

Heider, K. G. (1991). *Landscapes of emotion: Mapping three cultures of emotion in Indonesia.* Cambridge: Cambridge University Press.

Heise, D. R., & Calhan, C. (1995). Emotion norms in interpersonal events. *Social Psychology Quarterly, 58,* 223–240.

Heise, D. R., & O'Brien, J. (1993). Emotion expression in groups. In M. Lewis & J. M. Haviland (Eds.), *Handbook of emotions* (pp. 489–497). New York: Guilford Press.

Hess, U., Banse, R., & Kappas, A. (1995). The intensity of facial expression is determined by underlying affective state and social situation. *Journal of Personality and Social Psychology, 69,* 280–288.

Higgins, E. T. (1987). Self-discrepancy: A theory relating self and affect. *Psychological Review, 94,* 319–340.

Hillman, J. (1960/1997). *Emotion.* Evanston, IL: Northwestern University Press.

Hirsch, B. J. (1980). Natural support systems and coping with major life changes. *American Journal of Community Psychology, 8,* 159–172.

Hitch, P. J., Fielding, R. G., & Llewelyn, S. P. (1994). Effectiveness of self-help and support groups for cancer patients: A review. *Psychology and Health, 9,* 437–448.

Hochschild, A. R. (1979). Emotion work, feeling rules, and social structure. *American Journal of Sociology, 85,* 551–575.

Hochschild, A. R. (1983). *The managed heart: Commercialization of human feeling.* Berkeley: University of California Press.

Hochschild, A. R. (1989a). The economy of gratitude. In D. D. Franks & E. D. McCarthy (Eds.), *The sociology of emotions: Original essays and research papers* (pp. 95–113). Greenwich, CT: JAI Press.

Hochschild, A. R. (1990). Ideology and emotion management: A perspective and path for future research. In T. D. Kemper (Ed.), *Research agendas in the sociology of emotions* (pp. 117–142). Albany, NY: SUNY Press.

Hochschild, A. R., with Anne Machung. (1989b). *The second shift: Working parents and the revolution at home.* New York: Viking.

Hoffman, E. (1989). *Lost in translation.* New York: Dutton Press.

Hoffman, M. L. (1987). The contribution of empathy to justice and moral judgment. In N. Eisenberg & J. Strayer (Eds.) *Empathy and its development* (pp. 47–80). Cambridge: Cambridge University Press.

Hofstede, G. (1980). *Culture's consequences: International difference in work-related values.* Beverly Hills, CA: Sage.

Hooven, C., Gottman, J. M., & Katz, L. F. (1995). Parental meta-emotion structure predicts family and child outcomes. *Cognition and Emotion, 9,* 229–264.

Horowitz, M. J. (1991). Emotionality and schematic control processes. In M. J. Horowitz (Ed.), *Person schemas and maladaptive interpersonal patterns* (pp. 413–423). Chicago: University of Chicago Press.

Hsee, C. K., Hatfield, E., Carlson, J. G., & Chemtob, C. (1990). The effect of power on susceptibility to emotional contagion. *Cognition and Emotion, 4,* 327–340.

Hume, D. (1738/1995). On reason and the emotions: The fact/value distinction. In L. P. Pojman (Ed.), *Ethical theory: Classical and contemporary readings* (2nd ed., pp. 399–427). Belmont, CA: Wadsworth.

Hummel, R. P. (1987). *The bureaucratic experience* (3rd ed., pp. 123–175). New York: St. Martin's Press.

Huxley, A. (1932/1989). *Brave new world.* New York: Harper Perennial.

Iglesias, I. (1996). Vergüenza ajena. In R. Harré & W. G. Parrott (Eds.), *The emotions* (pp. 122–131). London: Sage.

Illouz, E. (1991). Reason within passion: Love in women's magazines. *Critical Studies in Mass Communication, 8,* 231–248.

Irvine, J. T. (1990). Registering affect: Heteroglossia in the linguistic expression of emotion. In C. A. Lutz & L. Abu-Lughod (Eds.), *Language and the politics of emotion* (pp. 126–161). Cambridge: Cambridge University Press.

Irvine, J. T. (1995). A sociolinguistic approach to emotion concepts in a Senegalese community. In J. A. Russell, J. M. Fernández-Dols, A. S. R. Manstead, & J. C. Wellenkamp (Eds.), *Everyday conceptions of emotion* (pp. 251–265). Dordrecht, the Netherlands: Kluwer.

Ito, K. L. (1985). Affective bonds: Hawaiian interrelationships of self. In. G. M. White & J. Kirkpatrick (Eds.), *Person, self, and experience* (pp. 301–327). Berkeley: University of California Press.

Izard, C. E. (1991). *The psychology of emotions.* New York: Plenum Press.

Jackal, R. (1988). *Moral mazes: The world of corporate managers.* New York: Oxford University Press.

Jacoby, S. (1983). *Wild justice: The evolution of revenge.* New York: Harper & Row.

Jakobs, E., Fischer, A. H., & Manstead, A. S. R. (1997). Emotional experience as a function of social context: The role of the other. *Journal of Nonverbal Behavior, 21,* 103–130.

James, W. (1884/1984). What is an emotion? Reprinted in C. Calhoun & R. C. Solomon (Eds.), *What is an emotion?* (pp. 127–141). New York: Oxford University Press.

Johnson, S. M., & Greenberg, L. S. (1994). *The heart of the matter: Perspectives on emotion in marital therapy.* New York: Brunner/Mazel.

Jones, E. E., & Pittman, T. S. (1982). Toward a general theory of strategic self-presentation. In J. Suls (Ed.), *Psychological perspectives on the self* (Vol. 1, pp. 231–262). Hillsdale, NJ: Erlbaum.

Jones, W. H., Hobbs, S. A., & Hockenbury, D. (1982). Loneliness and social skills deficits. *Journal of Personality and Social Psychology, 42,* 682–689.

Jorgensen, P. F. (1998). Affect, persuasion, and communication processes. In P. A. Andersen & L. K. Guerrero (Eds.), *The handbook of communication and emotion* (pp. 403–422). San Diego, CA: Academic Press.

Kahlbaugh, P. E., & Haviland, J. M. (1994). Nonverbal communication between parents and adolescents: A study of approach and avoidance behaviors. *Journal of Nonverbal Behavior, 18,* 91–113.

Kappas, A., Hess, U., & Scherer, K. R. (1991). Voice and emotion. In R. S. Feldman & B. Rimé (Eds), *Fundamentals of nonverbal behavior* (pp. 200–237). Cambridge: Cambridge University Press.

Karen, R. (1992, February). Shame. *The Atlantic Monthly,* 40–70.

Karim, W. J. (1990). Prelude to madness: The language of emotion in courtship and early marriage. In W. J. Karim (Ed.), *Emotions of culture: A Malay perspective* (pp. 21–63). Oxford: Oxford University Press.

Kaufman, G. (1992). *Shame: The power of caring* (3rd ed.). Rochester, VT: Schenkman Books.

Kelley, H. H. (1967). Attribution in social psychology. In D. L. Vine (Ed.), *Nebraska symposium on motivation* (pp. 192–238). Lincoln, NE: Academic Press.

Kelley, H. H., Berscheid, E., Christensen, A., Harvey, J. H., Huston, T. L., Levinger, G., McClintock, E., Peplau, L. A., & Peterson, D. R. (1983). *Close relationships.* New York: W. H. Freeman.

Kelley, H. H., & Michela, J. (1980). Attribution theory and research. *Annual Review of Psychology, 31,* 457–501.

Keltner, D., & Bonanno, G. A. (1997). A study of laughter and dissociation: Distinct correlates of laughter and smiling during bereavement. *Journal of Personality and Social Psychology, 73,* 687–702.

Kenny, M. G. (1990). Latah: The logic of fear. In W. J. Karim (Ed.), *Emotions of culture: A Malay perspective* (pp. 123–141). Oxford: Oxford University Press.

Kidd, V. (1975). Happily ever after and other relationship styles: Advice on interpersonal relations in popular magazines, 1951–1973. *Quarterly Journal of Speech, 61,* 31–39.

King, L. A., & Emmons, R. A. (1990). Conflict over emotional expression: Psychological and physical correlates. *Journal of Personality and Social Psychology, 58,* 864–877.

Klimes-Dougan, B., & Kistner, J. (1990). Physically abused preschoolers' responses to peers' distress. *Developmental Psychology 26,* 599–602.

Kochman, T. (1981). *Black and white styles in conflict.* Chicago: University of Chicago Press.

Kohlberg, L. (1981). *The philosophy of moral development.* San Francisco: Harper & Row.

Kohn, A. (1993). *Punished by rewards.* Boston: Houghton Mifflin.

Konradi, A. (1996). Preparing to testify: Rape survivors negotiating the criminal justice process. *Gender and Society, 10,* 404–432.

Kövecses, Z. (1990). *Emotion concepts.* New York: Springer-Verlag.

Kövecses, Z. (1995). Language and emotion concepts. In J. A. Russell, J. M. Fernandez-Dols, A. S. R. Manstead, & J. C. Wellenkamp (Eds.), *Everyday conceptions of emotion* (pp. 3–15). Dordrecht, the Netherlands: Kluwer.

Kraut, R. E., & Johnston, R. E. (1979). Social and emotional messages of smiling: An ethological approach. *Journal of Personality and Social Psychology, 37,* 1539–1553.

Kring, A. M., Smith, D. A., & Neale, J. M. (1994). Individual differences in dispositional expressiveness: Development and validation of the emotional expressivity scale. *Journal of Personality and Social Psychology, 66,* 934–949.

Kübler-Ross, E. (1969). *On death and dying.* New York: Macmillan.

Kunkel, A. W., & Burleson, B. R. (1998). Social support and the emotional lives of men and women: An assessment of the different cultures perspective In D. J. Canary & K. Dindia (Eds.), *Sex differences and similarities in communication* (pp. 101–125). Mahwah, NJ: Erlbaum.

Labouvie-Vief, G., Devoe, M., & Bulka, D. (1989). Speaking about feelings: Conceptions of emotion across the life-span. *Psychology and Aging, 4,* 425–437.

Landman, J. (1993). *Regret: The persistence of the possible.* New York: Oxford University Press.

Lang, P. J. (1988). What are the data of emotion? In V. Hamilton (Ed.), *Cognitive perspectives on emotion and motivation* (pp. 173–191). Dordrecht, the Netherlands: Kluwer.

Lanzetta, J. T., & Englis, B. G. (1989). Expectations of cooperation and competition and their effects on observers' vicarious emotional responses. *Journal of Personality and Social Psychology, 56,* 543–554.

Larsen, R. J., & Zarate, M. A. (1991). Extending reducer/augmenter theory into the emotion domain: The role of affect in regulating stimulation level. *Personality and Individual Differences, 12,* 713–723.

Lateiner, D. (1992). Affect displays in the epic poetry of Homer, Vergil, and Ovid. In F. Poyatos (Ed.), *Advances in nonverbal communication* (pp. 255–265). Amsterdam and Philadelphia: John Benjamins.

Laux, L., & Weber, H. (1991). Presentation of self in coping with anger and anxiety: An intentional approach. *Anxiety Research, 3,* 233–255.

Lazarus, R. S. (1982). Thoughts on the relations between emotion and cognition. *American Psychologist, 37,* 1019–1024.

Lazarus, R. S. (1984). On the primacy of cognition. *American Psychologist, 39,* 124–129.

Lazarus, R. S. (1991). *Emotion and adaptation.* New York: Oxford University Press.

Lazarus, R. S., & Lazarus, B. N. (1994). *Passion and reason: Making sense of our emotions.* Oxford: Oxford University Press.

Leary, M. R., Britt, T. W., Cutlip, W. D., II, & Templeton, J. L. (1992). Social blushing. *Psychological Bulletin, 112,* 446–460.

Leary, M. R., & Kowalski, R. M. (1995). *Social anxiety.* New York: Guilford Press.

Leary, M. R., & Meadows, S. (1991). Predictors, elicitors, and concomitants of social blushing. *Journal of Personality and Social Psychology, 60,* 254–262.

Leary, M. R., Rogers, P. A., Canfield, R. W., & Coe, C. (1986). Boredom in interpersonal encounters: Antecedents and social implications. *Journal of Personality and Social Psychology, 51,* 968–975.

Leavitt, J. (1996). Meaning and feeling in the anthropology of emotions. *American Ethnologist, 23,* 514–539.

LeDoux, J. E. (1994). The degree of emotional control depends on the kind of response system involved. In P. Ekman and R. J. Davidson (Eds.), *The nature of emotion* (pp. 270–272). New York: Oxford University Press.

Lee, D. H. (1988). The support group training project. In B. H. Gottlieb (Ed.), *Marshalling social support: Formats, processes, and effects* (pp. 135–163). Newbury Park, CA: Sage.

Leets, L., & Giles, H. (1997). Words as weapons – When do they wound? Investigations of harmful speech. *Human Communication Research, 24,* 260–301.

Lehman, D. R., Ellard, J. H., & Wortman, C. B. (1986). Social support for the bereaved: Recipients' and providers' perspectives on what is helpful. *Journal of Consulting and Clinical Psychology, 54,* 438–446.

Lehman, D. R., Wortman, C. B., & Williams, A. F. (1987). Long-term effects of losing a spouse or child in a motor vehicle crash. *Journal of Personality and Social Psychology, 52,* 218–231.

Le Poire, B. A., & Burgoon, J. K. (1994). Two contrasting explanations of involvement violations: Expectancy violations theory versus discrepancy arousal theory. *Human Communication Research, 20,* 560–591.

Lerner, M. J. (1980). *The belief in a just world: A fundamental delusion.* New York: Plenum Press.

Levenson, R. W., Carstensen, L. L., & Gottman, J. M. (1994). The influence of age and gender on affect, physiology, and their interrelations: A study of long-term marriages. *Journal of Personality and Social Psychology, 67,* 56–68.

Levenson, R. W., Ekman, P., Heider, K., & Friesen, W. V. (1992). Emotion and autonomic nervous system activity in the Minangkabau of West Sumatra. *Journal of Personality and Social Psychology, 62,* 972–988.

Levenson, R. W., & Gottman, J. M. (1983). Marital interaction: Physiological linkage and affective exchange. *Journal of Personality and Social Psychology, 3,* 587–597.

LeVine, R. A. (1992). Gusii funerals: Meanings of life and death in an African community. In L. A. Platt & V. R. Persico, Jr. (Eds.), *Grief in cross-cultural perspective: A casebook* (pp. 73–128). New York: Garland.

Levy, R. (1973). *Tahitians: Mind and experience in the Society Islands.* Chicago: University of Chicago Press.

Levy, R. I. (1984a). Emotion, knowing and culture. In R. A. Shweder & R. A. LeVine (Eds.), *Culture theory* (pp. 214–237). Cambridge: Cambridge University Press.

Levy, R. I. (1984b). The emotions in comparative perspective. In K. R. Scherer & P. Ekman (Eds.), *Approaches to emotion* (pp. 397–412). Hillsdale, NJ: Erlbaum.

Lewis, H. B. (1971). *Shame and guilt in neurosis.* New York: International Universities Press.

Lewis, H. B. (1987). Shame: The "sleeper" in psychopathology. In H. B. Lewis (Ed.), *The role of shame in symptom formation* (pp. 1–28). Hillsdale, NJ: Erlbaum.

Lewis, M. (1992). *Shame: The exposed self.* New York: Free Press.

Lewis, M. (1993). Self-conscious emotions: Embarrassment, pride, shame, and guilt. In M. Lewis & J. M. Haviland (Eds.), *Handbook of emotions* (pp. 563–573). New York: Guilford Press.

Lewis, M., & Haviland, J. M. (Eds.). (1993). *Handbook of emotions.* New York: Guilford Press.

Lewis, M., & Michalson, L. (1983). *Children's emotions and moods.* New York: Plenum Press.

Lief, H. I., & Fox, R. C. (1963). Training for "detached concern" in medical students. In H. I. Lief, V. F. Lief, & N. R. Lief (Eds.), *The psychological basis of medical practice* (pp. 12–35). New York: Harper & Row.

Lindsay-Hartz, J. (1984). Contrasting experiences of shame and guilt. *American Behavioral Scientist, 27,* 689–704.

Lofland, L. H. (1985). The social shaping of emotion: The case of grief. *Symbolic Interaction, 8,* 171–190.

Lutz, C. A. (1986). The domain of emotion words in Ifaluk. In R. Harré (Ed.), *The social construction of emotions* (pp. 267–288). Oxford: Basil Blackwell.

Lutz, C. A. (1988a). Ethnographic perspectives on the emotion lexicon. In V. Hamilton, G. H. Bower, & N. H. Frijda (Eds.), *Cognitive perspectives on emotion and motivation* (pp. 399–419). Dordrecht, the Netherlands: Kluwer.

Lutz, C. A. (1988b). *Unnatural emotions.* Chicago IL: University of Chicago Press.

Lutz, C., & White, G. M. (1986). The anthropology of emotions. *Annual Review of Anthropology, 15,* 405–436.

Malatesta-Magai, C. (1991). Development of emotion expression during infancy: General course and patterns of individual difference. In J. Garber & K. A. Dodge (Eds.), *The development of emotion regulation and dysregulation* (pp. 49–68). Cambridge: Cambridge University Press.

Mandler, G. (1984). *Mind and body.* New York: W. W. Norton.

Manstead, A. S. R. (1991). Expressiveness as an individual difference. In R. S. Feldman & B. Rimé (Eds.), *Fundamentals of nonverbal behavior* (pp. 285–328). Cambridge: Cambridge University Press.

Manstead, A. S. R. (1992). Gender differences in emotion. In A. Gale & M. W. Eysenck (Eds.), *Handbook of individual differences: Biological perspectives* (pp. 355–387). New York: Wiley.

Manstead, A. S. R. (1993). Children's representation of emotions. In C. Pratt & A. F. Garton (Eds.), *Systems of representation in children: Development and use* (pp. 185–210). New York: Wiley.

Manstead, A. S. R., & Edwards, R. (1992). Communicative aspects of children's emotional competence. In K. T. Strongman (Ed.), *International review of studies on emotion* (Vol. 2, pp. 167–195). Chichester: Wiley.

Markus, H. R., & Kitayama, S. (1991). Culture and the self: Implications for cognition, emotion, and motivation. *Psychological Review, 98,* 224–253.

Markus, H. R., & Kitayama, S. (1994). The cultural construction of self and emotion: Implications for social behavior. In S. Kitayama & H. R. Markus (Eds.), *Emotion and culture* (pp. 89–130). Washington, DC: American Psychological Association.

Martin, J., Knopoff, K., & Beckman, C. (1998). An alternative to bureaucratic impersonality and emotional labor: Bounded emotionality at the Body Shop. *Administrative Science Quarterly, 43,* 429–469.

Matsumoto, D., & Kudoh, T. (1993). American–Japanese cultural differences in attributions of personality based on smiles. *Journal of Nonverbal Behavior, 17,* 231–243.

Mayer, J., & Abramson, J. (1994). *Strange justice: The selling of Clarence Thomas.* Boston: Houghton Mifflin.

McCarthy, E. D. (1989). Emotions are social things: An essay in the sociology of emotions. In D. D. Franks & E. D. McCarthy (Eds.), *The sociology of emotions: Original essays and research papers* (pp. 51–72). Greenwich, CT: JAI Press.

McConnell, T. (1993). *Gratitude.* Philadelphia: Temple University Press.

McCroskey, J. C. (1982). Oral communication apprehension? A reconceptualization. In M. Burgoon (Ed.), *Communication yearbook 6* (pp. 136–170). Beverly Hills, CA: Sage.

McKeon, R. (1941). *The basic works of Aristotle.* New York: Random House.

McLuhan, M. (1964). *Understanding media.* New York: McGraw-Hill.

Mead, G. H. (1934). *Mind, self and society.* Chicago: University of Chicago Press.

Memmi, A. (1957/1990). *The colonizer and the colonized.* London: Earthscan Publications.

Menon, U., & Shweder, R. A. (1994). Kali's tongue: Cultural psychology and the power of shame in Orissa, India. In S. Kitayama & H. R. Markus (Eds.), *Emotion and culture* (pp. 241–284). Washington, DC: American Psychological Association.

Mesquita, B., & Frijda, N. H. (1992). Cultural variations in emotions: A review. *Psychological Bulletin, 112,* 179–204.

Meštrović, S. (1997). *Postemotional society.* London: Sage.

Metts, S. (1994). Face and facework: Implications for the study of personal relationships. In S. Duck (Ed.), *Handbook of personal relationships* (2nd ed., pp. 373–390). Chichester: Wiley.

Metts, S., & Bowers, J. W. (1994). Emotion in interpersonal communication. In M. L. Knapp & G. R. Miller (Eds.), *Handbook of interpersonal communication* (2nd ed., pp. 508–541). Beverly Hills, CA: Sage.

Metts, S., Sprecher, S., & Regan, P. C. (1998). Communication and sexual desire. In P. A. Andersen & L. K. Guerrero (Eds.), *The handbook of communication and emotion* (pp. 353–377). San Diego, CA: Academic Press.

Middleton, D. R. (1989). Emotional style: The cultural ordering of emotions. *Ethos, 17,* 187–201.

Mikula, G., Scherer, K. R., & Athenstaedt, U. (1998). The role of injustice in the elicitation of differential emotional reactions. *Personality and Social Psychology Bulletin, 24,* 769–783.

Miller, K. I., Stiff, J. B., & Ellis, B. H. (1988). Communication and empathy as precursors to burnout among human service workers. *Communication Monographs, 55,* 250–265.

Miller, L. C., & Berg, J. H. (1984). Selectivity and urgency in interpersonal exchange. In V. J. Derlega (Ed.), *Communication, intimacy, and close relationships* (pp. 161–205). New York: Academic Press.

Miller, R. S. (1987). Empathic embarrassment: Situational and personal determinants of reactions to the embarrassment of another. *Journal of Personality and Social Psychology, 53,* 1061–1069.

Miller, R. S. (1996). *Embarrassment: Poise and peril in everyday life.* New York: Guilford Press.

Miller, W. I. (1993). *Humiliation: And other essays on honor, social discomfort, and violence.* Ithaca, NY: Cornell University Press.

Miller, W. I. (1997). *The anatomy of disgust.* Cambridge, MA: Harvard University Press.

Mitchell, T. (1990). *Passional culture: Emotion, religion, and society in southern Spain.* Philadelphia: University of Pennsylvania Press.

Montepare, J. M., Goldstein, S. B., & Clausen, A. (1987). The identification of emotions from gait information. *Journal of Nonverbal Behavior, 11,* 33–42.

Moore, T. (1992). *The care of the soul.* New York: Harper/Collins.

Moreland, L. (1987). The formation of small groups. In C. Hendrick (Ed.), *Group processes: Review of personality and social psychology* (Vol. 8, pp. 80–110). Newbury Park, CA: Sage.

Morgen, S. (1983). Towards a politics of "feelings": Beyond the dialect of thought and action. *Women's Studies, 10,* 203–223.

Morgen, S. (1995). It was the best of times, it was the worst of times: Emotional discourse in the work cultures of feminist health clinics. In M. M. Ferree & P. Y. Martin (Eds.), *Feminist organizations: Harvest of the new women's movement* (pp. 234–247). Philadelphia: Temple University Press.

Motley, M. T., & Camden, C. T. (1988). Facial expression of emotion: A comparison of posed expressions versus spontaneous expressions in an interpersonal communication setting. *Western Journal of Speech Communication, 52,* 1–22.

Mumby, D. K., & Putnam, L. L. (1992). The politics of emotion: A feminist reading of bounded rationality. *Academy of Management Review, 17,* 465–486.

Myers, D. G. (1992). *The pursuit of happiness: Who is happy and why.* New York: William Morrow.

Myers, F. R. (1979). Emotions and the self: A theory of personhood and political order among Pintupi aborigines. *Ethos, 7,* 343–370.

Nathanson, D. L. (1987). Shaming systems in couples, families, and institutions. In D. L. Nathanson (Ed.), *The many faces of shame* (pp. 246–270). New York: Guilford Press.

Nathanson, D. L. (1992). *Shame and pride: Affect, sex and the birth of the self.* New York: W. W. Norton.

Nelson, T. J. (1996). Sacrifice of praise: Emotion and collective participation in an African-American worship service. *Sociology of Religion, 57,* 379–396.

Noesner, G. W., & Webster, M. (1997). Crisis intervention: Using active listening skills in negotiations. *The FBI Law Enforcement Bulletin, 66,* 13–19.

Noller, P. (1984). *Nonverbal communication and marital interaction.* Oxford: Pergamon Press.

Norton, R. (1983). *Communicator style: Theory, application, and measures.* Beverly Hills, CA: Sage.

Notarius, C. I., & Herrick, L. R. (1988). Listener response strategies to a distressed other. *Journal of Social and Personal Relationships, 5,* 97–108.

Nussbaum, M. C. (1986). *The fragility of goodness.* Cambridge: Cambridge University Press.

Oakley, J. (1992). *Morality and the emotions.* London: Routledge.

Oatley, K. (1992). *Best laid schemes.* Cambridge: Cambridge University Press.

Oatley, K. (1993). Social construction in emotions. In M. Lewis & J. M. Haviland (Eds.). *Handbook of emotions* (pp. 341–352). New York: Guilford Press.

Oatley, K., & Duncan, E. (1992). Incidents of emotion in daily life. In K. T. Strongman (Ed.), *International review of studies on emotion* (Vol. 2, pp. 249–293). Chichester: Wiley.

Oatley, K., & Jenkins, J. M. (1996). *Understanding emotions.* Cambridge, MA: Blackwell.

Oatley, K., & Larocque, L. (1995). Everyday concepts of emotions following every-other-day errors in joint plans. In J. A. Russell, J.-M. Fernandez-Dols, A. S. R. Manstead, & J. C. Wellenkamp (Eds.), *Everyday conceptions of emotion* (pp. 145–165). Dordrecht, the Netherlands: Kluwer.

O'Keefe, B. J. (1988). The logic of message design: Individual differences in reasoning about communication. *Communication Monographs, 55,* 80–103.

Omdahl, B. L. (1995). *Cognitive appraisal, emotion, and empathy.* Mahwah, NJ: Erlbaum.

Ong, W. J. (1982). *Orality and literacy: The technologizing of the world.* London: Methuen.

Ortony, A., Clore, G. L., & Collins, A. (1988). *The cognitive structure of emotions.* Cambridge: Cambridge University Press.

Owen, W. F. (1987). The verbal expression of love by women and men as a critical communication event in personal relationships. *Women's Studies in Communication, 10,* 15–24.

Parish, S. M. (1994). *Moral knowing in a Hindu sacred city.* New York: Columbia University Press.

Parkinson, B. (1991). Emotional stylists: Strategies of expressive management among trainee hairdressers. *Cognition and Emotion, 5,* 419–434.

Parkinson, B. (1995). *Ideas and realities of emotion.* New York: Routledge.

Parkinson, B. (1996). Emotions are social. *British Journal of Psychology, 87,* 663–684.

Parks, M. R. (1982). Ideology in interpersonal communication: Off the couch and into the world. In M. Burgoon (Ed.), *Communication yearbook 6.* New Brunswick, NJ: Transaction Books.

Parks, M. R. (1994). Communicative competence and interpersonal control. In M. L. Knapp & G. R. Miller (Eds.), *Handbook of interpersonal communication* (2nd ed., pp. 589–618). Thousand Oaks, CA: Sage.

Parrott, W. G. (1991). The emotional experiences of envy and jealousy. In P. Salovey (Ed.), *The psychology of jealousy and envy* (pp. 3–30). New York: Guilford Press.

Parrott, W. G. (1995). The heart and the head. In J. A. Russell, J.-M. Fernandez-Dols, A. S. R. Manstead, & J. C. Wellenkamp (Eds.), *Everyday conceptions of emotion* (pp. 72–84). Dordrecht, the Netherlands: Kluwer.

Parrott, W. G., & Harré, R. (1996). Embarrassment and the threat to character. In R. Harré & W. G. Parrott (Eds.), *The emotions* (pp. 39–56). London: Sage.

Patterson, M. L. (1983). *Nonverbal behavior: A functional perspective.* New York: Springer-Verlag.

Pennebaker, J. W. (1989). Confession, inhibition, and disease. In L. Berkowitz (Ed.), *Advances in experimental social psychology* (Vol. 22, pp. 211–244). New York: Academic Press.

Pennebaker, J. W. (1993a). Putting stress into words: Health, linguistic, and therapeutic implications. *Behaviour Research and Therapy, 6,* 539–548.

Pennebaker, J. W. (1993b). Social mechanisms of constraint. In D. M. Wegner & J. W. Pennebaker (Eds.), *Handbook of mental control* (pp. 200–219). Englewood Cliffs, NJ: Prentice-Hall.

Pennebaker, J. W. (1997). *Opening up: The healing power of expressing emotions* (rev. ed.). New York: Guilford Press.

Pennebaker, J. W., Mayne, T. J., & Francis, M. E. (1997). Linguistic predictors of adaptive bereavement. *Journal of Personality and Social Psychology, 72,* 863–871.

Pennebaker, J. W., Rimé, B., & Blankenship, V. E. (1996). Stereotypes of emotional expressiveness of Northerners and Southerners: A cross-cultural test of Montesquieu's hypotheses. *Journal of Personality and Social Psychology, 70,* 372–380.

Pennebaker, J. W., & Roberts, T.-A. (1992). Toward a his and hers theory of emotion: Gender differences in visceral perception. *Journal of Social and Clinical Psychology, 11,* 199–212.

Peters, J. D. (1989). John Locke, the individual, and the origin of communication. *Quarterly Journal of Speech, 75,* 387–399.

Peters, T. J., & Waterman, R. H., Jr. (1982). *In search of excellence: Lessons from American's best-run companies.* New York: Harper & Row.

Petty, R. E., & Cacioppo, J. T. (1986). *Communication and persuasion: Central and peripheral routes to attitude change.* New York: Springer-Verlag.

Philipsen, G. (1975). Speaking "like a man" in Teamsterville: Culture patterns of role enactment in an urban neighborhood, *Quarterly Journal of Speech, 61,* 13–22.

Philipsen, G. (1992). *Speaking culturally.* Albany, NY: Suny Press.

Pickens, J., & Field, T. (1993). Facial expressivity in infants of depressed mothers. *Developmental Psychology, 29,* 986–988.

Pittam, J., & Scherer, K. R. (1993). Vocal expression and communication of emotion. In M. Lewis & J. M. Haviland (Eds.), *Handbook of emotions* (pp. 185–197). New York: Guilford Press.

Planalp, S. (1998). Communicating emotion in everyday life: Cues, channels, and processes. In P. A. Andersen & L. K. Guerrero (Eds.), *Communication and emotion: Theory, research, and applications* (pp. 29–48). San Diego, CA: Academic Press.

Planalp, S., DeFrancisco, V., & Rutherford, D. (1996). Varieties of cues to emotion in naturally occurring situations. *Cognition and Emotion, 10,* 137–153.

Planalp, S., & Honeycutt, J. M. (1985). Events that increase uncertainty in personal relationships. *Human Communication Research, 11,* 593–604.

Planalp, S., Rutherford, D. K., & Honeycutt, J. M. (1988). Events that increase uncertainty in personal relationships II: Replication and extension. *Human Communication Research, 14,* 516–547.

Plutchik, R. (1987). Evolutionary bases of empathy. In N. Eisenberg & J. Strayer (Eds.), *Empathy and its development* (pp. 38–46). Cambridge: Cambridge University Press.

Potter, S. H. (1988). The cultural construction of emotion in rural Chinese social life. *Ethos, 16,* 181–208.

Provine, R. R. (1997). Yawns, laughs, smiles, tickles, and talking. In J. A. Russell & J.-M. Fernandez-Dols (Eds.), *The psychology of facial expression* (pp. 158–175). Paris: Cambridge University Press.

Putnam, L. L., & Mumby, D. K. (1993). Organizations, emotion, and the myth of rationality. In S. Fineman (Ed.), *Emotion in organizations* (pp. 36–57). London: Sage.

Rachman, S. J. (1990). *Fear and courage.* New York: W. H. Freeman.

Rafaeli, A., & Sutton, R. I. (1987). Expression of emotion as part of the work role. *Academy of Management Review, 12,* 23–37.

Rago, R. (1989). Finding the magic: Cognitive aspects of mood and emotion in advertising. *Review of Business, 11,* 9–11.

Rawlins, W. K. (1992). *Friendship matters: Communication, dialectics, and the life course.* New York: Aldine de Gruyter.

Rawls, J. (1971). *A theory of justice.* Cambridge, MA: Harvard University Press.

Reardon, K. K., & Buck, R. (1989). Emotion, reason, and communication in coping with cancer. *Health Communication, 1,* 41–54.

Reisenzein, R. (1983). The Schachter theory of emotion: Two decades later. *Psychological Bulletin, 94,* 239–264.

Retzinger, S. M. (1991). *Violent emotions.* Newbury Park, CA: Sage.

Retzinger, S. M. (1995). Shame and anger in personal relationships. In S. Duck & J. T. Wood (Eds.), *Confronting relationship challenges* (pp. 22–42). Thousand Oaks, CA: Sage.

Riesman, D. (1950). *The lonely crowd: A study of the changing American character.* New Haven, CT: Yale University Press.

Rimé, B. (1995). Mental rumination, social sharing, and the recovery from emotional exposure. In J. W. Pennebaker (Ed.), *Emotion, disclosure and health* (pp. 271–291). Washington, DC: American Psychological Association.

Rimé, B., Mesquita, B., Philippot, P., & Boca, S. (1991). Beyond the emotional event: Six studies of the social sharing of emotion. *Cognition and Emotion, 5,* 435–465.

Rimé, B., Philippot, P., & Cisamolo, D. (1990). Social schemata of peripheral changes in emotion. *Journal of Personality and Social Psychology, 59,* 38–49.

Romney, A. K., Moore, C. C., & Rusch, C. D. (1997). Cultural universals: Measuring the semantic structure of emotion terms in English and Japanese. *Proceedings of the National Academy of Science USA, 94,* 5489–5495.

Rorty, A. O. (Ed.). (1980). *Explaining emotions.* Berkeley CA: University of California Press.

Rosaldo, M. Z. (1980). *Knowledge and passion: Ilongot notions of self and social life.* New York: Cambridge University Press.

Roseman, I. J., Spindel, M. S., & Jose, P. E. (1990). Appraisals of emotion-eliciting events: Testing a theory of discrete emotions. *Journal of Personality and Social Psychology, 59,* 899–915.

Russell, J. A. (1994). Is there universal recognition of emotion from facial expression? A review of the cross-cultural studies. *Psychological Bulletin, 115,* 102–141.

Russell, J. A., & Sato, K. (1995). Comparing emotion words between languages. *Journal of Cross-Cultural Psychology, 26,* 384–391.

Saarni, C. (1990). Emotional competence: How emotions and relationships become integrated. In R. A. Thompson (Ed.), *Socioemotional development/Nebraska symposium on motivation* (Vol. 36, pp. 115–182). Lincoln: University of Nebraska Press.

Saarni, C. (1993). Socialization of emotion. In M. Lewis & J. M. Haviland (Eds.), *Handbook of emotions* (pp. 435–446). New York: Guilford Press.

Saarni, C., & Crowley, M. (1990). The development of emotion regulation: Effects on emotional state and expression. In E. Blechman (Ed.), *Emotions and the family* (pp. 53–73). Hillsdale, NJ: Erlbaum.

Saarni, C., & Harris, P. L. (Eds.). (1989). *Children's understanding of emotion.* New York: Cambridge University Press.

Salmond, A. (1991). *Two worlds: First meetings between Maori and Europeans 1642–1772.* Auckland, New Zealand: Viking.

Salovey, P. (1992). Mood-induced self-focused attention. *Journal of Personality and Social Psychology, 62,* 699–707.

Salovey, P., Hsee, C. K., & Mayer, J. D. (1993). Emotional intelligence and the self-regulation of affect. In D. M. Wegner & J. W. Pennebaker (Eds.), *Handbook of mental control* (pp. 258–277). Englewood Cliffs, NJ: Prentice-Hall.

Salovey, P., & Mayer, J. D. (1990). Emotional intelligence. *Imagination, Cognition and Personality, 9,* 185–211.

Salovey, P., Mayer, J. D., Goldman, S. L., Turvey, C., & Palfai, T. P. (1995). Emotional attention, clarity, and repair: Exploring emotional intelligence using the trait meta-mood scale. In J. W. Pennebaker (Ed.), *Emotion, disclo-*

sure and health (pp. 125–154). Washington, DC: American Psychological Association.

Sapir, E. (1921). *Language: An introduction to the study of speech.* New York: Harcourt, Brace & World.

Schachter, S. (1959). *The psychology of affiliation.* Stanford, CA: Stanford University Press.

Schachter, S., & Singer, J. (1962). Cognitive, social and physiological determinants of emotional state. *Psychological Review, 69,* 379–399.

Scheff, T. J. (1977). The distancing of emotion in ritual. *Current Anthropology, 18,* 483–505.

Scheff, T. J. (1979). *Catharsis in healing, ritual, and drama.* Berkeley: University of California Press.

Scheff, T. J. (1984). The taboo on coarse emotions. In P. Shaver (Ed.), *Review of personality and social psychology: Emotions, relationships, and health* (pp. 146–169). Beverly Hills, CA: Sage.

Scheff, T. J. (1990). *Microsociology: Discourse, emotion, and social structure.* Chicago: University of Chicago Press.

Scheff, T. J. (1994). *Bloody revenge.* Boulder, CO: Westview Press.

Scheff, T. J. (1995). Shame and related emotions: An overview. *American Behavioral Scientist, 38,* 1053–1059.

Scheff, T. J., & Retzinger, S. M. (1991). *Emotions and violence.* Lexington, MA: Lexington Books.

Scherer, K. R. (1986). Vocal affect expression: A review and a model for future research. *Psychological Bulletin, 99,* 143–165.

Scherer, K. R. (1988). Criteria for emotion-antecedent appraisal: A review. In V. Hamilton, G. H. Bower, & N. H. Frijda (Eds.), *Cognitive perspectives on emotion and motivation* (pp. 89–126). Dordrecht, the Netherlands: Kluwer.

Scherer, K. R. (1992a). Vocal affect expression as symptom, symbol, and appeal. In H. Papousek, U. Jurgens, & M. Papousek (Eds.), *Nonverbal vocal communication: Comparative and developmental approaches* (pp. 43–60). Cambridge: Cambridge University Press.

Scherer, K. R. (1992b). What does facial expression express? In K. T. Strongman (Ed.), *International review of studies on emotion* (Vol. 2, pp. 139–165). Chichester: Wiley.

Scherer, K. R. (1994). Affect bursts. In S. H. M. van Goozen, N. E. van de Poll, & J. A. Sergeant (Eds.), *Emotions: Essays on emotion theory* (pp. 161–193). Hillsdale, NJ: Erlbaum.

Scherer, K. R., & Wallbott, H. G. (1994). Evidence for universality and cultural variation of differential emotion response patterning. *Journal of Personality and Social Psychology, 66,* 310–328.

Scherer, K. R., Wallbott, H. G., Matsumoto, D., & Kudoh, T. (1988). Emotional experience in cultural context: A comparison between Europe, Japan, and the United States. In K. R. Scherer (Ed.), *Facets of emotion* (pp. 5–30). Hillsdale, NJ: Erlbaum.

Schoek, H. (1966). *Envy.* Indianapolis, IN: Liberty Press.

Schwartz, B. (1967). The social psychology of the gift. *American Journal of Sociology, 73,* 1–11.

Searle, J. R. (1969). *Speech acts.* Cambridge: Cambridge University Press.

Segrin, C. (1998). Interpersonal communication problems associated with depression and loneliness. In P. A. Andersen & L. K. Guerrero (Eds.), *The handbook of communication and emotion* (pp. 215–242). San Diego, CA: Academic Press.

Shannon, C., & Weaver, W. (1949). *The mathematical theory of communication.* Urbana: University of Illinois Press.

Sharpsteen, D. J. (1991). The organization of jealousy knowledge: Romantic jealousy as a blended emotion. In P. Salovey (Ed.), *The psychology of jealousy and envy* (pp. 31–51). New York: Guilford Press.

Shaver, P. R., Schwartz, J., Kirson, D., & O'Connor, C. (1987). Emotion knowledge: Further explorations of a prototype approach. *Journal of Personality and Social Psychology, 52,* 1061–1086.

Shaver, P. R., Wu, S., & Schwartz, J. C. (1992). Cross-cultural similarities and differences in emotion and its representation: A prototype approach. In M. S. Clark (Ed.), *Emotion* (pp. 175–212). Newbury Park, CA: Sage.

Shimanoff, S. B. (1985). Expressing emotions in words: Verbal patterns of interactions. *Journal of Communication, 35,* 16–31.

Shimanoff, S. B. (1987). Types of emotional disclosures and request compliance between spouses. *Communication Monographs, 54,* 85–100.

Shoda, Y., Mischel, W., & Peake, P. K. (1990). Predicting adolescent cognitive and self-regulatory competencies from preschool delay of gratification: Identifying diagnostic conditions. *Developmental Psychology, 26,* 978–986.

Shorter, E. (1977). *The making of the modern family.* New York: Basic Books.

Siegert, J. R., & Stamp, G. H. (1994). "Our first big fight" as a milestone in the development of close relationships. *Communication Monographs, 61,* 345–360.

Signorini, I. (1982). Patterns of fright: Multiple concepts of susto in a Nahua–Ladino community of the Sierra de Puebla (Mexico). *Ethnology, 21,* 313–323.

Sillars, A. L., & Weisberg, J. (1987). Conflict as a social skill. In M. E. Roloff & G. R. Miller (Eds.), *Interpersonal processes* (pp. 140–171). Newbury Park, CA: Sage.

Silver, R. L., Boon, C., & Stones, M. H. (1983). Searching for meaning in misfortune: Making sense of incest. *Journal of Social Issues, 39,* 81–102.

Simpson, J. A., Ickes, W., & Blackstone, T. (1995). When the head protects the heart: Empathic accuracy in dating relationships. *Journal of Personality and Social Psychology, 69,* 629–641.

Smith, A. C., III, & Kleinman, S. (1989). Managing emotions in medical school: Students' contacts with the living and the dead. *Social Psychology Quarterly, 52,* 56–69.

Smith, C. A., & Ellsworth, P. C. (1985). Patterns of cognitive appraisal in emotion. *Journal of Personality and Social Psychology, 48,* 813–838.

Smith, C. A., & Lazarus, R. S. (1993). Appraisal components, core themes, and the emotions. *Cognition and Emotion, 7,* 233–269.

Smith, R. A. (1991). Envy and the sense of injustice. In P. Salovey (Ed.), *The psychology of jealousy and envy* (pp. 79–99). New York: Guilford Press.

Solomon, R. C. (1980). Emotions and choice. In A. O. Rorty (Ed.), *Explaining emotions* (pp. 251–281). Berkeley: University of California Press.

Solomon, R. C. (1989). The emotions of justice. *Social Justice Research, 3,* 345–374.

Solomon, R. C. (1990). *A passion for justice.* Reading, MA: Addison-Wesley.

Solomon, R. C. (1993). The philosophy of emotion. In M. Lewis & J. M. Haviland (Eds.), *Handbook of emotions* (pp. 3–15). New York: Guilford Press.

Sommers, S. (1984a). Adults evaluating their emotions: A cross-cultural perspective. In C. Z. Malatesta & C. E. Izard (Eds.), *Emotion in adult development* (pp. 319–338). Beverly Hills, CA: Sage.

Sommers, S. (1984b). Reported emotions and conventions of emotionality among college students. *Journal of Personality and Social Psychology, 46,* 207–215.

Sorce, J. F., Emde, R. N., Campos, J., & Klinnert, M. D. (1985). Maternal emotional signaling: Its effect on the visual cliff behavior of 1-year-olds. *Developmental Psychology, 21,* 195–200.

Spiegel, D. (1993). *Living beyond limits.* New York: Ballantine Books.

Spiegel, D. (1995). How do you feel about concern now? – Survival and psychosocial support. *Public Health Reports, 110,* 298–300.

Spiegel, D., Bloom, J. R., Kraemer, H. C., & Gottheil, E. (1989). Effect of psychosocial treatment on survival of patients with metastatic breast cancer. *The Lancet, 2,* 888–891.

Spitzberg, B. H., & Cupach, W. R. (1984). *Interpersonal communication competence.* Beverly Hills, CA: Sage.

Stanton, A. L., Danoff-Burg, S., Cameron, C. L., & Ellis, A. P. (1994). Coping through emotional approach: Problems of conceptualization and confounding. *Journal of Personality and Social Psychology, 66,* 350–362.

Stearns, C. Z., & Stearns, P. N. (1986). *Anger: The struggle for emotional control in America's history.* Chicago: University of Chicago Press.

Stearns, P. N. (1989). *Jealousy: The evolution of an emotion in American history.* New York: New York University Press.

Stearns, P. N. (1994). *American cool: Constructing a twentieth-century emotional style.* New York: New York University Press.

Stearns, P. N., & Knapp, P. (1996). Historical perspectives on grief. In R. Harré & W. G. Parrott (Eds.), *The emotions* (pp. 132–150). London: Sage.

Stein, N. L., & Oatley, K. (1992). Basic emotions (Special issue). *Cognition and Emotion, 6,* 161–319.

Stein, N. L., Trabasso, T., & Liwag, M. (1993). The representation and organization of emotional experience: Unfolding the emotional episode. In M. Lewis & J. M. Haviland (Eds.), *Handbook of emotions* (pp. 279–300). New York: Guilford Press.

Stenberg, C. R., & Campos, J. J. (1990). Anger expressions in infancy. In N. L. Stein, B. Leventhal, & T. Trabasso (Eds.). *Psychological and biological approaches to emotion* (pp. 247–282). Hillsdale, NJ: Erlbaum.

Sternberg, R. J., & Barnes, M. L. (Eds.). (1988). *The psychology of love.* New Haven, CT: Yale University Press.

Stiles, W. B. (1987). "I have to talk to somebody": A fever model of disclosure. In V. J. Derlega & J. H. Berg (Eds.), *Self-disclosure: Theory, research, and therapy* (pp. 257–282). New York: Plenum Press.

Strongman, K. T., & Strongman, L. (1996). Maori emotion. In R. Harré & W. G. Parrott (Eds.), *The emotions: Social, cultural and biological dimensions* (pp. 200–203). London: Sage.

Sullins, E. S. (1991). Emotional contagion revisited: Effects of social comparison and expressive style on mood convergence. *Personality and Social Psychology Bulletin, 17,* 166–174.

Sullivan, P. A. (1990, February). *Patricia Schroeder and the ethic of care in political discourse.* Paper presented at the Western Speech Communication Association convention, Sacramento, CA.

Sullivan, P. A. (1993). Women's discourse and political communication: A case study of Congressperson Patricia Schroeder. *Western Journal of Communication, 57,* 530–545.

Sullivan, P. A., & Goldzwig, S. R. (1994). Constructing a postmodernist ethic: The feminist question for a new politics. In L. H. Turner & H. M. Sterk (Eds.), *Differences that make a difference: Examining the assumptions in gender research* (pp. 203–212). Westport, CT: Bergin & Garvey.

Summerfield, A. B., & Green, E. J. (1986). Categories of emotion-eliciting events: A qualitative overview. In K. R. Scherer, H. G. Wallbott, & A. B. Summerfield (Eds.), *Experiencing emotion: A cross-cultural study* (pp. 50–65). Cambridge: Cambridge University Press.

Sun, L. (1991). Contemporary Chinese culture: Structure and emotionality. *The Australian Journal of Chinese Affairs, 26,* 1–41.

Sunnafrank, M. (1984). A communication-based perspective on attitude similarity and interpersonal attraction in early acquaintance. *Communication Monographs, 51,* 372–380.

Sunoo, B. P. (1995). How fun flies at Southwest Airlines. *Personnel Journal, 74,* 62–72.

Sutton, R. I. (1991). Maintaining norms about expressed emotions: The case of bill collectors. *Administrative Science Quarterly, 36,* 245–268.

Sutton, R. I., & Rafaeli, A. (1988). Untangling the relationship between displayed emotions and organizational sales: The case of convenience store clerks. *Academy of Management Journal, 31,* 461–487.

Tait, R., & Silver, R. C. (1989). Coming to terms with major negative life events. In J. S. Uleman & J. A. Bargh (Eds.), *Unintended thought* (pp. 351–382). New York: Guilford Press.

Tangney, J. (1991). Moral affect: The good, the bad, and the ugly. *Journal of Personality and Social Psychology, 61,* 102–111.

Tannen, D. (1984). *Conversational style: Analyzing talk among friends.* Norwood, NJ: Ablex.

Tavris, C. (1984). On the wisdom of counting to ten: Personal and social dangers of anger expression. In P. Shaver (Ed.), *Review of personality and social psychology: Emotions, relationships, and health* (pp. 170–191). Beverly Hills, CA: Sage.

Tavris, C. (1989). *Anger: The misunderstood emotion* (pp. 48–69). New York: Simon & Schuster.

Tavuchis, N. (1991). *Mea culpa: A sociology of apology and reconciliation.* Stanford, CA: Stanford University Press.

Taylor, S. E. (1989). *Positive illusions.* New York: Basic Books.

Taylor, S. E., Falke, R. L., Mazel, R. M., & Hilsberg, B. L. (1988). Sources of satisfaction and dissatisfaction among members of cancer support groups. In B. H. Gottlieb (Ed.), *Marshalling social support: Formats, processes, and effects* (pp. 187–208). Newbury Park, CA: Sage.

Taylor, S. E., & Fiske, S. (1975). Point of view and perceptions of causality. *Journal of Personality and Social Psychology, 32,* 439–445.

Taylor, V. (1995). Watching for vibes: Bringing emotion into the study of feminist organizations. In M. M. Ferree & P. Y. Martin (Eds.), *Feminist organizations: Harvest of the new women's movement* (pp. 223–233). Philadelphia: Temple University Press.

Terkel, S. (1972). *Working: People talk about what they do all day and how they feel about what they do.* New York: Pantheon.

Thayer, R. E. (1996). *The origin of everyday moods: Managing energy, tension, and stress.* New York: Oxford University Press.

Thimm, C., & Kruse, L. (1993). The power–emotion relationship in discourse: Spontaneous expression of emotions in asymmetric dialogue. *Journal of Language and Social Interaction, 12,* 81–102.

Thoits, P. A. (1990). Emotional deviance: Research agendas. In T. D. Kemper (Ed.), *Research agendas in the sociology of emotions* (pp. 180–203). Albany, NY: SUNY Press.

Thomas, S. P., & Droppleman, P. (1997). Channeling nurses' anger into positive interventions. *Nursing Forum, 32,* 13–21.

Thompson, J., & Held, D. (Eds.). (1982). *Habermas: Critical debates.* Cambridge, MA: MIT Press.

Thompson, R. A. (1987). Empathy and emotional understanding: The early development of empathy. In N. Eisenberg & J. Strayer (Eds.), *Empathy and its development* (pp. 119–145). Cambridge: Cambridge University Press.

Tice, D. M., & Baumeister, R. F. (1993). Controlling anger: Self-induced emotion change. In D. M. Wegner & J. W. Pennebaker (Eds.), *Handbook of mental control* (pp. 393–409). Englewood Cliffs, NJ: Prentice-Hall.

Tomkins, S. S. (1963). *Affect, imagery, and consciousness: Vol. 2. The negative affects.* New York: Springer.

Tracy, S. J. (1998), November). *Smile, you're at sea: A Foucaultian-informed analysis of emotional management on a cruise ship.* Paper presented at the National Communication Association Conference, New York.

Tracy, S. J., & Tracy, K. (1998). Emotion labor at 911: A case study and theoretical critique. *Journal of Applied Communication Research, 26,* 1–22.

Turner, F. (1995). Shame, beauty, and the tragic view of history. *American Behavioral Scientist, 38,* 1060–1075.

Van Dijk, T. A., & Kintsch, W. (1983). *Strategies of discourse comprehension.* New York: Academic Press.

Van Hooft, S. (1994). Scheler on sharing emotions. *Philosophy Today, 38,* 18–29.

Van Maanen, J., & Kunda, G. (1989). "Real feelings": Emotional expression and organization culture. In L. L. Cummings, & B. M. Staw (Eds.), *Research in organization behavior* (Vol. 11, pp. 43–103). Greenwich, CT: JAI Press.

Vangelisti, A. L. (1994). Messages that hurt. In W. R. Cupach & B. H. Spitzberg (Eds.), *The dark side of interpersonal communication* (pp. 53–82). Hillsdale, NJ: Erlbaum.

Vangelisti, A. L., Daly, J. A., & Rudnick, J. R. (1991). Making people feel guilty in conversations: Techniques and correlates. *Human Communication Research, 18,* 3–39.

Vernon, P. (1941). Psychological effects of air raids. *Journal of Abnormal and Social Psychology, 36,* 457–476.

Vogel, G. (1997). Scientists probe feelings behind decision-making. *Science, 275,* 1269.

Wagner, H. L., MacDonald, C. J., & Manstead, A. S. R. (1986). Communication of individual emotions by spontaneous facial expressions. *Journal of Personality and Social Psychology, 50,* 737–743.

Wagner, P. M. (Producer and Director). (1993). Bill Moyers: Healing and the mind: Healing from within (Vol. 3). [videorecording] (Available from Ambrose Video Publishing, 1290 Avenue of the Americas, Suite 2245, New York, NY 10104).

Walden, T. A. (1991). Infant social referencing. In J. Garber & K. A. Dodge (Eds.), *The development of emotion regulation and dysregulation* (pp. 69–88). Cambridge: Cambridge University Press.

Waldron, V. R. (1994). Once more, *with feeling*: Reconsidering the role of emotion in work. In S. A. Deetz (Ed.), *Communication yearbook 17* (pp. 388–416). Thousand Oaks, CA: Sage.

Wallbott, H. G. (1988a). Faces in context: The relative importance of facial expression and context information in determining emotion attributions. In K. R. Scherer (Ed.), *Facets of emotion* (pp. 139–160). Hillsdale, NJ: Erlbaum.

Wallbott, H. G. (1988b). In and out of context: Influences of facial expression and context information on emotion attributions. *British Journal of Social Psychology, 27,* 357–369.

Wallbott, H. G., & Scherer, K. (1988). How universal and specific is emotional experience? Evidence from 27 countries and five continents. In K. R. Scherer (Ed.), *Facets of emotion* (pp. 31–56). Hillsdale, NJ: Erlbaum.

Wallerstein, J. S., & Blakeslee, S. (1989). *Second chances.* New York: Ticknor & Fields.

Wasielewski, P. L. (1985). The emotional basis of charisma. *Symbolic Interaction, 8,* 207–222.

Watson, D., Clark, L. A., McIntyre, C. W., & Hamaker, S. (1992). Affect, personality, and social activity. *Journal of Personality and Social Psychology, 63,* 1011–1025.

Watson-Gegeo, K. A., & White, G. M. (1990). *Disentangling: Conflict discourse in Pacific societies.* Stanford: Stanford University Press.

Watzlawick, P., Beavin, J. H., & Jackson, D. (1967). *Pragmatics of human communication.* New York: W. W. Norton.

Wegner, D. M. (1992). You can't always think what you want: Problems in the suppression of unwanted thoughts. In M. P. Zanna (Ed.), *Advances in experimental social psychology* (Vol. 25, pp. 193–225). New York: Academic Press.

Wegner, D. M., Erber, R., & Zanakos, S. (1993). Ironic processes in the mental control of mood and mood-related thought. *Journal of Personality and Social Psychology, 65,* 1093–1104.

Wegner, D. M., & Lane, J. D. (1995). From secrecy to psychopathology. In J. W. Pennebaker (Ed.), *Emotion, disclosure, and health* (pp. 25–46). Washington, DC: American Psychological Association.

Weinberg, N. (1995). Does apologizing help? The role of self-blame and making amends in recovery from bereavement. *Health and Social Work, 20,* 294–299.

Weiss, R. S. (1975). *Marital separation.* New York: Basic Books.

White, G. L., & Mullen, P. E. (1989). *Jealousy: Theory, research, and clinical strategies.* New York: Guilford Press.

White, G. M. (1990). Moral discourse and the rhetoric of emotions. In C. A. Lutz & L. Abu-Lughod (Eds.), *Language and the politics of emotion* (pp. 46–68). Cambridge: Cambridge University Press.

White, G. M. (1994). Affecting culture: Emotion and morality in everyday life. In S. Kitayama & H. R. Markus (Eds.), *Emotion and culture* (pp. 219–239). Washington, DC: American Psychological Association.

Whitehouse, H. (1996). Rites of terror: Emotion, metaphor and memory in Melanesian initiation cults. *Journal of the Royal Anthropological Institute, 2,* 703–716.

Whorf, B. L. (1956). *Language, thought and reality.* New York: Wiley.

Wiemann, J. M., & Knapp, M. L. (1975). Turn-taking in conversation. *Journal of Communication, 25,* 75–92.

Wierzbicka, A. (1994). Emotion, language, and cultural scripts. In S. Kitayama & H. R. Markus (Eds.), *Emotion and culture* (pp. 133–196). Washington, DC: American Psychological Association.

Wierzbicka, A. (1995). Everyday conceptions of emotion: A semantic perspective. In J. A. Russell, J.-M. Fernandez-Dols, A. S. R. Manstead, & J. C. Wellenkamp (Eds.), *Everyday conceptions of emotion* (pp. 19–47). Dordrecht, the Netherlands: Kluwer.

Wikan, U. (1990). *Managing turbulent hearts.* Chicago: University of Chicago Press.

Wills, T. A. (1990). Social support and the family. In E. Blechman (Eds.), *Emotions and the family* (pp. 75–98). Hillsdale, NJ: Erlbaum.

Wilmot, W. W., Hocker, J. L. (1998). *Interpersonal conflict* (5th ed.). Boston: McGraw-Hill.

Winzeler, R. (1990). Amok: Historical, psychological, and cultural perspectives. In W. J. Karim (Ed.), *Emotions of culture: A Malay perspective* (pp. 97–122). Oxford: Oxford University Press.

Wispé, L. (1991). *The psychology of sympathy.* New York: Plenum.

Witte, K. (1998). Fear as motivator, fear as inhibitor: Using the extended parallel process model to explain fear appeal successes and failures. In P. A. Andersen & L. K. Guerrero (Eds.), *The handbook of communication and emotion* (pp. 423–450). San Diego, CA: Academic Press.

Wood. L. A. (1986). Loneliness. In R. Harré (Ed.), *The social construction of emotion* (pp. 184–208). Oxford: Basil Blackwell.

Woodward, K. (1996). Global cooling and academic warming: Long-term shifts in emotional weather. *American Literary History, 8,* 759–779.

Wortman, C. B., & Dunkel-Schetter, C. (1979). Interpersonal relationships and cancer: A theoretical analysis. *Journal of Social Issues, 35,* 120–155.

Wortman, C. B., & Silver, R. C. (1989). The myths of coping with loss. *Journal of Consulting and Clinical Psychology, 57,* 349–357.

Wouters, C. (1989). The sociology of emotions and flight attendants: Hochschild's *Managed Heart. Theory, Culture and Society, 6,* 95–123.

Wurmser, L. (1995). *The mask of shame.* Northvale, NJ: Jason Aronson.

Younoszai, B. (1993). Mexican American perspectives related to death. In D. P. Irish, K. F. Lundquist, & V. J. Nelsen (Eds.), *Ethnic variations in dying, death, and grief* (pp. 67–78). Washington, DC: Taylor & Francis.

Zajonc, R. B. (1980). Feeling and thinking: Preferences need no inferences. *American Psychologist, 35,* 151–175.

Zajonc, R. B. (1984). On the primacy of affect. *American Psychologist, 39,* 117–123.

Zammuner, V. L., & Frijda, N. H. (1994). Felt and communicated emotions: Sadness and jealousy. *Cognition and Emotion, 8,* 37–53.

Zeman, J., & Garber, J. (1996). Display rules for anger, sadness, and pain: It depends on who is watching. *Child Development, 67,* 957–974.

Zeman, J., & Shipman, K. (1996). Children's expression of negative affect: Reasons and methods. *Developmental Psychology, 32,* 842–850.

Zillman, D. (1990). The interplay of cognition and excitation in aggravated conflict among intimates. In D. D. Cahn (Ed.), *Intimates in conflict* (pp. 187–208). Hillsdale, N.J.: Erlbaum.

Zillman, D. (1993). Mental control of angry aggression. In D. M. Wegner & J. W. Pennebaker (Eds.), *Handbook of mental control* (pp. 370–392). Englewood Cliffs, NJ: Prentice-Hall.

Author Index

Subject Index

Studies in Emotion and Social Interaction

First Series
Editors: Paul Ekman and Klaus R. Scherer